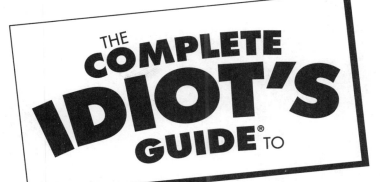

THE COMPLETE IDIOT'S GUIDE® TO

Simple Home Improvements

Illustrated

D1307073

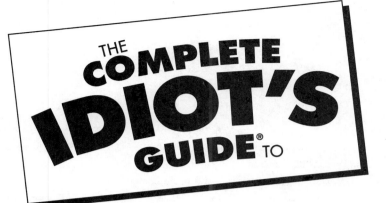

THE COMPLETE **IDIOT'S** GUIDE® TO

Simple Home Improvements
Illustrated

by David J. Tenenbaum

ALPHA

A member of Penguin Group (USA) Inc.

For Meg. She knows why!

ALPHA BOOKS

Published by the Penguin Group

Penguin Group (USA) Inc., 375 Hudson Street, New York, New York 10014, U.S.A.

Penguin Group (Canada), 10 Alcorn Avenue, Toronto, Ontario, Canada M4V 3B2 (a division of Pearson Penguin Canada Inc.)

Penguin Books Ltd, 80 Strand, London WC2R 0RL, England

Penguin Ireland, 25 St Stephen's Green, Dublin 2, Ireland (a division of Penguin Books Ltd)

Penguin Group (Australia), 250 Camberwell Road, Camberwell, Victoria 3124, Australia (a division of Pearson Australia Group Pty Ltd)

Penguin Books India Pvt Ltd, 11 Community Centre, Panchsheel Park, New Delhi—110 017, India

Penguin Group (NZ), cnr Airborne and Rosedale Roads, Albany, Auckland 1310, New Zealand (a division of Pearson New Zealand Ltd)

Penguin Books (South Africa) (Pty) Ltd, 24 Sturdee Avenue, Rosebank, Johannesburg 2196, South Africa

Penguin Books Ltd, Registered Offices: 80 Strand, London WC2R 0RL, England

International Standard Book Number: 1-59257-294-4
Library of Congress Catalog Card Number: 2004113216

06 05 04   8 7 6 5 4 3 2 1

Interpretation of the printing code: The rightmost number of the first series of numbers is the year of the book's printing; the rightmost number of the second series of numbers is the number of the book's printing. For example, a printing code of 04-1 shows that the first printing occurred in 2004.

Printed in the United States of America

Note: This publication contains the opinions and ideas of its author. It is intended to provide helpful and informative material on the subject matter covered. It is sold with the understanding that the author and publisher are not engaged in rendering professional services in the book. If the reader requires personal assistance or advice, a competent professional should be consulted.

The author and publisher specifically disclaim any responsibility for any liability, loss, or risk, personal or otherwise, which is incurred as a consequence, directly or indirectly, of the use and application of any of the contents of this book.

Most Alpha books are available at special quantity discounts for bulk purchases for sales promotions, premiums, fund-raising, or educational use. Special books, or book excerpts, can also be created to fit specific needs.

For details, write: Special Markets, Alpha Books, 375 Hudson Street, New York, NY 10014.

Publisher: *Marie Butler-Knight*
Product Manager: *Phil Kitchel*
Senior Managing Editor: *Jennifer Chisholm*
Senior Acquisitions Editor: *Mike Sanders*
Development Editor: *Lynn Northrup*
Production Editor: *Janette Lynn*

Copy Editor: *Keith Cline*
Illustrator: *Laura Robbins*
Cartoonist: *Chris Eliopoulos*
Cover/Book Designer: *Trina Wurst*
Indexer: *Julie Bess*
Layout: *Becky Harmon*
Proofreading: *John Etchison*

Contents at a Glance

Contents

Appendixes

Foreword

A user-friendly home improvement guide is finally here. David Tenenbaum has illustrated the basics to help us all examine our own abilities to repair, replace, or just improve our lives.

For the past 25 years, I have made my living by specializing in residential design. Raised in a family architectural business, I learned all phases of home construction and repair through firsthand experience. Improving aspects of an existing home is always my first recommendation before replacement or costly changes. As an owner of a residential design firm that specializes in every facet of renovation, interior design, and new home construction, my clients often misunderstand home repair challenges and lose the opportunity to restore what they already have.

This book is a quality guide that will encourage people to create improvements, maintain existing homes, and prevent unnecessary repairs. David Tenenbaum not only presents sensible solutions for homeowners, but I believe the content of this book is invaluable to a wide range of building professionals to carry out common-sense home repair and improvements. Each chapter provides a step-by-step approach that leads to success.

In the years I have known David, there isn't one project or skill that he has not been able to master. David examines every option when approaching a repair project. He has the uncanny gift to communicate information in a straightforward, rational manner to make complex situations understandable to the homeowner.

In the residential design business, I have seen a renewed interest on the part of my clients to understand their home repair challenges. So often I hear, "Can we improve what we have and not make a major change?" This book helps homeowners overcome their fears and become more self-confident to undertake any home improvement. I enthusiastically recommend this resource to many of my clients as a prerequisite in their renovation plans. Dave Tenenbaum delivers. Read this book and feel empowered to take control over your home improvements!

Mark Udvari-Solner
Udvari-Solner Design Company
Residential Design Architect, Associate A.I.A.

Introduction

When I'm photographing pro house-fixers at work, their first question is always the same: What makes you qualified to write about home improvement? My answer is simple: I've been making improvements, as a pro and then as an amateur, for more than 30 years.

I understand the skepticism: As a veteran of the building trades, I'm surprised when folks write about home repair and improvement without having served their time in the trenches. In the average home book, projects proceed step by step, as inevitably (and about as exciting) as the tax code. But to write a realistic book on home improvement, you must have a firsthand appreciation for the range of surprises you'll encounter in a real-world project.

How can you give good advice if you don't know when to improvise or break the rules?

But while home improvement can be confusing and frustrating, it can also be satisfying, gratifying, and profitable.

◆ The satisfaction of making a new type of improvement, like building your first stud wall.

◆ The gratification of working with a new type of material, such as tile or molding.

◆ The certainty that you can save a bundle almost every time you pick up your tools.

One of the key satisfactions is seldom mentioned: Home improvement requires you to learn on the job. Even "know-it-mosts" like myself are constantly encountering new situations, new materials, and new tools. Learning to deal with the novel and unknown is both a challenge and a delight.

I learned this from my father, Frank, an electronic engineer convinced he could do almost anything. His message was unstated but unmistakable: When you start a new project, you are your own best resource. If you don't have the tools, where can you get them? Where can you find the material?

Most of all, if you don't have the necessary expertise, where can you get it? Here. Finally, a home-improvement book written by someone who has actually improved houses is in your hands. Once you read the simple, realistic projects in *The Complete Idiot's Guide to Simple Home Improvements Illustrated*, you'll want to get started on a hobby that's satisfying, gratifying, and profitable.

Getting Oriented to This Book

This book is divided into 10 parts:

Part 1, "Getting Started," introduces you to the ideal mind-set for doing your own improvements: a can-do attitude, a tolerance for frustration, and the ability to learn and improvise. I also show you how to invest in some tools and build a basic workshop in which to hold them.

Part 2, "On the Walls," discusses what may be the single-most important part of your house. Whether it's building a new wall, applying drywall to an existing one, building an arch, or nailing up wainscoting, wall work is important work.

Part 3, "Windows and Doors," shows you how these areas are often the first victims of age and decay, and one of the sorest of sore spots for most aging houses. Here you'll find some simple techniques to help you replace doors and windows, and install a storm door.

Part 4, "Floors: Getting Underfoot," shows you how to keep your floors looking good. Whether it's hardwood, laminate, tile, or vinyl, floors require their own set of techniques, all explained and illustrated here.

Part 5, "Storage Solutions," introduces smart, attractive storage solutions for books, kitchen apparatus, and hand tools.

Part 6, "Kitchen Projects," includes ideas for giving your kitchen a face-lift, whether it's replacing the kitchen sink or tiling the counter and backsplash. I also show how to build and install drawers in your kitchen cabinets, and build and attach a new hardwood front to them.

Part 7, "Fun in the Bath," offers projects that range from simple (install towel racks) to necessary (replace a toilet). I also show you how to build a medicine cabinet and install a pedestal sink.

Part 8, "Electrical Matters," shows you how to replace or install built-in light fixtures, install lighting under a kitchen cabinet, install a safer electric outlet, and run TV cable through the walls and ceiling.

Part 9, "For Decoration or for Fun," gives you lots of ideas for improving the look of a room, including a good paint job and installing new molding around the windows, doors, and baseboard. For a sense of completion, consider adding crown molding around the ceiling. This part also explains how to replace a fireplace mantelpiece, install a sun tube to bring in the sunlight, and build a sleeping loft.

You'll also find two helpful appendixes. Appendix A defines the building terms found in *italics* throughout the text. Appendix B lists recommended books and online sites that will come in handy in your home-improvement journey.

Extras

I've also included two types of sidebars to help you solve common problems and highlight common dangers:

Building Smarts

Check these boxes for helpful tips that make for a smoother building experience.

Dave's Don'ts

These boxes warn you of dangers and common mistakes that may cost you time and money.

Acknowledgments

I wish to thank Ken Schuster of Schuster Construction, Karl Lorentz of Lorentz Plumbing, and TDS Custom Construction (all of Madison, Wisconsin) for letting me photograph their work. I also appreciate friends and neighbors Laurel, Ruedi, and Monika; Shana and Johan; Maureen and Tom; and Bill, Corliss, and Talia. They were kind enough—or foolish enough—to loan me their houses so we could photograph actual improvements.

Illustration Credits

Photography by David J. Tenenbaum, with Alexander Tenenbaum, Joshua Tenenbaum, and Meg Wise.

Computer illustrations by David J. Tenenbaum.

Photo props courtesy of Porter Cable, Delta Machinery, Robert Bosch Tool Corp., Dewalt Industrial Tool Co., Sears, Bucketboss (Fiskars Brands, Inc.), Senco Products Inc., and Paslode (a division of Illinois Tool Works).

Special Thanks to the Technical Reviewers

The Complete Idiot's Guide to Simple Home Improvements Illustrated was reviewed by experts who double-checked the accuracy of what you'll learn here, to help us ensure that this book gives you everything you need to know about making simple home improvements. Special thanks are extended to Doug Swayne, Karl Lorentz, and Fred Brown for lending their expertise.

Trademarks

All terms mentioned in this book that are known to be or are suspected of being trademarks or service marks have been appropriately capitalized. Alpha Books and Penguin Group (USA) Inc. cannot attest to the accuracy of this information. Use of a term in this book should not be regarded as affecting the validity of any trademark or service mark.

In This Part

Part 1

Getting Started

Most houses, whether they have faced a single winter or survived a century, can use improvement. Whether you want to upgrade a quasi-functional kitchen or replace a door that last closed in the Truman administration, you need a starting place. Chapter 1 describes the basic mind-set for home improvement: Can you deal with frustration? Can you spare the time? Do you like learning new skills? When you think about it, nobody is born knowing how to replace a window or a faucet. Everybody learns—or picks up the phone.

Then there is the question of having the right tools: Dull, entry-level tools seldom work. Chapter 2 describes a basic toolkit and some handy, but optional, tools. Tools call for a place to use and store them, so Chapter 3 describes the basic elements of a simple home workshop.

Ready? It's time to get started!

In This Chapter

Chapter **1**

Getting Oriented to Home Improvement

Got a bone to pick with the old home place? Been bugged beyond belief by the abysmal taste of former owners? Been hankering to rejuvenate/renovate/remodel the bathroom/kitchen/living room? Professional help is only a phone call—and a hefty check and some unexplained delays—away. My guess is that you're considering the path less traveled—doing it yourself.

Welcome to the field of home improvement—projects that are larger than home repair but smaller than remodeling. Home improvements make your home a nicer place to live in, without usually expanding the overall size or causing the valuation to skyrocket. Home improvements seldom require shiploads of capital or months of effort, and many projects in this book are modular: You can do one to satisfy a particular itch, or you can do several and renovate an entire room.

I'm convinced that many people who doubt their ability to work on their own houses can do a fine job, given enough time, tools, and advice. I can't give you time. I won't give you the actual tools, but I will give you plenty of advice. In the pages that follow, I reveal some of the tricks I've learned in 35 years of working on houses. I show you how the pros do it—but only when their technique is appropriate for a novice. I show you tricks that the pros disdain, but that you can use to do a better, faster, safer job.

Read on to learn how to make the home place a better place!

Suffering a major case of the homelies, this kitchen is screaming for some homeowner home improvement.

The completed area of the kitchen shows the payoff from four projects in this book: kitchen sink (Chapter 18), countertop (Chapter 19), kitchen storage (Chapter 20), and cabinet face (Chapter 21). Still to come: finishing the area to the right.

Your Skills and Your Project

Do you have the skills and tools for a given project? It's sometimes hard to know, because home work crosses boundaries. You work on some drywall, and suddenly you need to do some electrical work. You do some plumbing, and suddenly you're hauling out the drywall tools. You plan on some painting, then realize you need to repair walls or molding first.

If, after reading the relevant parts of this book, you're still foggy about what's required, read books focused on a particular topic, or talk with capable friends. Better yet, volunteer to help friends who know what they're doing on their projects. You'll learn buckets, and they'll get the benefit of a willing helper.

Spending Time, Spending Money

It's hard to anticipate the cost of any project. You may try to estimate the price of the major materials and incidentals, then multiply by two or three. You may come in under budget, but you are just as likely to spend more.

The same goes for time: Think about how many hours a project should require, then multiply that by two or three. After all, a memory lapse in the store will entail a return trip for those forgotten screws. A wiring snafu can set you back hours, as you, for example, move an electrical box to a better location. But here's a different way to think about time. You're learning something new—a skill that will pay back on the next project. And building, like other skilled work, can be fun!

The kitchen and the dining area now harmonize, courtesy of the cabinets described in Chapter 16 and the crown molding in Chapter 33.

A Matter of Temperament

Home improvement is not for everyone, and I'm not thinking only about physical strength or even building skill. I'm talking about disposition. Can you think ahead? Can you plan? Can you handle frustration? All of these are prerequisites for staying sane while doing your own improvements.

You'll need to plan the steps, the materials, the time, and the design. What materials, colors, and textures would look best in this particular room? How wide should the molding be? Although design questions are often overlooked in home-improvement books, they can be the most important—and rewarding—questions of all. That's why I've introduced many projects with some notes on design.

What about frustration? In books, tools never break. You never run out of wood or have to change plans because the spousal unit turned thumbs-down to your brilliant, half-finished design. You never have to clean up at the end

of the day and haul the tools back out in the morning. But all these frustrations are part of real-world home improvement.

Can you improvise? Ask anybody who does remodeling: Walls hide surprises, and the older the house, the more you may need to implement solutions to those surprises. In describing each project, I've discussed common issues you may confront, but given the huge range of construction details found in homes, there is no way I could cover them all. You may indeed need to learn some improvising skills.

The living room got a boost from three projects: the ceiling light (Chapter 27), crown molding (Chapter 33), and mantelpiece (Chapter 34).

Is This Project for You?

After you read a particular chapter in this book, answer the following questions to help you decide whether that project is right for you—and you are right for it:

◆ Are you good at solving problems in this field?

◆ Do you own—or can you borrow or rent—the necessary tools?

◆ Can you do the work alone? Will help be available if needed?

◆ How soon must the project be finished?

◆ Will bad weather hold you up?

◆ How much of your house will be out of commission?

A Family Affair

Think your project won't disrupt your family? Decommissioning a spare room, even a living room, is one thing, but placing the kitchen or the only bathroom off-limits can be tough on the kinfolk, particularly those who thrive on neatness and routine.

Home work is inevitably a family affair, and I promise to squelch my social advice after offering one suggestion: Keep the lines of communication open. Make sure your family knows—and, if necessary, approves—your plans. Don't schedule a major project the week before the in-laws arrive, or the day before your significant other has to finish a major project at work.

Building Codes and Your Project

It's hard to generalize about building codes, since localities make their own changes to the various standard codes, and there are three that apply in the United States. Others cover natural gas, electricity, plumbing, and heating, ventilating, air conditioning. You may need a building permit for a significant change, but not for a simple replacement. Thus you're usually okay putting in a new door, since that is replacing an existing feature. But you might need a permit to cut in a new door or window.

Only a local building inspector can tell you if your plans are permissible, if a licensed contractor must do the work, and if you need a building permit.

This living room benefited from two projects: molding replacement (Chapter 32) and a fresh coat of paint (Chapter 31).

A Few Final Thoughts

First, don't drive yourself to distraction. If you are a perfectionist, you might do better to hire a premium home-improvement contractor (and then hope you don't find an apprentice or a slacker working on your job). As you complete a project, learn to say, "It's perfect enough," or "That's the best I can do, and that makes it just fine."

Second, doing it yourself is all about control. You control the design, the schedule, the materials, the overall effect of the project. While some books stress saving money, I'm more interested in the satisfaction of making your own designs, and then carrying them out.

Want to do something unconventional? Want to break the rules?

It's your house. And once you learn to improve it, it will be, in all senses, even more *your* house.

In This Chapter

- ◆ Must-have tools
- ◆ Should-have tools
- ◆ Dream tools

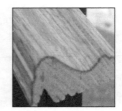

Your Tools

There are two categories of homeowners. Those who think the telephone is the ultimate home-improvement tool, and the rest of us. Some in the latter category, however, think it's possible to do home improvements with a few dull, outdated tools. Others (meet your author) believe any excuse to buy a tool is a good excuse.

I'm not sure whether you want to minimize or maximize your tool collection, so I've grouped tools in three categories: those you need, those you would do well to have, and some highlights of the boundless "I-want-'em" group.

Why is it better to own more tools? Because unforeseeable problems arise in the middle of a job, and you can solve most of these with the right tool. Recently, for example, I was fitting some molding against a cabinet face. It wasn't exactly a standard thing to do, but it wasn't a real oddball situation, either. I dragged out my belt sander, and in two minutes, angled the molding face. Having the right tool converted an awkward transition into an unnoticeable one, and did so quickly.

Although cost savings may not be your primary motivation for doing your own home improvements, those savings are real. I would advise investing some of that saving in tools. You'll get a double pay-off: Having the right tool for a project makes it faster, more accurate, and just *more fun*. And next time you need that tool, you won't have to buy or borrow it.

Must-Have Tools

You can't get by without some basic hand and power tools.

Hand Tools

Hand tools are still the starting point for home improvement work. If you keep these tools in the tool bucket, you should be able to complete an improvement without incessant tool-fetchit trips:

◆ Claw hammer

◆ ⅜" reversible, variable-speed, cordless drill

◆ Assortment of drill bits and screwdriver bits, in small bag

◆ Assorted screwdrivers

◆ Locking and needle-nose pliers

This bucket-style toolbag stays open, so the tools are always ready to work.

◆ Nailset

◆ Pencils

◆ Compass (a.k.a. divider, used for scribing)

◆ Torpedo level

◆ Utility knife

◆ Hand plane

◆ Wood chisel

◆ Margin trowel

◆ Magnetic stud finder

◆ Wire stripper-cutter

◆ Circuit tester

◆ Tape measure

◆ Small square

◆ A small container of screws and nails

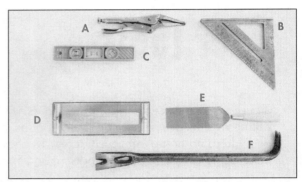

These obscure tools are fiendishly handy for home improvements.

A. Needle-nose locking pliers replace wire cutters, pliers, and locking pliers.

B. A small aluminum or plastic square guides a circular saw for a 90° cut. It's also handy for marking right angles and other angles.

C. A torpedo level can level or plumb electric boxes, shelves, pictures, and cabinets.

D. A sanding block grabs the sandpaper far better than a block of wood.

E. A mason's margin trowel is perfect for drywall and plaster work. I use mine to scrape paint and other crud, glaze windows, mix mortar, pry off molding, and protect walls from a prybar.

F. This rigid, hexagonal prybar disassembles stuff neatly because the flat tongue slips under the wood. And when you hammer it, it doesn't spring back.

Electric Drill

Your first power tool should be a ⅜", variable-speed, reversing drill. A drill makes holes in wood, metal, even tile, but it's equally useful for driving screws. Don't assume you need a battery drill; they are handy, but heavier and more expensive.

Clamps

Clamps may seem humdrum and optional, but it ain't so, Jo (or Joe). You need clamps almost any time you're gluing. They are also handy for holding pieces while nailing or screwing, and for stabilizing wood while sawing, drilling, sanding, or routing. See the discussion of the merits of various clamps in Chapter 16.

Jigsaw

Jigsaws are made to cut curves, but they will cut straight with a sharp blade. I use mine for cutting wood and drywall.

Jigsaws are handy and versatile.

Should-Have Tools

This large category of second-echelon tools is growing every year, as toolmakers probe our desires and whet our appetite for their unending inventions. Still, a few of these tools will make your work faster and more satisfying.

Power Miter Box

A power miter box makes accurate crosscuts and miter (angled) cuts. For more money, miter boxes also cut bevels or wider boards. If you plan to cut molding, pay a bit more for accuracy.

Fran insisted we unplug the power miter box before she touched it. Otherwise, she'd be wearing goggles and ear protectors.

Circular Saw

A circular saw makes crosscuts or rip cuts, and is especially handy for cutting plywood.

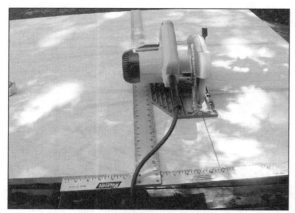

A square clamped to the plywood improves accuracy with a circular saw.

Orbital Sander

Orbital sanders make fast work of finishing wood. Not only are they less likely to gouge than a belt sander, they're also cheaper and lighter.

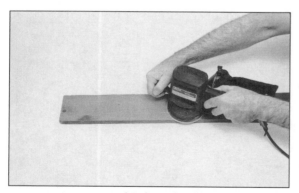

Orbital sander.

Dream Tools

Here we enter dangerous territory, at least for we toolophiles. I selected from the land of tool desire according to how often I used these tools to produce this book.

Plate Joiner

A plate joiner is a specialized tool that cuts slots for plates, commonly called "biscuits." It's handy for cabinetry, miter joints in molding, and repairs.

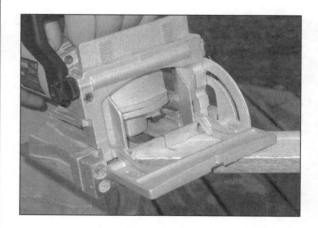

A plate joiner (top) makes a biscuit joint (bottom).

Table Saw

A table saw is best for rip-sawing, and handy for working on plywood, cabinetry, and general carpentry.

Table saw.

Power Planer

A power planer removes thin layers of wood. It's handy for fitting doors, smoothing saw cuts, making shims, and trimming edges to fit.

A power planer trims a door.

Router

A router shapes the edges and faces of boards, and is used in almost all our cabinets and shelving projects. A basic router will work fine; plan to buy a bit for each shape you want to cut. In the photo I'm using a router with a cove bit to make a half-round groove in the front of a cabinet door.

Router.

In This Chapter

- ◆ A working shop
- ◆ Storage solutions
- ◆ Time-saving tips

    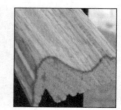 

Your Workshop

A workshop is a useful—but not exactly essential—part of home improvement. In truth, most of your work will occur on site: You can't build an archway in your basement or garage, and then tack it to the walls.

So your workshop can be plain or ornate, as long as it satisfies three basic functions: storing the junk you need so you can find it when you need it, giving you a place to work efficiently, and offering plenty of light and electrical outlets.

A Working Shop

Basements and garages are both candidates for the workshop location. A basement is warm, but may have too little air circulation for dusty projects or work with toxic chemicals, and may not be accessible for large projects. The garage may be hot in summer, cold in winter, and liable to usurpation by motor vehicles. Still, it's better than the basement for painting, sanding, noisy work, and large projects.

Whatever location you choose, the need for fast-in, fast-out access dictates the iron rule of organization—everything gets a place.

Workbench

The workbench should have a surface at least 2' deep and 6' wide. Don't buy a workbench—make one from 2 × 4s and ¾" plywood or an old door. Prevent sway with diagonal bracing or by fastening the workbench to the wall.

Get a vise to hold tools while you sharpen them, and to hold other objects while drilling, sawing, or filing.

Electrical Matters

You can't have too much light. Fluorescent lights are a cheap source of unbeatable no-shadow illumination. To save time, wire several lights to one switch.

Nor can you have too many electric outlets. Place an outlet every 4' along the wall behind the workbench, and double-check the grounding system.

Storage Solutions

The main reason to fuss with storage is because nobody likes searching for stuff. In the interest of saving money, I've suggested some low-rent storage solutions. But whatever you use, make it logical, make it handy, make it accessible—and use it.

This organizer set me back about $5. With more than a dozen fasteners at hand, I usually have what I need.

Can you use these kinds of storage?

Item	Storage Suggestion
Power tools	Cases, open shelves, or hooks.
Hand tools	Pegboard (see Chapter 17), toolbag or bucket, drawers, nails, or hooks for squares, levels, etc.
Clamps	Hanging on pegboard, beefy nails, or lag screws.
Health and safety	A closed box. (Store masks and equipment respirators in plastic bags.)
Extension cords	Nails or hooks. Coil the cord, wrap the last 3' around the hank, and tuck the end through the loops.
Fasteners	Cans, original packaging, narrow shelves, or plastic containers.

Narrow shelves are perfect for storing fasteners. Face the label out for fast action.

Time-Saving Tips

Because home improvements always seem to take too long, I always think about how I can save time. Here are some tips I've found helpful:

◆ Store tools intelligently. Use the kind of ready-to-go toolkit described in Chapter 2. Keep other tools in their places, where you can find them.

◆ Use labels. I keep a stack of adhesive mailing labels and a marker in the workshop, near some empty containers.

◆ To avoid extra trips to the store, keep extra, half-broken, and didn't-fit parts on hand. Buy extra hardware—it's usually cheaper than another trip to the store.

◆ Bring a list to the store so you don't forget anything.

◆ Know what you're doing—by reading this and other books, and by talking with people who should know. *The Complete Idiot's Guide to Home Repair and Maintenance Illustrated* (see Appendix B) offers valuable advice on maintenance and repair.

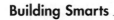

Building Smarts _____

When you buy a new tool, don't just throw the manual under the workbench. A file or folder will keep the manuals in good condition—where you can actually find them.

A tool belt will speed up your project, and is worth its weight for preventing stooping.

◆ Do projects in logical sequence: all the demolition, all the framing, all the electrical, all the drywall, and all the painting. This reduces tool hauling and helps you focus.

In This Part

On the Walls

Most of what you see in your house is drywall or plaster. Even if you don't spend your days staring at the walls, it's hard to ignore a wall that has failed its duty to be flat, smooth, and innocuous. And if you have dark paneling, the fastest way to lighten the room is to drywall right over the top, as explained in Chapter 4.

In Chapter 5, I describe how to make a drywall arch. In Chapter 6, we'll build and drywall a stud wall in the basement, and I explain how to build a wall in an easier, above-grade room. If wood is what you want to see, explore the simple installation of wainscot in Chapter 7.

In This Chapter

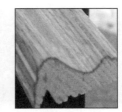

Chapter 4

Drywall an Existing Wall

It's handy to know how to use drywall when a wall has flubbed at its job of being flat, smooth, and paintable. It's also handy when you need to quickly and cheaply put a flat surface on a new stud wall. Drywalling is not something you'll do for entertainment, but it's an easy knack to learn, and a handy one to know.

In the photos in this chapter, we're hiding some primitive siding that a former owner (you reading, Pete?) once thought would make a good wall. His wife tells us the marriage almost foundered on this foolish obsession. We sided with Sue, and eventually decided to cover the funky siding with something more suave (or at least innocuous)—namely, drywall.

Step 1: Getting Started

First, assess your situation. If you're drywalling a new wall, add *nailers* (hunks of wood to hold your nails or screws) at inside corners to support both sides of corner joints.

Find the studs. (Drill through the existing wall if you have to.) Mark the center of the studs on the floor.

If you are fastening over ½" or thicker plywood, as in these photos, rescrew the plywood to the studs using 2" construction or drywall screws.

Building Smarts

Drywall is sold in sheets, 4' by 8', 9', or 10' and up. The 8' sheets are awkward enough; buy the larger sheets only if you are sure you can handle them. Drywall comes in three thicknesses:

- ⅜": Cheap, light, and fragile; it's suitable for covering a wall that's already in decent shape.
- ½": The standard drywall, used in most cases.
- ⅝": Premium stuff; quieter, heavier, and harder to handle.

Stripping Old Molding

To remove molding, pull off the top pieces, then the lower ones. Don't try to remove several pieces at once! If the molding doesn't budge, drive a few nails through the back with a nail punch, and then pry some more. You'll see photos showing how to remove door trim and baseboards in Chapter 32.

Dave's Don'ts

Drywalling is dusty work. To preserve domestic bliss, it's smart to protect your house and furnishings before you start. Tape plastic to within 1" of the wall.

After the molding is off, remove any old wall material that's higher than the wall surface.

Electrical Considerations

Switches and outlets can be a challenge. If the boxes seem to "float" in the wall, secure them according to the directions in Chapter 27.

Cut openings for electrical boxes in the new drywall, using either of these techniques:

- Measure the position and cut the drywall using a jigsaw or a hand drywall saw. (It's helpful to make the hole a hair larger than the box.)

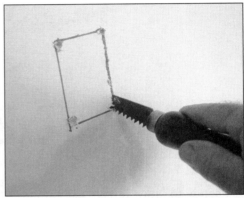

Hand drywall saws are one of the cheaper beauties on the tool rack. They leave less mess than a jigsaw or a RotoZip.

- Hold the sheet against the wall and trace the box outline with a RotoZip tool. (See Chapter 5 for details on using this tool.)

The front of electrical boxes should be no more than ¼" below the new wall surface. If any are deeper, slip in a box extender, making sure it does not touch wires.

This box extender increases box depth by ½", just enough for a new sheet of drywall.

Step 2: Cutting Drywall

With the prep work done, the pace should start to pick up. Hang panels horizontally or vertically, following these guidelines:

◆ Minimize the number of joints.

◆ Place vertical joints at the center of studs.

◆ Avoid joints at the top corners of windows or doors. Try to place a sheet surrounding the opening, in the form of an upside-down *U*.

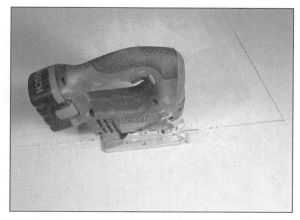

A jigsaw is great for cutting inside corners, as shown by the pencil line. A hand wood saw does a fine job of cutting drywall, if you use enough support to avoid breakage.

A sharp utility knife cuts one side of the drywall. (It's easiest to use a couple of strokes.) Fold the piece away from you and cut the far side. That handy guide is called a *drywall square*.

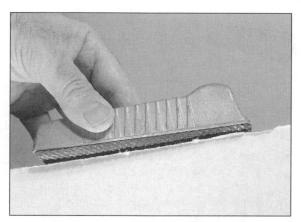

This *rasp* (rough-cutting file) smoothes cuts in drywall. If pieces are too tight, rasping the edges may save recutting.

Step 3: Hanging Rock (Fastening Drywall)

Once you have a few pieces cut, you'll start hanging rock—as drywallers call the fastening stage. Most people use screws, but traditionalists can still find phosphate-coated, rust-resistant drywall nails. Make a small dimple with the last hammer stroke, pushing the nail head below the surface.

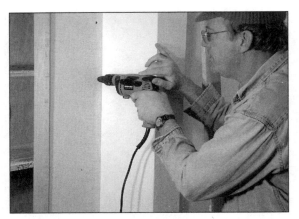

Take it from John: A *drywall screw gun* is ideal for hanging rock. These guns can be set to drive screws at any depth you want. A variable speed drill will work, but it's harder to control depth. For a big job, consider renting a screw gun.

Building Smarts

Drywall nails are tricky to use and almost obsolete. Screws hold the drywall tighter to the studs but cause less damage to nearby walls. Buy screws that bite ¾" into the studs—deeper is not better. Hide screws if you can: Place the bottom row under the baseboard. Screws around doors and windows can be hidden by the *casing*, the molding around an opening. The only trick with screws is to set them below the surface, but not deep enough to damage the panel. This is almost foolproof with a screw gun; it takes some practice with a variable-speed drill. Make sure to press the panel against the stud while screwing. Ideal screw locations are as follows:

◆ 12" apart on every ceiling joist

◆ 16" apart on every stud

◆ About ½" from panel edges

When screwing a corner, take account of the drywall on the adjacent wall. To hit the stud, this screw must be 1¼" from the corner.

When the sheets are in place, attach the *corner bead*, the L-shaped plastic used to cover outside corners.

Tack the corner bead in place. (We're using nails because their heads lie flatter than screws in this location.) When the bead is straight and slightly above the adjacent surfaces, pound the nails home.

Step 4: The Taping Ceremony

Before you tape the joints, attend to a couple of details:

1. Check that all screw and nail heads are below the surface by sliding a taping knife over the screw heads.

2. Fill any extra-deep areas with setting-type joint compound. This *mud*—the generic name for mortar and plaster compounds—fills deep areas better than standard drywall joint compound, and also sets faster.

Now it's time to tape. Drywall tape helps hide the joints between panels. You can buy paper or fiberglass tape. You place fiberglass tape directly on a dry joint. You embed paper tape in a fresh layer of joint compound, and then cover it with another layer of compound.

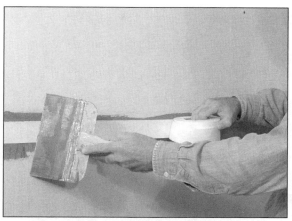

Quickly press the tape into the seam.

Lay a second coat of compound on the tape while the first coat is wet, smoothing the tape as you go.

Corners are a bit more difficult, especially inside corners. Work from the corner toward the flat sections, and take your time. A corner trowel is essential for inside corners.

Lay paper tape in fresh joint compound: Trowel a layer of compound along a seam.

Tape an inside corner much like a flat joint. First, place mud in the corner with a 4" knife. Then spread the mud with a corner trowel. Fold paper tape and use the corner trowel to press it into the mud. Don't try to get a perfect joint on the first coat.

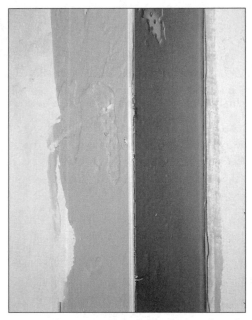

An outside corner after the first coat of mud. Although you can still see the perforations in the corner bead, the major holes are filled. That's the job of the first coat.

Use a small taping knife (4" model shown) to fill screw holes. Return for a second coat after the compound shrinks.

With the first coat of mud in place, let everything dry overnight.

Step 5: Finishing the Job

After the first coat has dried, scrape the ridges with a drywall knife. Sand other high spots with a drywall sanding screen. Use a dust mask and good floor covering at this dusty stage.

Drywall sanding screens won't clog with drywall dust, so they will work much longer than sandpaper.

After the high spots are leveled, apply a second coat of joint compound on the remaining voids.

This wide *drywall knife*—drywall trowel—is ideal for applying second and third coats of joint compound.

You'll probably need a third coat of drywall mud, but it should be thinner, easier to apply, and faster to dry. After the third coat, spackling, such as Patch 'n Paint, is ideal for filling any low spots.

Building Smarts

To make flaws jump out, hold a portable light near the wall. When your wall is smooth enough to pass this test, it will look perfect in ordinary light.

When the wall is dry, prime and paint, as described in Chapter 31, then restore the molding, as described in Chapter 32.

In This Chapter

Chapter 5

Build an Archway

Home fashions come and home fashions go, but ever since the Romans, arches have always been in style. Although drywall is flat as a frying pan, you can shape it into an arch—bend it to your will, if you will, using some tricks of the trade.

But first you must prepare an opening. Whether you're fixing an ugly arch or putting an arch in a doorway, the same techniques apply. If you're simply drywalling a wall that already has an arch, skip ahead to Step 6: Drywalling Over an Existing Arch.

The "before" shot. Shame on the carpenters who built the front arch without bothering to match the rear one! We're going to tear out and rebuild the front arch to match its more graceful neighbor.

Step 1: Making the Pattern

You have two choices in making a pattern: Either copy an existing arch, or make a new shape. In either case, make a half pattern, and then use it on both sides. That ensures that both sides are symmetrical.

Copying an Existing Arch

Board stiffener   Cardboard pattern   Clamp

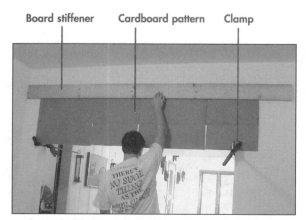

Alex is holding cardboard, stapled to a wood stiffener, across the archway we'll duplicate. To hold the pattern level, I measured up from the floor to find the starting point (arrows), and then traced the arch on the cardboard.

Drawing a New Pattern

If you don't have an arch to duplicate, draw the shape freehand or with homemade drawing tools, following these suggestions:

◆ Draw long-radius curves with a home-made compass. Tie a pencil to a string, have a helper stand on the other end of the string, and draw an arc. (Although few arches are fully circular, the arcs of a circle are helpful drawing guides.)

◆ Sketch lightly on cardboard until you find a curve you like.

◆ Cut the rough pattern (use a jigsaw, if you have one), hold it in place, and eyeball the shape.

Step 2: Demolition Derby

To prepare an interior doorway for an arch, first remove the door and *jambs*, the wood surrounding the door. Then remove trim, drywall, or plaster to expose the *framing* (the 2 × 4 or 2 × 6 structure). You'll find hints on removing trim in Chapter 32.

On a drywall or plaster corner, like the one in the photos, cut and remove the *corner bead* (the metal or plastic angle piece capping the corner).

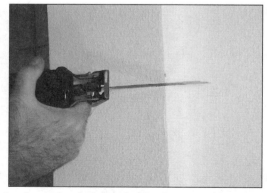

Cut the corner bead with a hacksaw or this recipro-cating saw, which should have a fine-toothed, metal-cutting blade.

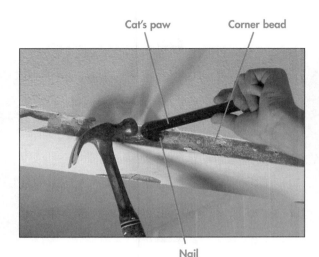

Pull the nails or screws fastening the corner bead. This "cat's paw" removes nails without harming the surroundings. Although we didn't use gloves to protect against cuts, that would be smart. Protect your eyes during demolition.

Measure up from the floor to the bottom of the arch (marked with arrows in the previous photo) and remove the drywall or plaster above that point.

Dave's Don'ts

Make every effort to minimize damage during demolition. Don't loosen, crack, or gouge any more wall than necessary. Work slowly. Cut around anything you remove so the wall surface breaks cleanly. You'll probably have some damage to repair, but less is definitely more.

Remove drywall around the opening, leaving a smooth, rectangular cutout.

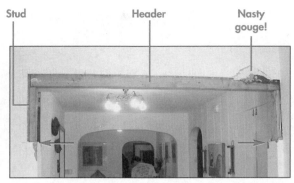

The *header*—that beam across the top of the opening—and studs are exposed after we removed corner beads and loose drywall. The arch starts at arrows, at the same height used while making the pattern. We'll fill that nasty gouge with patching compound.

Step 3: Making the Forms

My dictionary didn't include a good word for the plywood pieces that form the arch, so I will call them forms. Using the pattern, mark four arch forms on ¾" plywood or *OSB* (*oriented strand board*), which is a cheaper replacement for plywood.

Building Smarts

If the drywall is nailed directly to the studs, the forms will be the same size as the pattern. Each form will have one right angle and two pointy ends. If the wall surface is more than 1¼" thick, the forms will be nailed to the face of the studs, and the forms will be larger than the pattern, as shown in the following drawing. If the wall is even thicker than that, you may have to shim behind the forms.

A jigsaw makes short work of cutting forms. This is ¾" OSB, but ¾" plywood works equally well.

Step 4: Positioning and Attaching the Forms

Positioning the forms may be the most important part of this whole process. It is *critical* to place the forms one drywall thickness (usually ½") behind the finished wall surface.

If your drywall is fastened directly to the studs, the face of the form goes flush with the studs. For a 2 × 4 wall, you can achieve this by attaching a 2" *nailer* (piece added to hold nails) to the studs and the header. Taper the bottom of the nailer so that it doesn't push out the bottom of the arch. Then screw the forms to the nailer.

Now that you've chosen the form location, attach them:

1. Screw each form in place. Place a 2" construction screw every 4 to 6 inches.

2. Screw existing drywall near the joints.

3. Screw the 1 × 4 and 2 × 4 blocking into position. The blocking will support the curved drywall strip on the bottom of the arch.

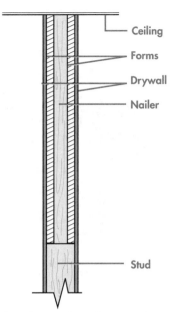

A 2" nailer and ¾" forms place the new drywall flush with existing drywall—on a standard wall.

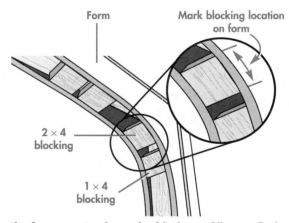

The forms are in place. The *blocking*—filler—is flush to the edge of the forms. Mark the blocking on the form to simplify nailing the drywall. Notice that to place the drywall at the correct level, I nailed the form to the edge of the stud. This was an unusually thick wall.

Step 5: Cutting and Attaching the Drywall

By now, you should be able to smell victory! If you've worked carefully, the drywall stage should be a snap. Just follow these steps:

1. Cut a strip of drywall for the underside of the arch, ¼" narrower than the width between the form faces. Dampen the back so the drywall can bend.

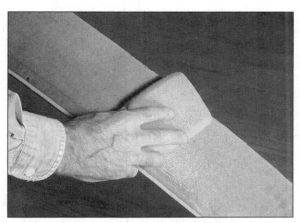

Wet the back of the drywall, wait half an hour, and then gradually bend it.

2. In tight curves, make parallel cuts on the back of the drywall, then fold it into place.

3. Starting at the bottom, push this strip tight against the forms and screw into place.

4. Mark the center of the arch. Hold a rectangle of drywall against one side of the arch, touching the center mark. From the back, mark the arch shape on the drywall.

5. With the drywall marked, cut the arch profile. Repeat for the other three forms.

Waste   Arch

A jigsaw makes short work of curves, but a hand drywall saw would suffice.

6. Screw each piece of drywall in place. If the existing wall is loose around the edges, screw it as well.

Nail this flexible corner bead every 4 inches or so. Smooth any imperfections that appear while you are nailing.

7. Nail flexible corner bead along both faces. Nails lie flatter than screws. Use rust-resistant, phosphate-coated drywall nails.

8. Make sure all nails or screws are below the surface. Run a trowel wherever you see fasteners. Drive raised fasteners deeper, and remove loose ones.

To finish the drywalling, skip down to Step 7: Finishing Up.

Step 6: Drywalling over an Existing Arch

You may need to cut an arch shape in drywall while drywalling an existing wall. If you have a rotary tool like a RotoZip, you can cut the drywall in place. Otherwise, have a helper hold drywall against the arch, mark the arch, and remove it while you cut it. (The general steps for drywalling an existing wall are covered in Chapter 4.)

Cutting with a Saw

To mark the drywall and cut with a saw, follow these steps:

1. Place the sheet of drywall in its final location. Try to span the entire arch with one sheet.
2. Have a helper hold the sheet against the wall, and mark the curve from behind. Then remove the sheet, support it carefully, and cut with a jigsaw or a hand drywall saw. Return the sheet to position and fasten.

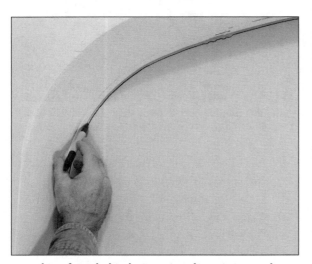

Working from behind, I'm using the existing arch to mark the drywall.

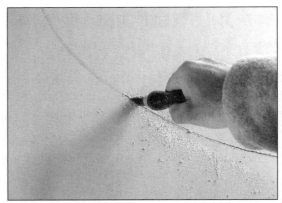

This drywall saw cuts curves and openings for electrical boxes.

Cutting with a Rotary Tool

The second way to cut an arch is slicker and faster—but only if you have a rotary cutting tool like a RotoZip. To use a rotary tool, follow these steps:

1. Mark a spot just inside the arch on the new drywall.
2. Screw the sheet in place.
3. Install a "guide point" bit. (These follow the shape of whatever is behind the new drywall.)
4. Adjust the cutting depth.

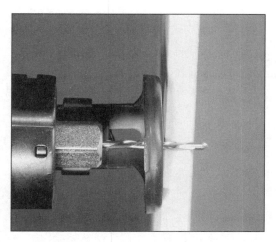

Set the rotary tool so it will poke ¼" through the new drywall.

5. Place a corner of the rotary tool at the mark from step 1. Start the tool and rotate it until the base lies flat on the drywall.

6. Move sideways until you feel the arch, and then follow the arch to make the cut.

The rotary tool follows the arch behind it.

Dave's Don'ts

The RotoZip is handy, but the dust will fly right through most vacuums (trust me on this one). Without a vacuum, much of the dust will fall to the floor for easy cleanup. Don't forget to wear ear and eye protection when operating a rotary tool.

7. After the cut, leave the sheet fastened to the wall.

Nail the flexible corner bead first to the underside of the arch, and then to the flat wall. If you use rigid corner bead on the flat stretch below the arch, make a smooth transition between the corner beads.

Step 7: Finishing Up

At this point, all you have to do is to finish the drywall. This process is explained thoroughly in Chapter 4.

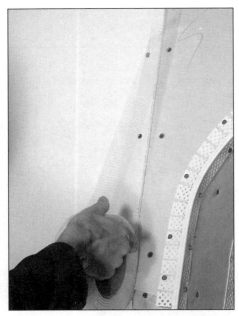

Easy-to-use, self-stick fiberglass tape bridges the joints. For small gaps, apply tape under patching material. Patch larger gaps first with quick-setting compound. After it dries, apply the tape.

I use two different patching compounds for most drywall work. Powdered, setting-type joint compound fills deep areas and sets quickly. Keep it below the final surface. Use normal drywall joint compound to smooth the wall.

I'm filling the underside of the arch with quick-setting compound. Half an hour later, I can trowel on drywall compound. Sanding and more drywall compound will blend this arch with the wall.

Fill the valley by troweling between the corner bead and the existing wall.

After a bit of a mess and a lot of careful marking and cutting, the reward is an arch that matches the prototype. It's an arch that looks as old as Rome.

In This Chapter

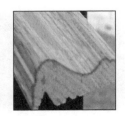

Chapter 6

Build a Stud Wall and Fasten Drywall

If good fences make good neighbors, good walls make good rooms. Stud walls—usually built of 2 × 4s—are the standard way to build home walls. Builders usually build walls flat on the floor, and then tilt them up into position. But existing homes usually don't have enough room, so it's necessary to build walls in place.

In this chapter, we'll show how to build a light-duty stud wall in place, piece by piece. And just to make things interesting, we'll build that wall in a heavily lived-in basement, where we confront the typical nightmares of basement construction: fastening to concrete, avoiding obstacles, and finding a way to build a straight wall more or less where it's wanted.

Step 1: Planning and Layout

You already have a general idea where you *want* to place the wall. Now let's get a realistic idea of where you *can* place it.

In this chapter, we describe a simple interior wall construction. While some of these methods apply to all walls, do not rely on these instructions if …

◆ The wall will be bearing significant weight. A *bearing wall* would need doubled top plates and stronger headers over doors or windows, among other things.

◆ The wall is on the exterior, either in the basement or above-grade. These walls face all sorts of insulation and moisture-barrier requirements that are too complicated for us to handle here.

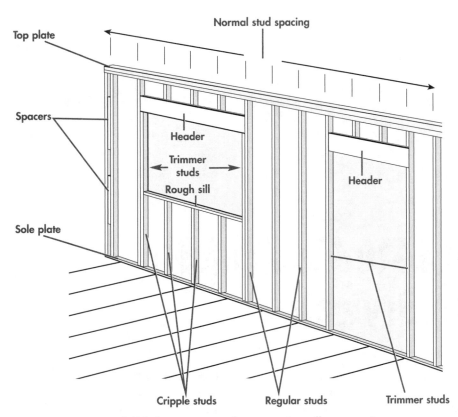

Top plate

Normal stud spacing

Spacers

Header

Trimmer studs

Rough sill

Header

Sole plate

Cripple studs   Regular studs   Trimmer studs

A little jargon goes a long way in wall construction.

Your decisions about wall placement depend on whether you plan to build in the basement or on a wood floor.

Building Smarts

A 4' level is handy in this project, but it won't reach from floor to ceiling. Instead of springing for a super-long level, hold a shorter level against a straight 2 × 4 to *plumb* from floor to ceiling.

In the Basement

Try to place walls that run parallel to the *joists*—framing under a floor—directly under a joist. Otherwise, build a bridge of 2 × 4 between the joists, and screw the *top plate* to it, as shown in later photos.

Walls that cross joists can be screwed to the joists—if you can reach them. If pipes or ducts block your way, piece in the top plate, and build the wall around the obstacles. As we'll see later, in really crowded circumstances, you may not need a top plate.

Obstacles are the key problem in basements. In newer houses, the ceiling may be fairly clear, but in older places, ducts, pipes, wires, and who knows what else can interfere with placing the top plate. In our example, we decided to attach blocking—spacers—to the joist, and then attach the top plate under the blocking. By dropping the top plate, spacers can make it easy to fasten a dropped ceiling, if you choose to install one.

Basement Posts

Posts, and the beams they support, offer a great location for a wall. If the posts are wood, use them as studs. If the posts are metal, attach a stud to one or both sides with 3/8" carriage bolts spaced 2' apart. If the post (either metal or wood) is more than 3-1/2" across and you plan to drywall both sides, shim one side of the studs. Use 3/4" × 1-1/2" furring strips or scraps of wood or plywood.

The beam above a post makes a perfect support for the top plate. You may even be able to skip the top plate and toe screw the studs to the beam. Place the face of the studs flush to the beam, then run the drywall up the side of the beam.

In the Rest of the House

The picture changes considerably when you're building on a wood floor. If the *walls run perpendicular to the joists*, screw the sole plate to the floor joists, and the top plate to the ceiling joists. (Don't know where the joists are? See the sidebar.)

Building Smarts

To build a wall, you need to know where the joists are, and which direction they run. Normally, joists run in the same direction on every floor of the house, so look first in the basement. Joists usually run across the shorter dimension of a room. If there's a center beam in the basement, the joists run perpendicular to it.

To secure the plates on *walls that parallel the joists*, follow these suggestions:

◆ Sole plate: Lag bolt the sole plate to a joist directly below. If you are not over a joist, screw the sole plate to the subflooring, as described later in this chapter.

◆ Top plate: Lag bolt the top plate to a joist directly above it. If you are not under a joist, use the blocking technique described later in this chapter. Place one blocking 6" in from the corners and then every 4' along the top plate.

Attach the new wall to studs in the existing walls if possible. Otherwise, add a blocking at the center of the stud. Remove the drywall between the studs adjacent to the new wall location, screw a block of 2 × 4 between the studs (keep the face flush to the studs), and replace the drywall.

Starting the Layout

Start the wall layout from a reference wall, such as an exterior wall, which was used to lay out the house. Measure at two places to locate a line parallel to the reference wall. Use a 3-4-5 (or 6-8-10) triangle to place a wall square to the reference wall. Don't be shy about checking your layout—pencil marks are easier to move than anchor bolts!

First wall is parallel to reference wall   **Second wall is square to first wall**

We measured from our first wall to draw a triangle 3' on one side, 4' on the second, and 5' at the hypotenuse. A "3-4-5 triangle" acts like a big square for accurate layout.

Locate corners and doorways (see the diagram later in the chapter to see how to arrange studs at corners). Corner construction varies depending on whether the walls will get drywall on one or two faces. Wherever you want drywall, give it something to nail to—drywall can't just hang in the breeze!

Use a chalk line, a long board, or a string to mark the walls on the floor. Remove any baseboard or other molding that will interfere with the wall, using the techniques described in Chapter 32.

Step 2: Fastening the Sole Plates

Start the wall with the sole plates—the flat 2 × 4s that support the bottom of the wall.

Building Smarts

In a bare, unobstructed room, you may be able to build the wall on the floor and then tilt it into place. Building "tilt-up" fashion is faster than the "stick-built" approach described here, because you can nail through the plates into the studs. Make a tilt-up wall ½" shorter than the ceiling, so it has room to tilt into place. After tilting, attach the sole plate to the floor, as described later in this chapter. Slip cedar or plywood shims in the gap at the top, and then fasten the top plate.

Sole Plates on Concrete

It's no fun fastening to concrete—unless you rent a rotary hammer. These brutes pound their way through concrete with so much verve that you don't even need to lean on them. Our rented drill made ½" holes in a minute apiece, so a four-hour rental should buy a lot of fastening, if you lay out the walls in advance.

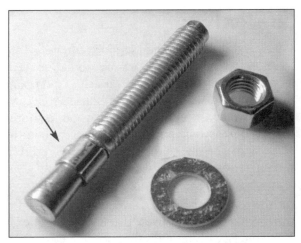

These ½" × 3¾" wedge-type anchors grab like crazy in a ½" hole. That slip ring (arrow) seizes the concrete when you tighten the nut.

Locate anchors about 2' apart on the sole plates, and about 8" from the ends. Plan ahead: don't put anchors under the stud locations. Read on for suggestions on stud placement.

This rented rotary hammer drilled right through the sole plate into the concrete. The rod (arrow) gauges when you've drilled deep enough. Insert an anchor before starting the next hole so the sole plate doesn't wander.

Before you return the rotary hammer, use it to fasten any studs to concrete walls. Two anchors should be plenty if a stud is fastened to the plates at top and bottom. On concrete-block walls, drill into the block, not the mortar.

A healthy whack places the anchors. These wedge-type anchors aren't threaded to the end, so Maureen won't wreck any threads with this Neanderthal routine.

An adjustable wrench tightens the anchors. The corner studs will not go on top of this anchor because only the closer side will get drywall. If dry-walling both sides, place the anchor 2" further from the corner. *X* marks the spot for another anchor.

Sole Plates on Wood

If the sole plates will cross the joists, find the joists and screw a $\frac{5}{16}$" × 4" lag bolt into every other joist. As before, avoid future stud locations when placing the lag bolts. If necessary, countersink the bolt head to avoid obstructing a stud.

If a nonbearing wall runs parallel but between the joists, it's probably safe to screw the sole plate to the subfloor. Drill $\frac{3}{16}$" holes in the sole plates, about 1' apart, in a zigzag pattern. Drill the first hole 1" from one edge of the sole plate, and the next 1" from the other edge, and so on. Then drive 3" deck or construction screws into the floor. (Depending on the floor construction, you may have to drill a small pilot hole in the floor first.) Lots of smaller screws make a stronger attachment to subfloor than a few lag bolts.

Step 3: Attaching the Top Plate

With the sole plates in place, plumb upward with a straight board and a level to locate the top plate. In the basement we worked in, the top plate was the toughest part, due to a spaghetti of conduit, pipes, and ducts.

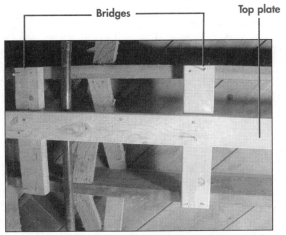

To run a wall parallel to the joists, but not directly underneath a joist, screw a 2 × 4 *bridge* every 2' to 3' to the joists. Screw the top plate to the bridges.

If you have no pipes at the ceiling, screw the bridge between the joists rather than under them.

We opted to build the wall directly below a joist, so we didn't bother with bridges. To allow clearance for pipes and conduit, we screwed blocks of 2 × 4 to the joist, and then attached the top plate to the blocks.

Blocking Maneuver

While placing blocking at the ceiling was the key to this basement wall, the job called for some monkeying around, and the use of 4½" lag bolts. You may have to loosen some pipe clamps to move pipes closer to the ceiling. Although this sounds hazardous, most long sections of pipe have some flexibility once you disconnect the straps.

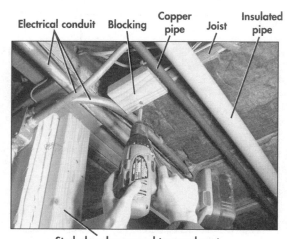

Electrical conduit   Blocking   Copper pipe   Joist   Insulated pipe

Stud already screwed to wood post

With 2½" screws, we're attaching blocking under the joist to make room for all these obstructions.

With the blocking in place, attach the top plate beneath it with lag bolts. To prepare for ⁵⁄₁₆" × 4½" lag bolts, use two long drill bits: drill a ⁵⁄₁₆" hole through the top plate and blocking, and a ¼" hole in the joist. Lag bolts have a reputation for being tough customers, but the threads only need to grab in the joist, not the blocking or plate. The ⁵⁄₁₆" hole lets the bolt slip through the blocking and top plate while grabbing only the joist.

This socket wrench makes fast work of the lag bolts. Don't overtighten, or you'll break the bolt or strip the hole!

Even the blocking did not prevent this curvy electrical conduit from bumping against the top plate, so we gouged the top plate with a saw and a chisel. Improvising comes with the territory when you're building a basement wall!

The pipe slips through the blocking, and the top plate gives a flat attachment for the studs.

Step 4: Laying the Studs

Positioning the plates is the hard part; the work gets easier as we start fastening the studs. Place one stud at each wall (they should already be in place against concrete walls) and one at the edge of each doorway.

Normally, studs are placed 16" O.C. (on center), which leaves 14½" gaps between studs. But if you start a stud against an adjoining wall, the first stud should not be 16" O.C. Otherwise, the center of the fourth stud will be 48¾" from the adjoining wall—too wide for a 48" sheet of drywall. You may be able to skirt this problem by running the drywall sheets horizontally. See the drawing for spacing of studs near a corner, and make sure you have studs at all drywall joints.

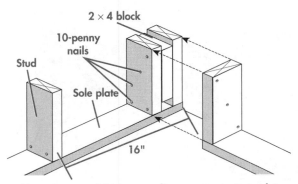

Use spacers and extra studs at a corner, to make good support for the drywall.

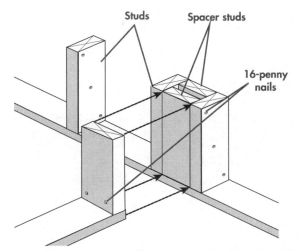

Tee intersections must include nailing surfaces for the finish walls.

Marking the Layout

Now that you've figured out where each stud will go, mark the stud locations on the sole plate.

A 4' level checks for plumb. If the top plate is plumb above the sole plate, check only for side-to-side plumbness.

Fascinating Fastening

If you will tilt the wall up, nail through the plates into the studs. (The nails will be vertical when the wall is placed.)

This hammer, with its monstrous, patterned head, is perfect for driving hefty nails.

If you will build the wall in place, there are three options for fastening studs to a sole plate or top plate:

If the plates are already in position, attach the studs using one of the following three methods:

1. *Toenailing.* This is a traditional, but difficult, method. Start the nail at almost 90° to the stud, and then start driving steeply toward the plate. Use two 8-penny nails on each side of the stud. (Don't nail on the faces that will get drywalled.)

Temporary spacer

A 14½" temporary spacer of 2 × 4 holds the stud against its neighbor as we toenail. Pros would call this cheating. I call it smart!

2. *Toe screw.* Drill a pilot hole and drive three 2½" screws in the sides of the studs.

Duct   Block   Clamp

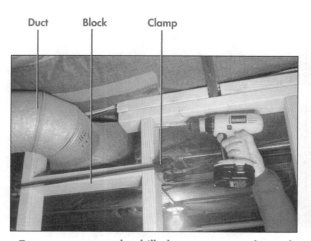

To toe screw, start the drill almost square to the stud. Once the hole is started, drill steeply toward the top plate. A clamp holds the stud during nailing; the block will hold the end of the drywall sheet.

3. *Truss plates.* These sheet-metal plates, sold in endless sizes and shapes, are conveniently covered with nail holes. They may seem like another Tenenbaum cheat, but truss plates are stronger than toe-nailing, call for less skill, and can be attached in impossibly tight quarters. Attach the truss plates with special 1½" nails sold for the purpose. No need to fill all those holes: Four nails on each side of the joint (eight per plate) is plenty. Buy flat, 3" × 5" truss plates. If you don't need them flat, bend them into an L shape.

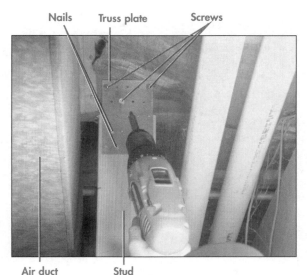

A truss plate attaches a stud to a sole plate. We toe-nailed the second stud at this doorway, because the nails would be farther from the end of the sole plate, and less likely to split it.

In a basement, you may run into places where you can't even place a top plate. If the wall runs perpendicular to the ceiling joists, attach each stud to a joist using a truss plate.

In these tight quarters, there's no room to toenail, but in the gap between a heating duct and the furnace's air supply, you can attach a stud. Use 1½" screws in tough-to-reach spots like this.

With the studs in place, nail up headers over the doorways. For these nonbearing walls, two 2 × 4s placed flat should work fine. On a bearing wall, the header would rest on a shorter stud.

After nailing through the stud into the header, we'll double up the stud.

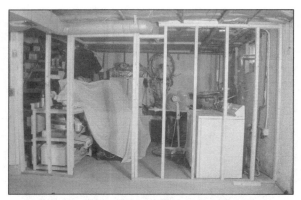

Finally, the studs and header are in place, and it's time to ponder the drywall dilemma.

Screwdriving Made Simple

It's sheer idiocy to do home improvement without power-driven screws. Strong, less destructive than nails, and *removable when you screw up,* screws have revolutionized home work. But driving big screws with a variable-speed drill can be a tough knack to learn. Try these tips:

◆ Frank T's trick: Drag the screw through a bar of damp hand soap. A bit of grease makes all the difference.

Hand soap: It's for screws, not just screwball kids!

◆ Drill a pilot hole most of the way through the joint.

◆ Drill a bigger hole through the outer board—screw threads only need to grab the *substrate*—the wood behind whatever you're fastening.

◆ Don't try to grab more than 1½" of sub-strate. Longer screws take too much work!

◆ Use screws that fit a square screwdriver bit, which gets a better grab than a Philips bit.

◆ Use a new screwdriver bit, and make sure it's the right size.

◆ If your power screwdriver starts to slip, immediately stop. Reverse the drill and pull the screw out a bit before driving it back in.

◆ If the screw head gets mangled, replace the screw before it gets stuck.

◆ Use plenty of pressure on the drill. Driving big screws is not a one-handed job.

◆ Don't overdrive the screw. Get ready to release the trigger just before the screw is home.

Step 5: Drywalling Season

I've already described how to drywall a less-obstructed room in Chapter 4, which covers the basics of cutting, fitting, and attaching drywall. A basement is more difficult, due to those obstructions. If you have pipes against the ceiling, as we did, end the drywall just below the pipes instead of making endless cutouts.

Building Smarts

If your basement is damp, consider using the moisture-resistant drywall sold for bathrooms.

To cut drywall around complicated obstructions, make a cardboard pattern. When the pattern fits, mark the drywall from it.

Pattern goes this far from edge of sheet

The tape measure tells me how far from the edge of the drywall I must place the pattern for this duct cutout.

A jigsaw makes a great cutter for curves, as around this round duct.

With an unseen helper, Maureen the Drywall Queen is muscling a sheet of drywall into place. Good thing only one sheet needed this degree of cutting and fitting!

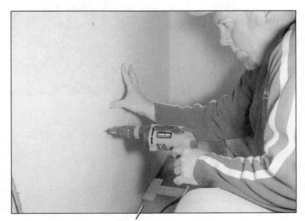

Shims

Tom finally gets to work! Notice the ½" plywood shims that hoist the drywall off the floor—necessary in a basement, but not above grade.

A slick drywall trick: Fasten an oversize piece in position, then cut it off at a doorway (shown) or a corner. Guide the utility knife along the stud.

To match drywall against an irregular surface, use a trick called *scribing.* Hold the drywall vertical, place the pencil in the notch and drag it *and* the cardboard along the irregular edge. After we cut at the line, the sheet will slide left toward the post. Then will we cut the right-hand edge.

It may not be art, but it's a step in the right direction. With some taping and mudding, this wall will go to work hiding the washing machine and blocking its roar.

From here, read Chapter 4 for information on finishing drywall. For information on hanging a prehung door in that doorway, see Chapter 9. Chapters 31 and 32 explain how to paint a room and install molding.

In This Chapter

- Step 1: Layout and prep made easy
- Step 2: Getting support: Meet the nailers
- Step 3: Nails, anybody?
- Step 4: Finishing the job

Chapter 7

Wainscot a Wall

Wainscot is a traditional wall dress-up. Although it's often used in dining rooms, in this chapter we used it to enliven a drab bathroom. The only unusual things about our installation were the desire to keep the wood dry, and to preserve a course of tiles along the bottom of the wall.

You can buy bogus "wainscot" in large panels, but it looks as fake as it is. We used the real stuff: ¼"-thick oak boards with a decorative bead down the center. Each board covers 3⅛" of wall. An overlap along one edge covers the joint.

Because wainscot can shrink with time, stain or paint all board faces beforehand so that the area revealed by shrinkage will resemble the face. Manufacturers recommend that you put sealer on the back to stabilize the boards, but because we didn't seal the front, we saw no reason to seal the back.

Step 1: Layout and Prep Made Easy

Unlike many home improvements, this one won't be consumed by hours of preparation. You just need to mark the top of the wainscot and cut the starting board.

Mark the Top Line

Mark the top of the wainscot and nailer—the board you'll nail the wainscot to. If you will not finish the bottom with baseboard, measure 32"—one wainscot length—up from the lowest point of the floor. If you will use baseboard, measure up 32" from the highest point on the floor. (The baseboard will cover gaps below the short boards.)

Mark a level line through your mark, across the whole wall. The wainscot and the nailer, described shortly, will both touch this line.

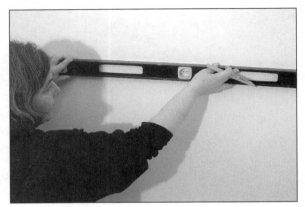

Laurel is marking a level line for the top.

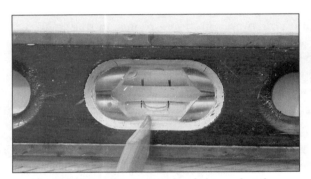

The bubble on this "spirit" level shows that the right side is slightly high. We'll adjust the level before marking.

Cut the Starting Board

To avoid having an extremely narrow last board, divide the length of the wall by the width of a board. Compare the remainder to the width of the wainscot. If the last board would be too short, follow these steps:

1. Add the remainder just calculated to the width of a whole board.

2. Divide by 2 to get the width of the first board.

For example, if you're using $3\frac{1}{8}$" wainscot, and the last board calculates to $1\frac{1}{4}$":

$$3\frac{1}{8}" + 1\frac{1}{4}" = 4\frac{3}{8}"$$

$$4\frac{3}{8}" / 2 = 2\frac{3}{16}" \text{ (width of first board)}$$

Point the first underlap away from the corner so the overlap on the new boards covers each joint.

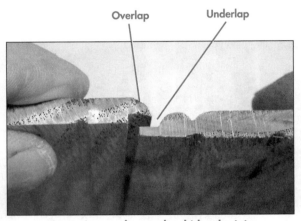

On wainscot, the overlap hides the joint.

Ideally you'll start in the straightest, most visible, corner. If that corner is crooked or not vertical, *scribe* the starting piece:

1. Hold the board vertical, touching the corner.

2. Measure the biggest gap between the board and the wall.

3. Set a divider ("compass") to this measurement.

4. Hold the divider horizontal and "scribe" down the wall.

5. Cut this line with a jigsaw, and then fit the board against the wall.

Building Smarts

Scribing is handy for adjusting ideal things that you're building with (like new wainscot) to the non-ideal things they should meet (like your house). Hold the board in the correct orientation (that is, vertical), measure how far it must move to reach the desired location, set the divider to that length, and scribe the cutting line.

Step 2: Getting Support: Meet the Nailers

Unfortunately, you can't nail wainscot to drywall or plaster without a nailer, such as 1 × 4. Instead, to hold the wainscot closer to the wall, we used ½"-thick strips of recycled hardwood molding, although 6" strips of ½" plywood would also work.

To find the studs for attaching the nailer, don't be afraid to drill through the plaster—after all, you'll be hiding the holes!

Countersink the screw heads flush to the nailer so the wainscot lies flat. Screw the top nailer to the studs, using screws that get at least 1" of "purchase," or grab, on the stud. We used 2" screws (½" nailer + ½" drywall + 1" purchase = 2").

If the baseboard is the same thickness as the top nailer, baseboard can serve as the bottom nailer. Remove the base shoe and nail the bottom of the wainscot to the baseboard. Otherwise, remove the baseboard and screw the bottom nailer to the studs, as before.

Because this wainscot was in a bathroom, we stopped it ½" above the floor, to keep the wood dry. Although that's unconventional, the gap is hardly noticeable.

Screw a nailer to the studs, using one screw per stud. Nails are weaker and harmful to the wall.

Step 3: Nails, Anybody?

The preliminaries are over, and it's time to nail the wainscot. These suggestions will help get it right:

- To prevent the hammer from slipping off the nail heads, clean the hammer face with sandpaper.
- Attach the wainscot with 1" panel nails. They have rings for a good grip, and if you choose the right color, they will almost disappear on the finished wall.
- Pre-drill holes in hardwood wainscot.
- Don't try to hide nails by nailing through the underlap: This risks splitting.
- Place the upper nails about 1½" from the top, where they will be covered by the chair rail (the top molding).

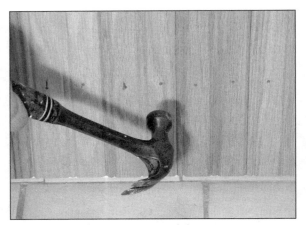

Easy does it as you nail the wainscot.

Cut the last board by scribing: Hold the board vertical and place it against the corner. Measure the overlap on the next-to-last board. Set the divider to this dimension, scribe the last board, and cut with a jigsaw.

Step 4: Finishing the Job

With the wainscot in place, turn your attention to molding. We used a variety called chair rail to finish off the wainscot. First we fastened a $\frac{1}{4}" \times \frac{3}{4}"$ hardwood spacer to cover the ends of the wainscot.

The Spacing Game

The hardwood spacer will be visible behind the chair rail, so you've got to place it perfectly level. (It goes just above the original line used to locate the nailer.)

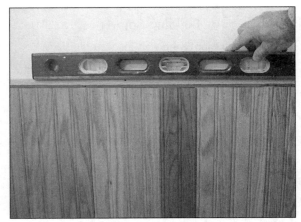

As you level the spacer, don't worry if it doesn't touch the wainscot everywhere—the chair rail will cover the gap.

Because the spacer will be covered, we attached it with 2½" screws, countersunk so the chair rail will rest tight against the spacer. If you don't have this nifty countersink bit, use a large, regular drill bit to make room for the screw head. Then drill a smaller hole for the screw shank.

Fastening the Chair Rail

With the spacer in place, fasten the chair rail flush to the top of the spacer. Make outside corners in the chair rail with outside miter joints. Cut both pieces at 45°. (To be safe, make them ⅛" long until you get the hang of these cuts.) You can see an example of an outside miter joint in Chapter 33.

An inside corner, as shown here, must be *coped*, or cut with a coping saw. Miter one end at 45°, with the front of the molding cut shorter than the back. Then cut down the new cut edge with a hand coping saw.

Cut along this edge

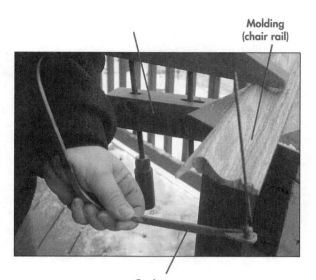

Molding (chair rail)

Coping saw

Angle the saw so the front of the board is slightly longer than the rear.

We miter cut this chair rail to prepare for the coping cut.

Building Smarts

Coping makes an inside corner joint that won't pull apart with time. Although it's easier than it sounds, it helps to practice on scrap wood. Coping is also useful for installing baseboard and crown molding.

Here's the chair rail after coping. Test fit it in the corner and adjust with a wood file if needed. When the joint fits, cut the other end to length.

A slight upward angle on the nail places the head flat on the sloping face of the molding. Place pairs of nails every 16 inches, preferably above the studs, where they will be easier to drive. Drill hardwood molding before nailing.

A nailset makes the finishing touch on any molding job.

A coped joint resembles an inside miter joint, but it won't pull apart!

Treated with a coat of Danish oil finish, the wainscot makes a beautiful wall, without screaming "look at me!"

In This Part

Part 3

Windows and Doors

You could solve a lot of problems by designing a house without windows or doors, but it's a gloomy prospect. When doors and windows have problems—and they always do—it may be time for replacement.

In some cases, the best choice is to install a new door in the existing jambs (Chapter 8). But when you're building a new wall, it's better to install a prehung door (Chapter 9). Combination storm-screen doors are a one-afternoon project, as Chapter 10 demonstrates. Finally, while it's tough to put in an entire window, Chapter 11 introduces a dandy, two-hour window replacement.

In This Chapter

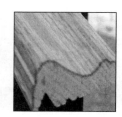

Chapter 8

Hang a Door in the Existing Jambs

Is your door doggone dragging? Splintered, saggy, unglued, butt-ugly, or a mismatch for other doors in your house? If you're determined to replace its miserable self, you have two options: Install a prehung door (a door already hinged to the *jambs*—the edgewise boards that frame the doorway—or hang a new door in the existing jambs.

Although prehung doors (see Chapter 9) are easier to hang, they require you to remove and replace the molding and the jambs. That's why it's often better to hang a new door in existing jambs, as described in this chapter. Remember, however, that "new" may not mean "fresh-from-the-box." You may be lucky enough to find a decent door on the curb, or at a salvage or resale shop. In fact, to match an older style, recycled may be your only option.

Step 1: Size Your Door

Door fitting is a tricky business. If your existing door is a good fit, use it as a template for the new door. Mark the face and top. Then remove the door and all hardware. Lay the new door on sawhorses, place the old door on top, and mark the outline—the face, top, and hinge side.

If the existing door is a poor fit—or absent—take a close look at the door opening. Ideally, the side jambs are plumb (vertical) and the sill and top jamb are level. To check, use a square or a level. (A jamb that's vertical must be square to a sill that's horizontal.)

The following procedure assumes that angle A is square; if a different corner is square, use it as a starting point.

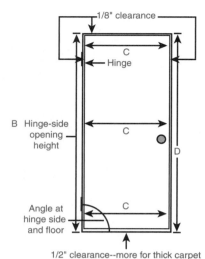

1/8" clearance

C
Hinge

B Hinge-side opening height
C

D

Angle at hinge side and floor
C

1/2" clearance--more for thick carpet

Analyzing door fit. Suggested clearances are for interior doors.

Follow these steps to mark and cut your door:

1. Measure the hinge-side opening height, B on the illustration. Subtract ⅝" for the top and bottom clearances to get the hinge-side door dimension (but see the following sidebar regarding bottom clearances). Measure from the door bottom and mark this height on the door's hinge side.

Building Smarts

The bottom clearance can present special problems. Carpet, or a badly sloped floor, can require a larger gap at the bottom. If the house has forced-air heating and cooling, but the room does not have a *supply* and a *return* duct, it's wise to leave 1' bottom clearance so air can circulate.

2. Measure across the top, middle, and bottom of the door opening, C. Subtract ¼" and use these measurements to cut the latch side. (If you are using a *hollow-core door*, see Chapter 16 for suggestions on cutting panels.) Set your circular saw for a

3° relief (or plane the edge after sawing). Don't remove too much wood—you can always replane the door.

3°

This subtle angle helps a door close smoothly.

3. Repeat on the latch side to get the latch-side height (D).

4. Check your measurements, and then saw the top and test the door fit. Use a plane to smooth your cuts and remove extra wood.

A hand plane will work along the sides of a door.

A power planer is the best tool for moderate door trimming, and is essential for planing end grain. Rent a planer if necessary.

Step 2: Mount the Hinges

When the door fits, fasten the hinges to the jamb. Use the existing hinge mortises if possible. Otherwise, locate the hinges to match other doors in the room, or use measurements from the following drawing. Mark the hinge location with a utility knife; it's more accurate than a pencil. If you must fill old hinge mortises (after changing the way a door opens, for example), consult *The Complete Idiot's Guide to Home Repair and Maintenance Illustrated* (see Appendix B).

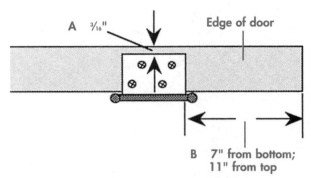

A   ³⁄₁₆"   Edge of door

B   7" from bottom;
     11" from top

If you don't want to use other doors in your room as a guide to hinge location, use these typical measurements.

To cut hinge mortises, use the technique for cutting a mortise for a door latch, shown later in this chapter.

To revive the stripped screw holes in old hinge mortises, try this old farmer's trick: Fill the holes with glue, stick in wooden matches, and break off the matches after the glue dries.

Hold the hinge plate in the mortise and dent the center of each screw hole with a nail so the drill centers in the hole. Drill pilot holes into these dents and fasten the hinge plates. If the attachment is weak, use 2½" screws, which grab the stud behind the jamb.

Dent the center of the screw hole so the drill will slip into position. Try to fasten the hinge perfectly vertical.

Step 3: Position and Attach the Door

Once the hinges are attached to the jamb, hold the door in position, using the cedar shims sold for mounting doors and windows. Use the top and bottom clearances from the above drawing—don't worry about side-to-side position yet. Carefully mark the location of each hinge on the door edge. Remove the door from the opening and chisel mortises on the edge. Affix the hinges and attach the door.

Cedar shims allow precise vertical placement of the door. A utility knife marks the hinge location.

Step 4: Install the Doorknob

To install a doorknob, you need a ⅞" bit, a 1½" bit, and a beefy drill. It may be cheaper to buy the hole saw shown in the following photos.

Tape the template supplied with the latch to the door. Bore in from the edge of the door with the ⅞" bit to about a 2" depth. Hold the bit square to the door.

With a ⅞" hole saw on a right-angle drill, I'm boring a hole for the latch mechanism. A big, battery-powered drill would also work.

Drill a 1½" hole for the doorknob assembly. When the bit starts to show through the far side, finish the hole from the other side to prevent splintering.

A 1½" hole saw cuts the hole for the doorknob assembly.

Slip the lock mechanism in the ⅞" hole and carefully trace its outline on the edge of the door. (Some mechanisms slip directly in the hole and need no chiseling.)

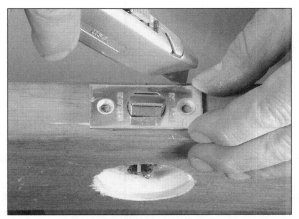

A utility knife beats a pencil for accuracy. Hold the latch plate straight on the door edge.

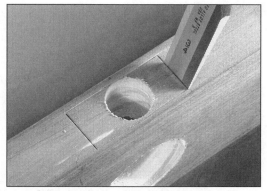

Carefully chisel along the line, deep enough to receive the latch plate.

Drill holes for the two screws holding the plate, using a nail or awl as before to center the drill. Screw the plate tight.

Assemble the mechanism per instructions, making sure the knob moves smoothly.

Put a blob of toothpaste or lipstick on the end of the latch, turn the knob, close the door, and release the knob to mark the jamb.

Carefully position the striker plate over the mark and outline the mortise with a utility knife. Chisel out a mortise for the plate, and then drill and chisel a deeper hole for the latch. Screw the plate into place and test the latch.

If the striker plate is accurately located, the door should latch perfectly. You may have to file a bit of metal off the striker plate to improve the alignment.

In This Chapter

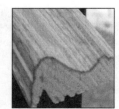

Chapter 9

Install a Prehung Door

A "prehung" door is sold attached to its jambs. Anybody who has hung a door to existing jambs (see Chapter 8) recognizes the miracle that is the prehung door. Instead of worrying about an error of $\frac{1}{16}$" here or $\frac{1}{8}$" there, prehung doors come perfectly fitted. Your main challenge is to avoid ruining that perfect alignment during installation.

Prehungs have one major limitation: You must remove and replace the casing molding on both sides of the doorway. Sometimes, like near the end of a remodeling project, there's no molding to remove. Sometimes, as with an exterior door, the advantages of a tight fit outweigh the molding work. One caution: Due to the many combinations of size, finish, and style, your particular door may well be a special-order item. Plan ahead.

Step 1: Prepare the Opening

Prehung doors are generally sold by the rough opening—the size of the hole in your wall, as described later. To measure the rough opening accurately, strip off the old door. Remove the trim (molding), as described in Chapter 32.

Remove the jambs starting from the bottom. Slip a prybar behind the jambs and pry against the stud. If the jamb is stuck behind some flooring, pry at the middle and saw through the jamb. Any damage to the nearby wall should be covered by trim.

This doorway has already lost the trim and jambs. After some inspection and repair, it will be ready for a prehung door.

Move level here to check that wall is plumb

Stud

Level

With a 4' level, I am checking that the stud is plumb. Next I will check if the stubby wall is plumb by moving the level as shown.

Although it's hard to enlarge an opening, it's easy to narrow or shorten one. Nail 2 × 4 spacers against the stud or header, and then nail the jambs to the spacers. Plan on some drywall repair when you cover these spacers at the end.

Step 2: Buy the Right Door

To buy a door, you need to know the swing and the size.

Swing Music

Which way should your door swing? Stand where the door should swing toward you. If the hinges should be on the left, you need a "hinge-left" door. If they should be on the right, you need a "hinge-right" door. Simple as that—so long as you're pulling the imaginary door toward you!

Check the Doorway

Place a long level (or a short level taped to a straight board) against the inside of the studs. If the studs are more than ¼" out of plumb, compensate by ordering a door for a smaller rough opening, as described in the next section.

Place the level against the wall, near the doorway, to check if the wall is plumb. It's hard to correct a wall that's tilted; but at least you'll understand why the door swings on its own!

Sizing the Door

Most interior doors are 1⅜" thick; exterior doors are usually 1¾" thick. The most common door size is 30" × 80"—2'6" × 6'8" in lumber jargon.

As I mentioned, more important than door size is rough opening size. To find the rough opening width, measure the narrowest point between the studs and subtract ½" for shims. To find the rough opening height, measure from the top (head) jamb to the floor and subtract ¼" for shims.

Measure wall thickness. If it's more than 4½",
order wider jambs or buy jamb *extenders* (narrow strips of wood you nail to the edge of the
jambs to make them flush with the wall).

You may find that a previous owner (like the
professor who once lived in this house) did
some carpentry-butchery. With the framing
exposed, it's easy to make repairs so the new
door can have a long, sturdy lifetime.

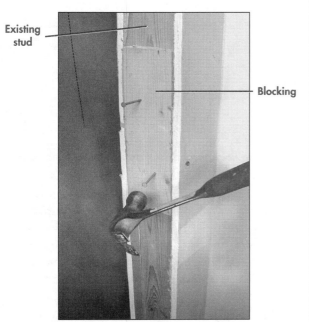

To strengthen the door jamb, we pried off scraps of
wood and nailed 2 × 4 blocking to the stud. A single
2 × 4 would be stronger, but harder to slip into place.

Step 3: Position and
Fasten the Jambs

Place the door assembly in the opening (with
the hinges where you want), and check that it
can sit plumb:

1. Check the gap between the jamb and the
   framing—ideally, it's about ¼" all around.

The gaps allow room for shims, which
will hold the door plumb. If the gap is
much larger, cut a hunk of plywood and
nail it behind your shims.

2. Check that the jambs are flush with (or at
   most ⅛" above) the drywall around the
   opening.

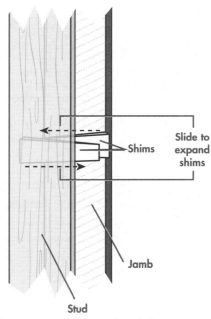

Pairs of shims precisely locate the jambs.

3. If the jambs are not flush, tack the jamb
   extenders mentioned earlier to the edge
   of the jambs. If that makes the jambs too
   wide, attach the jamb with the extenders
   flush to one wall, and hang the original
   jamb beyond the other wall, where you
   can plane it afterward. In this position,
   the plane won't hit a nail.

A level (or a straight piece of wood) checks that the door is flush in the opening. Do this often while positioning the door.

4. Check for at least ¼" bottom clearance when the jambs rest on the floor (but see sidebar).

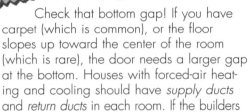

Building Smarts

Check that bottom gap! If you have carpet (which is common), or the floor slopes up toward the center of the room (which is rare), the door needs a larger gap at the bottom. Houses with forced-air heating and cooling should have *supply ducts* and *return ducts* in each room. If the builders cut the door bottoms short so air can circulate in the absence of a return duct, cut the new door to match the previous one.

5. With the jambs resting on the floor and flush to the walls, insert a pair of hinges between the jamb and the stud, behind the top hinge. Hold the level against the jamb, checking that it is plumb all the way to the floor. Check that the opposite jamb has room for shims.

6. Drill through the hinge jamb and *tack* through the shims with two 2½" finishing nails. (Keep the heads up in case you need to pull the nails.)

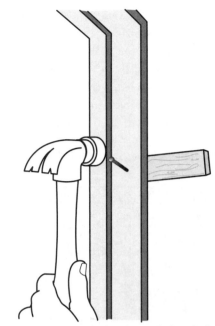

Drill two holes through the shims and tack the jamb into place.

Slide shims behind the center hinge. Move the shims in and out until the jamb is plumb, and tack through the shims. Repeat at bottom hinge, near the floor, and at the top of the hinge jamb. Keep checking that the jamb is plumb and flush to the walls. If necessary, pull the nails, adjust the shims, and readjust.

Check that the top jamb is level, and repeat the shimming-and-leveling ceremony on the opposite jamb. Again, start from the top and plumb downward with the level. While testing for plumbness before nailing, push the jamb tight against the shims and stud.

When all shims are tacked into place, check that …

◆ The door has equal gaps at the sides and top.

◆ The jambs are tight to the shims.

◆ The jambs are plumb and flush to the walls.

Now pound in the nails and set the heads.

A sharp utility knife (top) cuts the shims flush to the jambs. Cut halfway through and break the shim off. This thick shim may benefit from the tough love of a wood chisel (bottom).

Opening smoothly, closing with a satisfying "thunk," this door is set for years of easy operation. Maggie's pleased!

Step 4: Finish the Door

If your door is grazing the floor, remove the hinge pins, lay the door on sawhorses, and saw across the bottom, using a square or a piece of wood to guide the saw. To reduce splintering, score the door veneer exactly on the cut line with a utility knife before sawing.

The door may come predrilled for the doorknob and latch. Otherwise, see Chapter 8 for details on drilling and installing the hardware. To attach the molding, see Chapter 32.

In This Chapter

- ◆ Step 1: Choosing a storm door
- ◆ Step 2: Attachment theory
- ◆ Step 3: A little hardware and you're done!

Chapter **10**

Install a New Combination Storm-Screen Door

Storm doors may try to put on airs, but their basic job is simple: keeping out airs—and other annoyances, like mosquitoes. If your storm door is AWOL, bandaged with duct tape, or swinging in the breeze, attaching a new aluminum door is one of the simplest home improvements imaginable. You'll need an electric drill and a few hand tools; but unless the doorway is savaged or seriously out-of-square, it's a one-afternoon project, and a short one, at that.

Aluminum storm doors are sold hinged to an aluminum frame, painted white or whatever other color happens to be trendy. The door should come with instructions, which helps because you may have to adjust the following process to mount your particular door.

Step 1: Choosing a Storm Door

Durability, appearance, and a good seal are the three considerations in choosing a door. Although storm doors are pretty basic, you may have some choices, especially in the upper price ranges:

◆ Whether to buy a wooden-core door, which is stronger, quieter, and more costly

◆ Where the door will store the glass in summer

◆ Whether to spring for a spring-loaded, retractable screen, which will improve your winter view (but be another part to break down the line)

Recognizing that even duct tape won't hold his door together much longer, Johan gets ready to mount a new storm door. This beater is a hinge-right door.

Size is critical. Most doors fit an opening that is between 80" and 81", or 84" and 85" in height, by 32" or 36" wide. If you need a custom size, expect to spend a fortune, and to wait while your door is made. Also decide if you need a "hinge-right" or a "hinge-left" door—depending on where the hinge is when you pull the door toward you—in this case, when you're standing outside the house.

Almost all aluminum storm doors are surface-mounted, meant to be screwed to the outside face of the door opening (generally the jamb

edge, although this can vary). The beauty is that the door need not exactly fit the opening. The opening does need a flat surface, at least 1" wide, on the top and both sides of the opening, for the screws to grab. If the jambs are recessed, as shown in the diagram, the flat parts of the recesses must be at least 1" wide.

 Building Smarts _____

It's a rare doorway that is not marred by signs of old hinges or hardware. With the storm door removed, it's relatively easy to make repairs. To fill an old mortise for a hinge or a door latch, using a filler like Plastic Wood, and follow these steps:

1. Scrape and gouge to remove loose and protruding junk, and improve the filler's grip.
2. Apply enough filler to fill the bulk of the mortise. Don't worry about getting it level.
3. Briefly sand to make sure nothing builds above the final surface level.
4. Add more filler.
5. Sand with a sanding block or power sander to make everything flush.
6. Prime and paint.

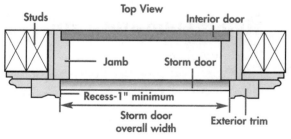

A slight recess is fine, if you have that critical 1" flat surface for mounting the door frame.

Measure the horizontal gap between the brick mold at three places, and the vertical gap from the brick mold to the threshold in two places. Bring these dimensions, and the hinge-left or hinge-right information, to the store when you buy your door. (It doesn't hurt to demonstrate what you mean, because a hinge-left door is not the same thing as a "left-hand" door.)

Step 2: Attachment Theory

With the door on hand, remove the storms and screens to lighten it. Now prepare the opening. Strip off any existing door and frame and check that the opening is square and plumb. Don't assume you're lucky enough to have such an opening—check with a level!

Hold the hinge-side frame in position and mark the height. The side frame should hold the top (head) frame close to the head jamb, with some clearance for vertical adjustment.

After removing the screws in the aluminum door frame, the old assembly should fall right off.

This door frame was sold oversize, so we followed instructions and cut the hinge side to fit. If your opening is regular, both side frames will be the same length.

Cut the side frame to length with a hacksaw. Cutting near the sawhorse reduces annoying vibration.

Position the hinge side and screw it to the jamb. Drill before the first few screws so the door doesn't move. Remove the glass and screen to reduce weight—and the chance of disaster!

Screw the hinge, which came mounted on the hinge-side frame on our door, to the door. With the door in place, screw your way across the top frame and down the latch side. Always check for an even gap between the frame and the door. Test that the door swings freely.

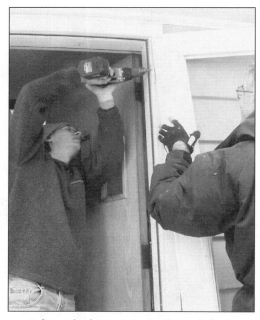

To reinforce the hinges, screw through the hinge side frame sideways. The screws in the front of the frame are already in place.

Slip the expander over the door bottom so the door will glide over the threshold while still sealing out the outdoors.

Step 3: A Little Hardware and You're Done!

With the door frame attached and the door moving freely, turn your attention to hardware, starting with the door latch. Tape the latch template to the door at a comfortable height *where it will not interfere with the doorknob.*

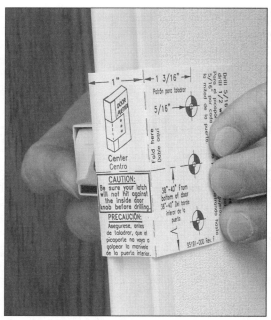

Tape the template to the edge of the door to locate three drill holes, marked by the bull's-eyes on the right. We don't know why, but Johan is holding the inside handle against the inside of the door.

The template is marked on both sides, because it's more accurate to drill from both sides. To prevent the drill from wandering, indent the door at the marks with a center punch or a big nail.

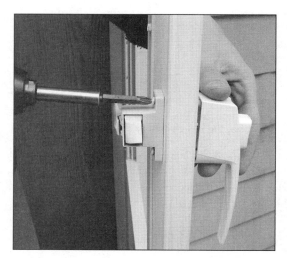

Stick the rectangular latch bar through the door to connect the inside and outside handles, and screw the latches together from inside.

Before mounting the striker, check that the shims push the striker out far enough to catch the latch. If the supplied shims are too thin, cut more from plywood or paneling.

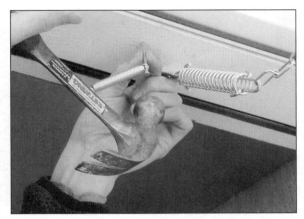

The safety chain prevents wind from ruining your new door. The spring prevents the safety chain from snagging your hair. Mount the spring so it retracts the chain; no tape measure needed!

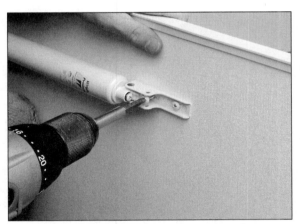

Screw the door closer bracket to the jamb, following instructions. Then screw the other bracket to the door. Put the closer in place, restore the glass and screens, and adjust the closer screw to control closing speed.

Now Johan's got a smile of accomplishment! The only loser in this deal is his natural gas company, which will be selling a lot less gas to this customer!

In This Chapter

- ◆ Step 1: Planning the installation
- ◆ Step 2: Delicious demolition
- ◆ Step 3: Puttin' it all together

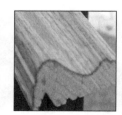

Install a Tilt-In Window in the Old Jambs

May we talk about your leaky, clanky, clunky double-hung windows? Windows are weak spots in many houses, especially the common double-hung variety—with sashes that slide vertically. Double-hungs that once were good have turned bad. Windows that started life with a quality disadvantage have only gotten worse.

Replacing windows can be a nightmare, if you have to replace the *jambs*—the frame around the window. More often, it's the moving parts, not the jambs, that have failed. If you've got good jambs, you can buy a kit to cure what ails your windows. You strip out the junk, install the kit, and renail or replace one small molding. Among many advantages: You don't touch the casing molding around the window, and you leave the storm window in place.

The Marvin Tilt-Pac kit I used in this chapter had insulated glass, a "tilt-in" feature allowing easy cleaning, and aluminum cladding on the outside to resist weathering. I installed the window in two hours, even though this was my first experience with these windows, and I was taking the photos seen here. Replacing the entire window would have been far more expensive, and could have taken five times as long.

Step 1: Planning the Installation

First of all, are your jambs in good shape? Is there rot, which usually starts at the bottom? Are the side jambs reasonably vertical? Are the sill and head (top) jamb reasonably horizontal? ("Reasonably" is hard to quantify, but let's say within ¼".)

If your jambs pass these tests, measure your windows. Each particular company may have its own instructions, but in general, you measure the width between the jambs, the height, and the sill angle. Marvin said to measure height on the inside, from the sill to the head (top) jamb.

Measure carefully. Measure again. Measure until your measurements agree. Then place your order. When I used this foolishly redundant but foolproof technique, the kit fit perfectly.

Use a sliding bevel to measure sill angle. The spacer is needed because the bevel could not touch the sill.

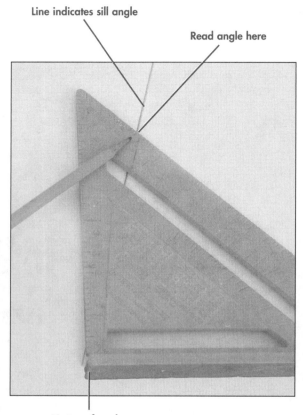

Transfer the angle from the sliding bevel to paper, then measure the angle with a plastic square. 14°, shown here, is standard.

Step 2: Delicious Demolition

Start by removing the outer stops, sash, and any hardware that would interfere with the new window.

 Building Smarts

Double-hung windows have their own lingo. *Sash* refers to the moving wooden frame that holds the glass. *Stops* are wooden molding that hold the sash in their channels. The *outer stop* holds the lower sash. The *parting stop* separates the two sashes. The *blind stop* is found behind the upper sash.

Remove the Outer Stops

After the replacement kit arrives, remove the moving parts of your window. Remove the outer stop gently if you plan to reuse it. If the molding refuses to move, drive some nails through with a nail set, and then pry as described here.

Margin trowel   Parting stop   Side jamb

Crowbar   Storm window frame

Once the parting stop is free at the bottom, add a crowbar to your arsenal. Pry against the inside of the jamb, not the outside, so your marks can be covered by the vinyl jamb liner.

Outer stop

To start removing the outer stop, slip in a margin trowel. Pry outward until a small crowbar fits behind the outer stop.

To reuse the outer stop, pull the nails through the back with locking pliers. (Hammering the nails from behind makes big divots in the face.)

Remove the Parting Stops

Pry out and discard the parting stops between the sashes. Hammer a trowel into the slot near one end and pry—the stop should be jammed, not fastened, into place. Remove the inner sash and any sash-lifting hardware. Remove the top parting stop.

Clean splinters and loose crud from the jambs. The demolition is done, and the window is ready for the replacement kit.

Step 3: Puttin' It All Together

Hard to believe, but half the job is done! Now you'll nail the jamb liner clips to the jambs, attach the vinyl jamb liners, and insert the sash in the liners.

Attach the Jamb Liners

Use 1" roofing nails to attach the jamb clips.

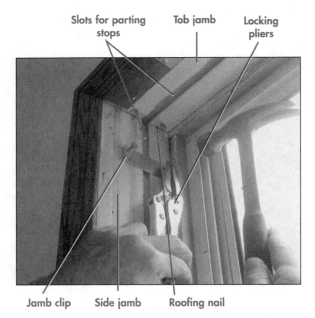

Slots for parting stops   Tob jamb   Locking pliers

Jamb clip   Side jamb   Roofing nail

I'm holding the nail in locking pliers as I nail a clip to the jamb. Pliers save fingers when driving short nails.

Now insert the vinyl jamb liners into the jamb liner clips. Note: The clips don't hold the liners tight to the jambs. The liners rest on foam that causes them to float ¼" above the jamb so you can compress the jamb liner to slip the sliding sash into the track.

Push the jamb liners against the jamb to engage the clips. This is the only tricky part of the installation—if the liner slips onto the wrong side of the clip, it won't engage.

Slip the new top jamb parting stop into the channel left by the old top jamb parting stop. Fasten with three small finishing nails.

Push the sash lifters toward the bottom of the jamb-liner tracks with a screwdriver. Then turn the screwdriver so the lifter will seize in the track.

Installing the Sash

It's payday on the window crew. Hold the sash upside down, and insert the pin on the inner sash into the track. With the pin above the lifting mechanism, push down to release the lifter.

Rotate the sash upward and press it into the track.

Upper sash in place

Exterior face   Sash pin engages lifter

With the sash upside down and inside out, slip the sash pins into the channel, above the lifting mechanism. Press down to engage the lifters.

Push the jamb liner back and press the window into its track.

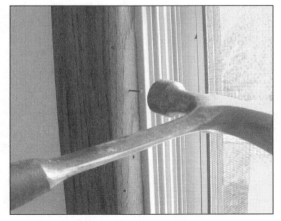

Renail the stops. Painless, eh?

In This Part

Part 4

Floors: Getting Underfoot

When the carpet wears out, do you march like a lemming to the carpet store instead of considering such options as solid hardwood, laminate, tile, or vinyl? Flooring scares many novice do-it-yourselfers, but it's usually a straightforward process, especially if your subfloor is sound.

If you are interested in affordability, vinyl (Chapter 14) and laminate (Chapter 12) are the best options. But even the premium materials—solid hardwood (Chapter 12) and tile (Chapter 13)—become affordable if you do the installation. Long after that "new" carpet is hauled to the curb, hardwood and tile will look as good as the day you installed them.

In This Chapter

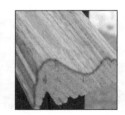

Install Wood Strip or Laminate Flooring

I'd imagine that ever since the invention of the sawmill, hardwood floors have been an essential part of homebuilding. Many houses built over the past couple of decades "feature" carpet over plywood or oriented strand board; when the carpet wears out, homeowners start thinking about something more durable, and hardwood flooring usually makes the short list.

In days of yore, unfinished "strip" flooring with tongue-and-groove edges (which hold the boards together and hide the nails) was your only choice. Now, however, you can buy tongue-and-groove prefinished. Although this stuff is extremely durable, there are fewer color options, and it's difficult to sand out high spots or damage during installation.

You'll also see a number of other ways to get a floor that looks like a traditional strip floor:

◆ **Engineered plank floor** is hardwood veneer on plywood. One key advantage is that the planks are more stable. With changes in humidity, strip flooring swells and shrinks, but this stuff is supposed to be so stable that at least one manufacturer says it can go directly over concrete. One disadvantage is durability: Whereas you can sand a strip floor several times, giving a half-century or more of wear, sanding can be risky over the thin veneer.

◆ **Longstrip flooring** is like engineered plank flooring, except each separate piece actually looks like several strips. The occasional joints across several strips are a dead giveaway that this is not strip flooring.

◆ **Laminate flooring** is a wood look-alike (more or less). A plastic film is printed with a wood pattern and glued to a backing. Quick to install, and said to be tough, it's not something you'd want to "fix" with a floor sander! But it does have major advantages in terms of easy installation. See Step 7: Laminate Flooring Installation at the end of this chapter for details.

Step 1: Preparing to Get Floored

Despite the many new wrinkles, we opted for a lesson in unfinished, ¾"-thick, 2¾" wide tongue-and-groove hardwood from two ace carpenters with TDS Custom Construction, Madison, Wisconsin.

The Substrate

Strip flooring requires a solid, flat base, at least ¾" plywood or oriented strand board. If you floor on top of this stuff, you can leave it alone, so long as adding ¾" of floor won't cause trouble with doors or room transitions. Caution: Older flooring often contained asbestos; it pays to get an asbestos test before ripping it out.

To check flatness, hold a 4' level or a straight 1 × 4 along the floor and look for spots that are more than ⅛" or so above or below the surroundings. Sand, chisel, or otherwise remove the high spots, and trowel on floor-leveling compound (made for tile preparation) on the low spots. You may have to scrape the floor if the room has recently been drywalled or has seen other major construction.

To check that the room is square and select the best starting point, see Chapter 13. Generally, it's smart to orient the boards parallel to the longest wall.

Floor Installation Basics

These suggestions will lead to a solid, tight, and attractive hardwood strip floor:

◆ To prevent sag, run the flooring perpendicular to the joists. If this is impossible and you have access to the underside of the floor, fasten 2 × 4 "blocking" between joists on 16" centers. This job is so time-consuming and likely to run afoul of ducts or pipes that you'll probably change your mind about the ideal direction for the flooring!

◆ Remove the baseboard and base shoe before starting (see Chapter 32 for details on this process). Base trim (baseboard and base shoe) can hide some flaws near the walls, but the room will look best if the base trim rests on good, flat flooring.

◆ Aim your nails into the joists. Draw lines or use a chalkline to mark the joists.

◆ A rented pneumatic flooring nailer, as shown in the photos, eases arm strain. You'll save money, but suffer more arm fatigue, by renting a manual nailer. Both nailers do the same thing in one stroke: Push the strip tight to its neighbor, and put the nail in a place where it will be hidden by the next strip.

◆ Allow flooring to adjust to your room conditions for a few days before starting. The flooring package should give details on the time required.

Step 2: The First Boards

Having chosen a starting point and assembled your tools, it's time to get some floor on the floor.

A Matter of Width

Before nailing the first board, divide the dimension across the room by the width of the flooring. If you would have a skinny closing strip—say less than 1"—it's best to ripsaw the starting strips first.

To give the starting and finishing boards the same width, calculate the width of the last board, add this amount to the width of a full board, and divide by 2. Assuming the last board would be $\frac{3}{4}$", here's the math:

$$\frac{3}{4}" + 2\frac{3}{4}" = 3\frac{1}{2}"$$
$$3\frac{1}{2}" / 2 = 1\frac{3}{4}" = \text{width of first and last board}$$

If the first wall is not straight, see the sidebar on scribing at the end of the chapter for a fast way to adjust the first board to fit.

Nailing Floor

Finally, the preparations are over. To make a starting line, measure one board width (either $2\frac{3}{4}$" or whatever you calculated for the starting board) from the wall and draw a line.

Measure one board width from the wall to find your starting line.

The chalkline marks the inside edge of the starting strip. Don't be tempted to snug the first strip against the wall—a string makes a straighter starting line.

It's critical to get the first line of boards right. If the wall bulges toward your string, move the line slightly to compensate.

Following the chalkline, Mike is nailing the first row of boards. If you don't have this kind of pneumatic nailer, drill holes and nail 2" finishing nails. I'd guess that in a few years Mike will wish he'd been wearing kneepads.

Step 3: Working Across the Floor

Work speeds up when you get away from the starting line. Craig and Mike were using a pneumatic (air-powered) floor nailer. You'll have to rent either a manual or pneumatic nailer. It's impossible to nail a floor right without one or the other: Nailers not only put the nail in the right place, they also snug the strips at the same time.

With a tap of his hammer, Mike is engaging the groove of the new board with the tongue of the previous one. Those loose boards are lying in the right orientation to make the job go faster.

Tight fit is critical. To slam a board into place, pound on a scrap of flooring; don't mash the flooring with your hammer. If it still won't fit, the board may be too warped to use whole, though you may be able to cut it and use part of it.

A chop saw cuts the last board in every row to length—⅛" less than the actual measurement to the end wall.

Before nailing, make sure every board is tight to its neighbor—you won't get a second chance. This mallet comes with a rented nailer; the rubber face whacks the pneumatic nailer (as you'll see in a later photo). The steel face snugs boards without damage.

Once Craig starts to use the floor nailer, the work speeds up. Even though this nailer is air-powered, it still needs a good whack to get a tight fit.

As you work your way across the room, measure to the far wall to make sure you're still parallel to it. When you no longer have room for the floor nailer, return to face nailing, taking extra care that the boards fit tight.

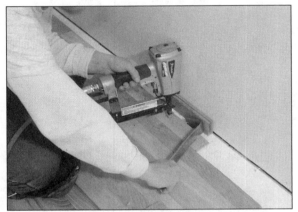

A flat prybar pushes against a block that protects the drywall to tighten this board for nailing.

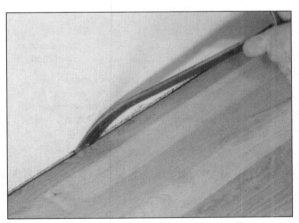

Craig cut this strip just wide enough to slip into place. Either leave a ¼" gap to the wall or trim off the bottom of one groove with a table saw or a chisel. Notice how tight the joints are?

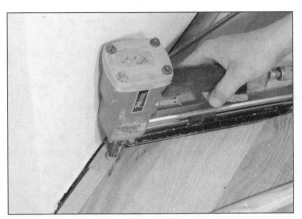

The finishing touch! The nailer sets the nails deep enough to leave room for wood filler. You can do the same thing with a nailset.

Step 4: So Your Room Isn't So Simple?

Up to now, we've floored a room without complications. But rooms tend to be connected to other rooms, and that makes matters more difficult. What do you do if the new floor …

◆ **Meets a carpet?** Place some extra padding—or a strip of ¼" plywood—under the edge to raise the carpet closer to floor level. Tack down a metal strip to hold the carpet.

◆ **Meets an existing strip floor?** The simplest, but least attractive, solution is to make a straight seam across the doorway. Consider using a *plate joiner*, a tool that cuts slots for plates that strengthen a joint, to make a strong glue joint between the new and old floors. But if the doorway is visually important—say a wide doorway that connects two rooms—you'll have to work harder. Remove a few boards from the finished floor by sawing down the center with a circular saw. Insert some new boards into the existing floor that are long enough to stretch into the new room. Use them to start the layout for the new room, using the same technique described below.

If the new floor turns a corner into an alcove or closet, how can you continue the pattern into the smaller room? By using one board from the pattern in the larger room to guide work in the smaller room.

Because this guide board will be in the center of the smaller room, you'll have to change direction so the board has, in effect, tongues on both sides. (You could say it will be speaking out of both sides of its mouth, but the point is that you can work the smaller room from the center toward the walls—opposite from the usual tactic.)

To change direction, place a spline—a rip-sawed piece of oak that fits the groove—into a board so it has two tongues.

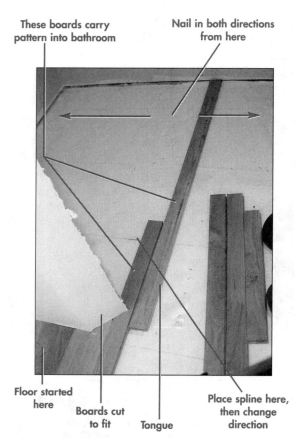

To carry a flooring pattern into an adjacent room, nail one or two boards across the transition. Slip a spline into the groove and change direction so the tongues face both directions. Now you can work toward both walls from these starting strips.

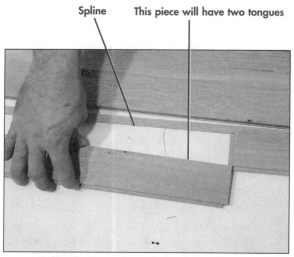

A spline lets you reverse direction to floor an adjacent room.

Step 5: Floor Sanding Made Simple

Unless you installed prefinished flooring, it's time to rent some floor-sanding equipment—or hire a floor finisher. The key hazard of sanding is gouging the floor, which usually happens when you lower a stationary sander with the drum rotating onto the floor. *Don't do this!*

(Photo by Essex Silver-Line Corporation)

A *drum sander* rotates a wide piece of sandpaper on the floor. This is your main tool, used everywhere except the edges.

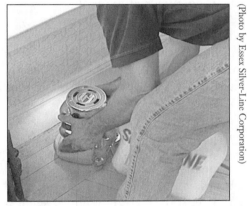

(Photo by Essex Silver-Line Corporation)

Sand the edges with a *disk sander,* a heavy-duty version of an orbital sander.

Use the drum sander to sand anywhere you can sand more or less parallel to the grain. Then work the edges with the disk sander.

Dave's Don'ts

Never put a running sander down unless it's moving across the floor—this leaves gouges.

Observe these *do's and don'ts* on floor sanding (see more details online at www.nofma.org/finishing.htm):

- ◆ *Do* protect yourself and the rest of the house from sawdust.
- ◆ *Do* move the sander at a steady pace across the floor.
- ◆ *Do* each pass twice—lift the sander as you reach the wall, start moving backward, and lower the sander. Move sideways (with the sander in the air) at the middle of the room.
- ◆ *Do* start with the least aggressive grit that will level and smooth the floor. 40 grit might be a good general starting point for a newly laid floor. Change sandpaper on both sanders in unison.
- ◆ *Do* work your way down through the grits—through 40, 60, and 100. If you skip too fast to finer grit, you won't remove marks left by the coarser paper.
- ◆ *Don't* let the abrasive get clogged—that can burn wood. Change sandpaper when needed.
- ◆ *Do* hold a light close to the floor to look for reflections from rough areas. These hidden blemishes may become painfully obvious after staining.
- ◆ *Do* scrape with a sharp chisel or wood scraper in the corners, where the disk sander won't reach.

Step 6: Finishing Up

The onerous task of sanding is followed by the more enjoyable process of staining and varnishing. To prevent damage, finish the floor as soon as the dust settles.

Stain is only necessary for esthetic reasons. Test stain colors on a scrap from the flooring, and if you don't like the premixed stains, ask a paint store to mix one for you.

Most do-it-yourselfers protect floors with polyurethane varnish, which comes in various levels of gloss. "Poly" is applied with a wide brush or a paint pad—a roller will leave hideous bubbles. Read the can before mucking around with any floor finish. In some cases, you must recoat within a certain period, or the finish will become too hard for the next coat of varnish to adhere.

Before starting, vacuum the room, including dust catchers like windowsills, and then wipe the floor with a rag dampened with mineral spirits.

After the first coat of varnish is dry, remove bubbles and dust by lightly hand-sanding with extra-fine sandpaper. Vacuum, tack-cloth, and recoat.

When using solvent-based varnish, use good ventilation; an organic solvent respirator is a smart move, especially in close quarters. The fumes—combined with the nasty solvent cleanup—are good reasons to consider water-based poly varnish. You may need more coats, but the varnish dries faster, so the finish traps less dust. Although waterborne finishes have less resistance to heat and chemicals than a solvent-based one, they are about equal in all-important scratch resistance.

Because many varnishes get stronger with age, hold off from walking on your beautiful new floor as long as possible.

Finally, reattach or replace base trim as described in Chapter 32, and you're done!

Strip flooring brings out the beauty in this kitchen.

Step 7: Laminate Flooring Installation

Laminate flooring is a fast, easy way to produce the look of wood, with major advantages in terms of a fast, almost tool-free installation (aside from a good carbide blade in your circular saw or miter box). We'll describe Armstrong's locking laminate floor, a material that can be applied over concrete (unlike traditional strip floor). Before buying any manufactured flooring, study the specifications about moisture conditions, subfloor construction, and installation details.

Armstrong's laminate, like other "floating" floors, is not attached to the underlayment, and it needs a ¼" gap on all sides (and near anything fixed, like a post or kitchen island) to allow for expansion. Unlike many products, however, this material needs no glue at the joints, saving a messy and time-consuming part of installation.

Getting Started

Find the starting point for the installation using the guidelines described for strip flooring. If the last board will be too narrow, cut the first board lengthwise. If the starting wall is irregular, mark and cut the edge of the first board by *scribing*, as described in the sidebar.

Building Smarts

Scribing is a trick for adjusting to the real world of irregular buildings. Hold the first board parallel to the starting wall, measure how far it must move to reach the desired location, set a divider (compass) to that length, and scribe the cutting line by dragging the divider along the wall and marking the board. The divider must be square to the wall while you mark.

Joining the Boards

Instead of gluing the joint, this locking floor has edges that simply lock together.

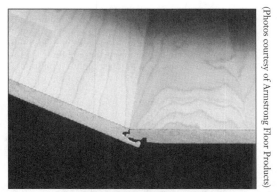

To lock a side joint, hold the new board angled up, engage the mechanism, and press down. The tongue is on the right board, the groove is on the left board.

Continue joining the boards. Pull boards from several cartons and inspect each before use. Test-fit an entire row before locking it into place. After locking each row, walk on the floor to press it down.

To engage the end joint, hold the new board at an angle. Lift the already-set boards, engage the side joint, and press down.

Finishing Up

The last board must be either ripsawed or scribed to width. In either case, be sure to remove an extra ¼" so the flooring does not jam against the wall.

When you're done, replace the base trim as described in Chapter 32.

Here's the finished joint. Notice the shims, used to create a ¼" gap at the wall.

In This Chapter

13

Lay a Ceramic Tile Floor

When it comes to flooring, tile is about as ancient—and attractive—as it gets. Nothing beats tile for a smooth, tough, carefree floor in a kitchen or bathroom, especially with such a wide array of ceramic and stone tiles on the market.

Ceramic, marble, and granite all make great floors. Although they are similar to work with, ultra-hard granite is the toughest to shape, and soft ceramic is the easiest. However, a rented tile saw, or wet saw, will cut any of these materials, so difficulty in cutting should not be a deciding factor in material selection. Price, however, may be; ceramic is at the bottom of the price heap, granite is at the top, and marble is midway in between.

Step 1: Preparing to Tile

Tiling, like its big brother, masonry, requires a unique frame of mind. It's a permanent material, and that means you must be wise in your choice of color, material, surface, and design. You have to work carefully and get it right the first time, because repairs are difficult if not impossible. Most importantly, you must let the mortar and grout set the pace. When they are hurrying to set, you have to hurry as well. When they are sluggish, you've gotta hit the brakes.

The choice of tile and grout is largely a matter of taste. Larger tiles are faster to lay and grout, but they may make a small room feel cramped. Tile size also affects joint width. Wide joints (say ¼") make sense with big tiles. Narrow joints can magnify tiny discrepancies in tile size or placement.

Dave's Don'ts

Tiling is hard on the knees. I highly recommend using kneepads to protect this useful anatomical joint. And use rubber gloves to protect your hands—mortar and grout will dry them out pronto!

Tile needs a firm base, the stronger the better. Ideally, your existing floor is 1¼"-thick plywood or oriented strand board, supported by joists placed on 16" centers—16" from center to center. To be on the safe side, I start by rescrewing the plywood to the joists with 2" construction screws, placed every 12" or so.

Cleaning Out the Old

Preparation starts by removing appliances, furniture, and molding (as described in Chapter 32 on molding replacement). Strip up any previous flooring that comes up relatively easily. If you can't strip securely glued flooring, lay the cement board onto lines of construction glue. The lines should be 8" apart, on top of each joist, and centered between the joists.

After some heavy peel-back work, this floor is ready for underlayment.

Cutting the Underlayment

Cement board, sold as WonderBoard and Ducock, is an excellent base for tile: rigid, waterproof, cheap, and flat. The only disadvantage: It instantly dulls knife blades. Stagger the joints so four corners don't meet, and place joints on top of the joists where possible.

Bill is using a jumbo drywall square, a utility knife, and *plenty* of blades to cut cement board. Cut one side (the label tells which), fold and break the board, and cut the other side.

The ¼" underlayment boards are cut and laid in position, ready to mortar.

Mortaring the Underlayment

The whole point of underlayment is to make a flat, stable base for the tiles. Underlayment gets laid in the same mortar bed you'll use for the tiles.

Once the boards are cut, mix thinset tile mortar and start laying underlayment:

1. Trowel mortar onto the plywood, following the same procedure used to mortar tiles.

2. Working quickly, lay the boards down, taking care to press the edges down. Don't wait too long, or the boards might rest not depress the mortar uniformly.

3. Screw the boards with 1¼" cement-board screws, placed about 8" apart. If the screws are hard to drive, drill quick *pilot holes* for them. Don't drive the screws too deep; that damages the cement board.

4. Use a straightedge to check flatness as you work.

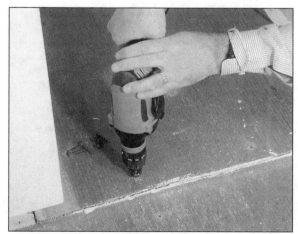

We're screwing underlayment with a screw gun, which shuts off when the screw reaches the right depth, but an electric drill would also work.

5. Fill joints between boards with mortar.

Step 2: Where to Start Tiling?

Finding the starting line can be the toughest part of tiling. It's helpful to start tiling in a corner. A triangle 3' × 4' × 5' is a right triangle. Measure a "3-4-5" triangle in your starting corner to check if it's square. You can get into big trouble by assuming your starting corner is square.

There are two methods for finding a starting line, depending on how the tile fits the room. In the next section we'll take a look at both.

Dave's Don'ts

Don't step on tiles during layout, when they are not supported by mortar. Don't mortar anything until every tile has been cut and test-fitted!

Choose Your Method

In *Method A*, you start on a center line. Place a joint along the center of the longer dimension of the room. Measure outward and calculate the width of the last row of tiles at the walls. If you will have pieces narrower than 2" or 3" (which are hard to lay but easy to damage), try Method B.

Corner

	10	5
9	4
8	3
7	2
6	1

Starting line (center line)　　Guide board

Method A: Place your starting line at the center of the room. Begin by screwing a guide board (described in the following sidebar) to the floor. After tiles 1 through 9 are set in place, break the guide board at cut A and lay tiles 10 through 21.

In *Method B*, you start parallel to a straight wall. Lay the first row along the longest straight wall, and let the chips (in this case, the smaller tiles) fall where they may.

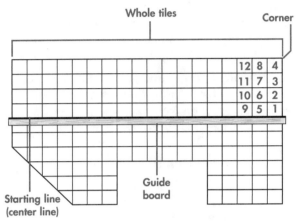

Method B: Start parallel to a straight wall. Lay in the order shown. After one side of the room is laid, remove the guide board and lay the other side.

Building Smarts

Pro tilers mark tile layouts with chalklines. But the rest of us notice that chalklines disappear as soon as we lay down mortar. To tile as straight as the pros, use a straight 1 × 4 guide board that's as long as your starting line.

Screwing the guide board into place.

1. Screw the guide board to the floor along the starting line, as shown in the diagram for Method A or B.

2. Start laying tile against the board.

3. When tiles on one side of the board are set (resistant to moving), unscrew and remove the board, without disturbing tiles. Lay the other side.

Here's a related cheat: Screw straight scraps of wood where tile meets carpet. Snug the tile against the wood to make a straight outside edge.

Here's a real-world example of using a guide board to start a layout using Method A. We are still cutting tiles; nothing is mortared yet. The guide board is screwed to the floor along the starting line. These 18"-square tiles cover a floor in a hurry.

Plastic spacers are a good way to keep the layout honest, both while testing fit and while laying. You're supposed to place the spacers flat on the floor, at the corners, but they're easier to place and remove in the standing position, as shown.

A wet saw can't cut curves, but you can approximate by making these parallel cuts, then breaking out the scrap. This hole is for a gas pipe behind the stove, and it's "good enough for where it's for," as builders sometimes say.

Cutting the Tile

I've already described how to choose a cutting technique. You can break most ceramic tiles with a tile breaker, which scores the tile and then presses it down across the score line. We rented a wet saw—which uses water to cool a diamond blade, because it's easier to use and can trim hairline amounts from the edge of tiles. Try to place cut edges toward the walls, because they will be either sharp (from a saw) or rough (from a tile breaker).

Step 3: Laying Tile

With a good bed of mortar and accurate cuts, it's tough to lay a bad tile. Tiling has these basic steps:

1. Lay down mortar.
2. Place each tile position in the mud and rotate into position.
3. Beat (tap firmly on) the tile with a 12" block of 2 × 4.

Shimmying and rotation both push the tile into the mortar.

A wet saw is best for cutting tiles. Keep your fingers away from that blade—it's sharp enough to cut stone!

Building Smarts

Tile trowels have a toothed side to lay out an even bed of mortar. When you set a tile into toothed mortar, the mortar cushions the tile, allowing precise height placement. Bigger teeth are used with bigger tiles; bags of tile mortar explain which trowel to use for your tile size.

First, Bill pushes mortar against floor with the flat side of the trowel, to get good adhesion.

Then he "tooths" the mortar with the toothed edge of the trowel. He's toothing slowly to lay out an even mortar bed.

Use the beating block (shown in a later photo) to check that each tile is level with its neighbors. Work fast to make adjustments before the mortar sets, and don't kill yourself aiming for thousandth-of-an-inch accuracy; $\frac{1}{16}$" accuracy is just fine.

After you level the tiles, place the spacers to set the joint width.

After you lay a few tiles, check the level with a straight 1 × 4. If you work quickly, the mortar will be soft enough to adjust the tile level. Continue checking the level as you work: The straightedge never lies!

As you set tiles, don't let mortar build up in the joints. Use a screwdriver and a wet rag to clear out mortar so none remains above the surface after you grout.

Almost done! This oddball (the tile, not the tile setter!) will complete the tile-laying phase.

I beat the last tile into place with this 2 × 4. Now I'm using the beater to check that the tile is level with its neighbors.

Step 4: Great Grout

Once the tiles are laid, give the mortar 24 hours to set. Assemble your grouting tools. It pays to have a range of trowels on hand to fill the joints. Some people prefer using the straight edge of a toothed tiling trowel. I prefer a drywall knife, sometimes assisted by a second trowel, as shown. The goal is to find a fast system that completely fills the joints.

Mix the grout, allow it to rest 10 minutes, and mix again.

I'm using a drywall knife and a tuckpointing trowel to grout the joints.

A drywall knife may work better by itself.

If the grout starts getting too stiff, it won't go into the joints. Throw it out and mix more.

Keep an eye on how the grout is setting. After five minutes, test the consistency to see if your finger can shape it.

Use your finger to smooth the partly set grout in the joint.

You may be tempted to buy a jointing tool to form the grout lines, but fingers often work better. Jointing tools tend to dig too deep in a wide joint, and ride up in a narrow one. A gloved finger, on the other hand, adapts nicely to varying widths. You may need to run your finger back and forth to smooth the joint. In a few minutes, scrape diagonally across the surface with a wide trowel to remove spilled grout.

Building Smarts

People who haven't worked with mortar resent letting the mortar run the show, but you've got to prevent the grout from "getting away from you." The various steps of grouting—placing the grout, forming the joint, and removing the excess—must be done when the grout has set up to the right consistency. If you get the timing right, the job will be fast, easy, and attractive.

As the grout sets, you can clean the floor more vigorously without harming the joint.

When the grout is sufficiently set, sponge diagonally across the entire floor to remove smeared grout. Talia will clean the sponge in the bucket but keep it relatively dry. Cleaning goes fast if you catch the grout at the right degree of setting.

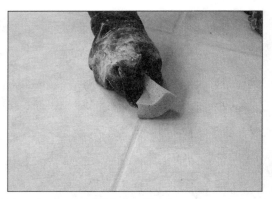

When the grout is fairly hard, a damp sponge does a final smoothing. Run it along the joint, adding a bit of water if necessary to smooth out the joint. Don't overwork the joint—stop when it's smooth enough.

After the grouting is done, leave everything alone for 24 hours so the grout can harden. After a few weeks, a silicon grout treatment can reduce staining, but it's not mandatory.

A sight for sore eyes (and backs)! The kitchen is reclaimed, and renewed! All that remains is to replace the molding, as described in Chapter 32.

In This Chapter

◆ Step 1: Prepare for your floor

◆ Step 2: Making the template

◆ Step 3: Cut and fasten the underlayment

◆ Step 4: Sticking it down

    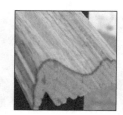 

14

Lay a Vinyl Floor

Is your kitchen or bathroom floor shot? Have generations of clodhoppers carved a path between the fridge and the sink? Then you're a candidate for vinyl flooring. As a quick means to erase bad taste, eradicate gouges, and enhance decor, vinyl is especially useful in bathrooms, kitchens, and entryways.

With the right preparation, vinyl can go over most flooring materials—wood, concrete, and older vinyl. The only trick is making the *template*—a pattern used to cut the flooring. In the example we've shown in this chapter, the vinyl itself served as a template, but it's faster and easier to use a paper template. Stand by for details.

Step 1: Prepare for Your Floor

Vinyl comes in many grades, colors, and styles. In terms of installation, what matters is how it's bonded to the subfloor. Full-adhesive floors, like the one shown here, require mastic, or adhesive, on the whole subfloor. Perimeter bonding gets a few inches of mastic around the edges; the flooring then shrinks and tightens. Self-adhesive flooring has a protective backing that you remove to expose the gummy stuff.

Building Smarts

To floor a bathroom right, remove the toilet; don't try to cut around it. Shut off the water supply, loosen the toilet-mounting bolts around the base, remove the toilet, and shove a rag into the drain to control odors. After the flooring is done, place a new seal into the drain and secure the toilet with new mounting bolts. This whole process is described in Chapter 24.

Remove the base trim. If the baseboard is in good shape, leave it in place. If the baseboard needs replacement, remove it as well. Chapter 32 describes how to remove and replace this molding.

It would be nice if you could put vinyl over a junky floor, but vinyl is thin, and it's got to rest on a solid, flat, clean subfloor. These steps will prepare your subfloor for action:

◆ Old *vinyl* must be securely stuck, with no loose spots, tears, wide seams, or cuts.

◆ Check *plywood* for loose panels, wide joints, knots, nail holes, or other damage.

Don't take chances with your subfloor—rescrew it. Drive 2" screws about every 8" in each joist. Don't let the heads stick up.

◆ Remove dirt, dust, and moisture from concrete or ceramic tile. Check for cracks, scaling, or other damage. Stone or ceramic tile must be tightly bonded.

◆ A quarter inch of plywood makes a good underlayment to strengthen and level the subfloor, but any doors must clear the floor as they swing.

◆ Avoid placing vinyl on floors that are constantly wet.

◆ Trowel on floor leveling compound to raise dips in the subfloor.

◆ Prime plywood, ceramic, or concrete with a product intended to prepare for vinyl.

Step 2: Making the Template

The key step in vinyl flooring is the template. Normally it's made from a wide roll of Kraft paper, but the guys from Schuster Construction (Madison, Wisconsin) shown in this chapter did not have paper on hand, so they used the flooring itself for a template. Again departing from standard procedure, they used the template to mark the ¼" plywood underlayment for this cramped entryway. Although we don't recommend making a pattern of vinyl, it does show one way to make a template—and the value of improvisation in home improvement.

Mark the template for any obstructions that would prevent the floor from moving into position.

When making a paper template, follow these hints:

◆ Make triangular cutouts in the template. Place tape over the cutouts to hold the template to the subfloor as you work with it.

◆ Press the paper into the corners and cut with a utility knife.

Although he's making the template from flooring rather than paper, Ken's showing how to cut the template near a wall. He's folded the vinyl up against the wall and is cutting at the fold. Cut so the vinyl edge will be hidden under the base shoe.

◆ To work around irregular objects, like plumbing or built-ins, build up your pattern from pieces of paper. Tape them together to make the template.

Step 3: Cut and Fasten the Underlayment

The hard work is over once the template is cut. In the tight entryway we photographed, it was impossible to position a whole sheet of underlayment and cut it to fit. (You'll run across the same problem in bathrooms.) Instead, Ken chose to use the template to mark the underlayment—more testimony to the value of thinking on your feet.

Saw the underlayment to size, making it about ¼" short in each dimension. If you try to get it just so, it might wedge into position, and I guarantee you'll have to monkey with it more than any piece of underlayment deserves!

Fasten the underlayment with power-driven staples, or 1¼" ring-shank underlayment nails. Place a nail about every 6".

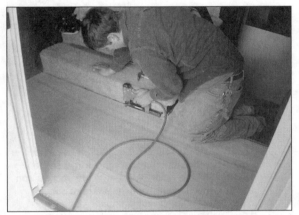

With an air-powered stapler, Seth is fastening the underlayment. No matter how you do this, make sure the fasteners don't stick up! A bit of carpenter's or construction glue underneath helps prevent squeaks.

Step 4: Sticking It Down

With all the preparation out of the way, it's time to get the flooring in place.

Cut the Flooring

Because we cut the vinyl in place, we skipped this step. If you made a paper template, unroll the flooring in a clean location and tape the template right-side up on top. Place a carpenter's square along the lines and cut without marking. *Always make these cuts with a sharp utility knife.* Place scrap wood underneath and try to cut all the way through on the first stroke of the knife.

Apply the Adhesive

Bring the flooring into the room, rolled up in a way that makes it easy to unroll. Spread adhesive across the floor with a notched trowel.

Smear an even coat of adhesive on a large section—say one half—of the floor. Work quickly so you can position the flooring before the glue sets.

Gently lay the first side into the adhesive and immediately shift it into its final location.

Push the floor into position, tight to the walls.

Press the floor down with your hands, and then move to a roller.

Roll the floor, with either a rented floor roller or a kitchen rolling pin. Look closely for bulges and concentrate on them. Let the floor set as indicated on the adhesive label.

Replace the base trim as described in Chapter 32, and you're done!

In This Part

Part 5

Storage Solutions

Got too much stuff? Join the club! The junk in most houses seems to grow by the hour. But the need for more smart, attractive storage has a brighter side: It's an excuse to buy some nice material and some nice tools.

Chapter 15 shows how to build strong, attractive, built-in bookshelves from affordable wood. If you're lucky enough to have space for a wall-mounted cabinet—or already have one, with a homely face—Chapter 16 explains how to build a new, hardwood front with doors. And if you have a concrete wall that *should* be storing your tools, Chapter 17 describes a highly functional pegboard-on-concrete project.

In This Chapter

Chapter 15

Build and Install Built-In Bookshelves

When you consider that bookshelves can hold artwork, bric-a-brac, or even records or books, who doesn't need more of them? You could buy units made of glued-up sawdust sandwiched between white plastic, but they are, well, kinda boring and predictable. Instead, you can build bookshelves from ¾", veneered plywood. Sure, it costs a bit more than melamine-coated particle board, but when you build right, veneer plywood looks as good as solid wood, and it's much cheaper and a lot less likely to warp. I used oak plywood in this chapter, but birch is also commonly available.

Step 1: Before You Start

You can make this project your own by adapting it to your situation and your tastes. Consider these options:

◆ Choose a veneer material and stain to match your décor.
◆ Select different moldings.
◆ Make the top of solid wood, or tile it.
◆ Change the overall size.
◆ Change the shelf spacing. If you make shelves with varying heights, taller shelves generally look best at the bottom.

Step 2: A Matter of Size

The location and use of your bookshelf will determine the dimensions of the shelves. For paperbacks, 9" of height may be sufficient in shelves that are 8" or 9" deep. For hardbound books, 12" height by 10" depth are good starting points, although art books may need even more room.

The materials listed in the table will make a bookcase 29¼" high × 54½" wide (plus twice the width of edge molding, 1¼" in this example), with two 12" high × 11" deep shelves.

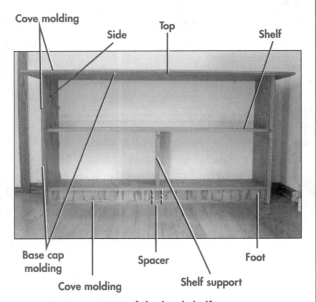

Parts of the bookshelf.

Name	Dimensions	# Used	Notes
Side	12" × 28¾"	2	Grain should be vertical.
Shelf	11" × 47½"	2	Grain should run horizontal.

Name	Dimensions	# Used	Notes
Top	14" × 54½"	1	Grain runs side to side.
Shelf support	12½" high × 9" deep	1	Make after cutting dadoes in sides.
Foot	3" × 47½"	1	
Spacer	3" × 9¼"	1	Any scrap will do.
Base cap molding	⅝" × ¾"	32' needed	
Cove molding	¾"	16' needed	

Depending on what you will be putting on the shelves, shelves longer than about 24" need the shelf support. The support looks better if it's recessed slightly behind the shelves, which are, in turn, recessed behind the sides.

Once you've determined the size of all parts, prepare a plywood cutting layout. The bookshelf shown needed considerably less than one 4' × 8' sheet of plywood.

Step 3: Preparing the Pieces

Cutting plywood can be tricky. Even with a good table saw, it's easier to start cutting a full sheet with a circular saw. If you're short of tools, a home center can cut the parts for you. Their panel saws are quick, accurate, and cheaper than buying a saw! Or have the store make some starting cuts, so it's easier to haul the plywood home.

A nice, big table saw makes fast work of cutting the plywood. A fine-toothed plywood blade reduces splintering.

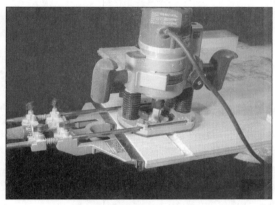

A router with a ¾" straight bit and an edge guide makes short work of cutting the top and bottom dadoes on the sides. Either clamp both pieces side by side, or cut the dadoes before rip-sawing the pieces to width.

You can also cut dadoes by guiding a router along a straight piece of wood.

 Building Smarts

Most joints in this shelf use *dadoes* (rectangular cutouts) measuring ¾" wide × ¼" deep. Dadoes join the shelves to the sides, the sides to the top, and the spacer to the shelves. Dadoes are not so easy to cut, but they offer a big payoff in terms of better alignment, easier gluing, and stronger joints. If you don't have a router, cut the dadoes with a table saw or a circular saw. Set the saw to cut ¼" deep. Guide a circular along a straight piece of wood, clamped as shown for the router. Move the guide to make three or four passes with the saw. Check the fit with scrap wood so the dado fits snugly. Remove remaining wood with a chisel.

After cutting the dadoes, sand all parts. Sandpaper comes in many roughnesses, called "grits." For this project, start with medium grit and work your way through fine and extra-fine sandpaper. Don't be tempted to skip a grit; you won't be able to remove the gouges left from the previous grit. With a random orbital sander, sanding should take less than half an hour.

Following label directions, apply stain with a rag or brush, wait a while, and wipe the boards dry.

Stain brings out the grain. Left: unstained oak veneered plywood. Middle: Immediately after applying stain, you might think you've made matters worse. Right: Not so! After wiping, proof that good stain shows off the grain of fine wood.

Step 4: Assembly

As usual, assembly takes less time than preparation. But you do need to work fast to get everything assembled before the glue sets—usually 10 minutes or so.

Get a web clamp or a light rope ready to hold the pieces together. Apply the glue, spread it quickly with a scrap of wood or an old toothbrush. First assemble the shelves to the sides, and then put the top on the sides. Mop up spilled glue with a wet rag before it sets. An assistant is always handy for this type of assembly.

The scrap brace is nailed to the top, and clamped to the side. The square kept everything kosher while I adjusted the brace.

When the glue sets, nail on the shelf support, foot, and spacer. These parts need no gluing.

Step 5: Finishing Up

All that remains at this point is to trim the shelf and fasten it to the wall. I used a "base cap" molding to hide the raw edges of the plywood. The base cap meets at outside miter joints at the front corners of the top.

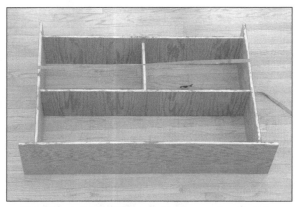

Working quickly, I've spread glue and nailed the shelves, using three 2" finishing nails per joint. The web clamp hold pieces while nailing.

Clamp the base cap molding over a small amount of glue, then drill and nail it with one 1½" finishing nail every 12".

A square helps you hit the center of the plywood with the nails. Don't let the nails break through the edge.

Sometimes it's easier to cut a piece in place. You can't cut this molding exactly 1" too short!

Remove base trim from the wall (see Chapter 32) and position the shelf. Locate the studs and screw diagonally through the top into the studs. Drive screws about 12" apart, but close enough to the wall to be covered by the cove molding.

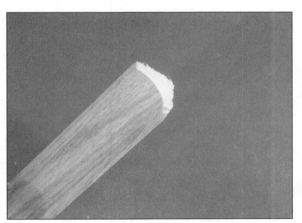

Cove molding visually bonds the bookshelf to the wall and floor.

Bevel each end of the top molding and nail it to the top with 1" finishing nails. Cut other moldings with beveled or square ends to meet adjacent surfaces. You may have to cut some finishing nails with pliers so they don't come through the plywood.

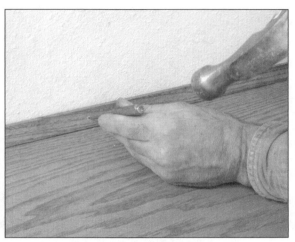

Use a nailset to drive nails under the surface. Fill holes with putty.

Replace the baseboard and base shoe to meet the edges of the bookshelf. Set all nails and putty the holes. Fill the exposed ends of the dadoes with wood filler, and sand smooth. Stain the putty, and you're done!

This shelf looks like it comes with the territory, as indeed it does.

In This Chapter

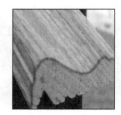

Chapter 16

Build a Front for an Existing Wall Cabinet

Did a previous owner leave you a mixed blessing—a built-in wall cabinet with a way-too-ugly face? Do you have a closet that could be turned into a good-looking cabinet? Are you interested in building an attractive china cabinet in a dining-room wall?

If so, keep reading to learn how to make a hardwood cabinet face and doors. Although you'll have to work accurately, the process is straightforward: Strip off the old face, if there is one, make a new hardwood face, and then make doors to match. I'll explain how to make doors with wood panels and glass inserts.

Step 1: Make the Face and Frame

Start by removing the old doors, molding, and face, following suggestions in Chapter 32. Then plan your course of attack. The cabinet shown here is surrounded by four edgewise pieces I call jambs, for their resemblance to window jambs. Before attaching the jambs, I narrowed the opening so the new doors would be more graceful than the old. I divided the opening into four smaller openings with rails. After building the face, I attached drywall to the ugly plywood seen in the early photos.

You may have to improvise to attach the face. If, like me, you have an existing cabinet, the jamb attachment should be obvious. Otherwise, as shown in the diagram, attach the side jambs to the studs at the edges of the cabinet.

Building Smarts

In this project, I've listed the ideal tools for each step. Here are a few alternative techniques if you don't have those tools:

◆ Make the doors with the simplified design shown in Chapter 21, using corner moldings and plywood. You'll save a ton of time. Definitely choose this option if you don't own and can't borrow a bunch of clamps.

◆ Instead of routing the dado for plywood and/or the rabbet for glass (shown in figures later in this chapter), cut them on a table saw.

◆ Instead of cutting the door parts with a power miter box, use the table saw's miter gauge (the angled gadget that rides in a slot on the table).

Install the Jambs

The jambs must be wide enough to hide the framing, and extend 1¼" above the finished wall surface. That leaves ½" protruding past the ¾" cove molding that joins the jambs to the wall.

The top jamb must be wide enough to cover the header above the cabinet. Fasten the top jamb with 2" hardened trim screws. As with all screw holes in this project, *countersink* the screw head so it will rest below the surface. At the end, hide these heads with wood filler.

Dave's Don'ts

Accuracy is everything in this project, and that starts with the jamb installation. Don't rush. Take your time, and make sure the frame is rectangular. The easiest way to do this is to set the jambs plumb and level, using shims if necessary.

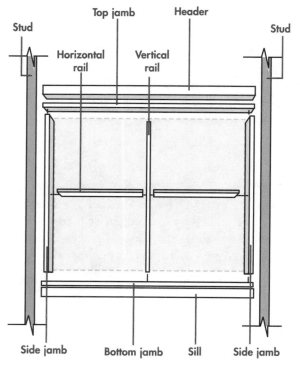

This exploded view shows four jambs and three rails; the framework for four doors. All pieces are ¾" hardwood except for the studs.

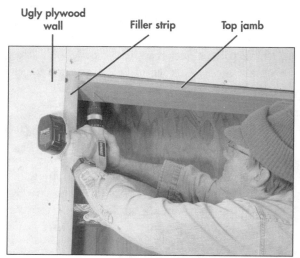

John is screwing the top jamb to the header. You can't see the cedar shims we used to level the jamb. The filler strip reduced the opening width.

Cut the ends of the side jambs square, and butt them under the top jamb. Check that the side jambs are plumb and screw about every 16" into the studs and/or filler strip.

Cut and fasten the bottom jamb under the side jambs.

Install the Rails

With the jambs in place, cut and install the horizontal and vertical rails. I used a plate joiner (also called a biscuit cutter) to hold the rails to the plywood shelves, but trim screws would also work. Plate joiners cut a slot in both pieces you will join. After you glue in a plate, the joint becomes extremely strong.

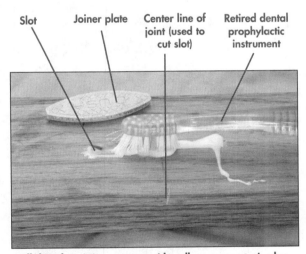

Fill the plate-joiner cutout with yellow carpenter's glue.

Like the jambs, the rails get a simple butt joint at the corners. Cut the ends for a snug fit, clamp the parts flush, and screw through the joint.

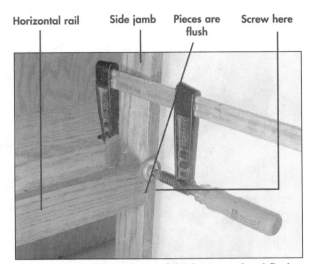

The clamp holds the front of the horizontal rail flush to the front of the side jamb.

Screw through the side jamb into the center rail with a 2¼" trim screw. This screw will hide under the cove molding.

Trim the Face

With the face done, nail ¾" cove molding around the edges. Use outside miter joints, as described for baseboards in Chapter 33. (Note: If the drywall is not yet attached, nail the cove molding after it is.)

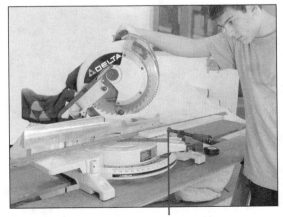

Clamp and board hold molding

Take it from Alex: Cut the cove molding slowly on the miter box.

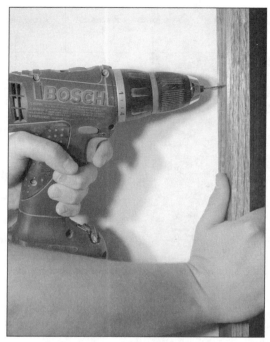

To attach the cove molding, drill and then drive a regular finish nail. Hardened trim nails generally don't need a pilot hole.

A pneumatic brad nailer makes short work of attaching this molding. Drive 1", 18-gauge nails at an angle so they don't come through the jamb.

Step 2: Cut the Doors

With the face and jambs in place, size and cut the doors. In the example, all doors are the same width, but the top and bottom were a different height. Each door is 1" wider, and 1" taller, than its opening, so they overlap the jambs by ½".

I used 1 × 4 hardwood for the door parts; 1 × 3 would work on smaller doors. Test the proportions with cardboard, which is a lot cheaper than hardwood!

Don't be a fool: Check that the design of your new doors will please *your* eye.

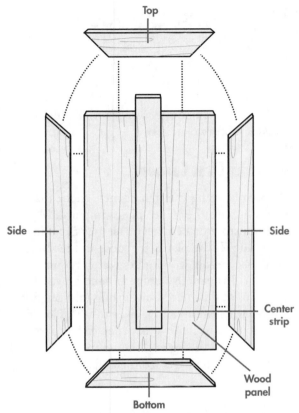

Top

Side

Side

Center strip

Wood panel

Bottom

Here's an exploded view of a wood-panel door.

Cut the door parts from hardwood, using a power miter box, if you have one, or a table saw or a hand miter box. Read your saw manual. If it's safe to cut two parts in a stack, cut both sides for each door together, label them, and glue them into the same door. The reason? Better accuracy yields tighter joints.

Cutting door parts on a power miter box. The two laser lines (highlighted) mark the edge of the cut; I'll use the piece on the right.

Cut the Joints

If you have—or can rent—a plate joiner, cut plate joints in the end of the door parts. Otherwise, put polyurethane glue—Gorilla Glue or PL Premium Construction Adhesive are two popular brands—in the joint. Clamp the parts exactly in position, and drive two 2¼" trim screws at each joint. Drill a slightly larger hole through the outer piece, and a smaller one in the inner piece. Polyurethane sets slowly, giving you time to get the joints right.

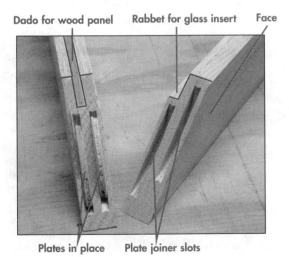

Dado for wood panel   Rabbet for glass insert   Face

Plates in place   Plate joiner slots

Two plate slots in each miter joint make a strong joint. Notice the difference between door parts for a wood panel and a glass insert.

From here on, your technique will depend on whether your doors will get glass inserts or plywood panels:

◆ Doors with glass get a *rabbet*—a two-sided rectangular cutout.

◆ Doors with plywood panels get a *dado*—a three-sided rectangular cutout.

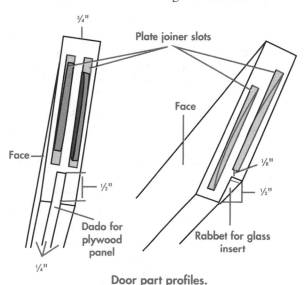

Door part profiles.

Rout a dado or rabbet on the inside of each door part, depending on whether it will get a wood panel or glass insert.

Alex is routing a rabbet on the inside of a part for a glass-insert door, using a ¼" straight router bit. Featherboards are springy gadgets that hold the wood against the fence and table.

Step 3: Glue the Doors

Now for some fun—it's door-clamping time. You've worked accurately so far, but it's no time to let your guard down. Clamp the doors square and flat in a clamping jig built from ¼" plywood, with one square corner. Then glue the doors in two stages.

Glue the First Corner

Before clamping the first corner, check that all joints fit with the joiner plates in place. Make any adjustments before you slather the joints with glue! If the plates are loose in the slots, don't use yellow wood glue, which requires a tight fit. Instead, use polyurethane glue, which fills gaps and is incredibly strong (although it is harder to clean up and slower to set). Cover your glue joints with wax paper so the parts don't stick to the jig and the scrap-wood blocks that protect the parts from clamps.

Building Smarts

You can't have enough clamps! I've identified some of the most useful types in these photos. Buy clamps in pairs, but get an assortment. Different clamps have different virtues:

◆ C-clamps are strong, with a deep reach, but adjust slowly.

◆ Pipe clamps are long, easy to adjust, and strong. But they're clumsy, and have a shallow reach.

◆ Bar clamps have a longer reach, but usually are weaker than pipe clamps.

◆ Handscrews are strong, won't damage wood, and have a long reach. But they are slow to adjust and expensive.

◆ Quick-adjusting, one-hand bar clamps are, well, quick to adjust, but they are weaker than many other clamps.

It's tempting to glue the entire door at once, but that's foolhardy. It's much easier to get a rectangle if you glue one joint first.

Here's a trick for clamping parts with mitered ends: Dry-assemble the whole door, and then clamp the whole door to tighten the first joint, as shown in the following photos.

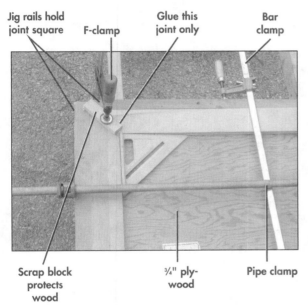

Jig rails hold joint square F-clamp Glue this joint only Bar clamp

Scrap block protects wood ¾" ply-wood Pipe clamp

Clamp the door in the clamping jig, holding the joint tight, square, and flat. Notice that the jig is screwed to 2 × 4s that hold it flat. *Glue only this one corner.* Clean spilled carpenter's glue with a wet rag.

As you tighten the clamps, *always* check that:

◆ The miters meet exactly at the corners.

◆ The miter joints are closed.

◆ The miter joints are compressed so the joints and the door are flat.

◆ The door parts touch the rails on the gluing jig.

◆ You've cleaned up extra glue.

Tighten the clamps gradually, making sure the door stays square.

When the glue is set (30 minutes for carpenter's glue, longer for polyurethane), remove the clamps.

Finish Gluing the Door

When the first joint is finished, glue the other three miter joints, add the joiner plates, and clamp. Insert a wood panel in the door before assembly. Insert glass when the door is finished, as described later. If you're using a ¼" veneer plywood panel, squirt glue into the dado on each door part and insert the panel. If the plywood is loose in the dado, flip the door over and press nails into the back.

Push loose plywood toward the front of the dado with a 4-penny finish nail every 4" or so. Remove the nails after the glue dries.

Turn the door right side up and clamp as described earlier in the chapter.

Quickly assemble the door, before the glue sets. See the earlier discussion for important clamping considerations.

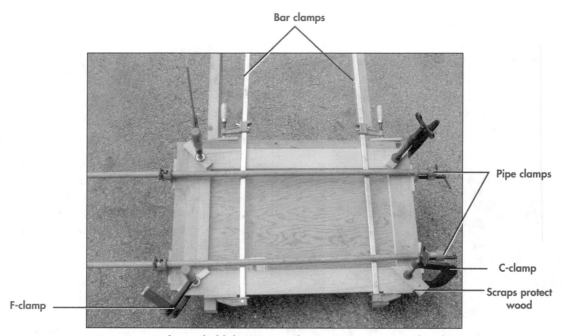

Four C- or F-clamps hold the joints to the jig. (One corner is already glued; the fourth clamp holds the door flat.) Four long clamps compress the joints. This door will get a glass insert; a plywood panel would already be in place.

Step 4: Dress Up the Doors

Once the clamping is done, it's time to dress up the edges, and, if necessary, insert the glass.

Finish the Doors

The best tool for dressing up the door edges is a router. A cove bit makes a nice, subtle design; much improved over a square corner, in my humble opinion.

If you don't have a router, try the following:

◆ Round the edges with sandpaper.

◆ Cut an angled *bevel* on the outside with a hand plane.

◆ Cut parallel, decorative grooves with a table saw.

In any case, don't remove too much wood at the edges, or your hinge screws may come through the front.

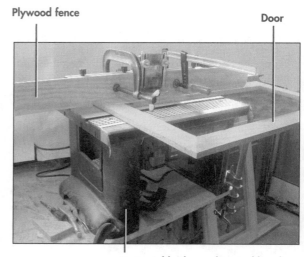

If you're lucky enough to have a router table, clamp a plywood fence to the table fence so the door will slide smoothly past the router bit.

Push wood filler into any gaps at the miter joints, wait a minute, and wipe it off with a solvent-filled rag. (Use water for water-soluble filler.)

A random orbital sander is perfect for sanding the doors. Use medium, fine, and then extra-fine sandpaper.

Hand-sand the door edges.

If you want, sand, screw and lightly glue a decorative strip to the panel. I used a ³/₁₆" thick molding called mullion casing.

Countersink a hole and drive ³/₈" × #4 flat-head brass screws in a regular pattern to fasten the center strip. Finally, stain the doors.

Glass Comes Last

It's finally time to lay glass in a glass-panel door. Measure the opening, and have a glass company cut a piece of ⅛" glass. Silicone caulking (buy a type that sticks to glass and wood) holds the glass in the rabbet.

Silicone caulking grabs the glass. Don't slobber caulking onto the front.

Carefully lay in the glass, clean caulking off the front, and let the caulk set.

Step 5: Mount the Doors

At last, victory is in sight! If you've worked carefully, the doors should practically fall into place. Almost.

After some experimentation, I settled on ½" overlay hinges, which placed the doors on top of ½" of the jambs. I bought brass-plated hinges because they include brass-plated screws, which are strong enough to work in hardwood. The solid-brass screws supplied with solid-brass hinges strip easily in hardwood.

Vertical adjust-
ment slot   Door

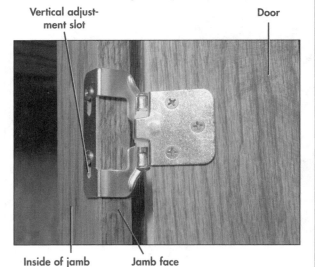

Inside of jamb   Jamb face

These overlay hinges line up the door. Screw them
to the door, then to the jambs.

Knobs make a real difference in appearance, so choose them carefully. These round solid-brass knobs had the classic look I wanted.

Turn the knob tightly onto its screw.

The completed cabinet, with its wood-panel and
glass doors, marks a major improvement over its
"ain't-I-crude?" predecessor.

In This Chapter

Chapter 17

Install Pegboard on a Concrete Wall

Pegboard is such cool stuff that I wish I'd invented it myself. Sold in 4' × 8' sheets, ⅛" or ¼" thick, it has holes about every inch. For decades, pegboard has been the one-size-fits-almost-all solution to storing tools where you can find and grab them quickly.

Pegboard is cheap, but you'll have to spend some bucks for the clever hangers for screwdrivers, clamps, hammers, files, and all the rest.

There are only three complications with pegboard. First, it needs at least ½" of space behind it to give room for hook end of the hangers. Second, you'll be deprived of any excuse for chaos in the tool room.

And third? Pegboard is often attached to a concrete wall. Bummer. Although attaching to concrete is never simple, we'll describe two of the least painful methods, and mention a nifty trick to minimize the need for fasteners.

Step 1: Lay Out the Nailers

Pegboard is fastened to *nailers*, horizontal strips of 1 × 2 that leave room for the hanger hooks. Place a nailer about every 2': three for a 4'-tall sheet of pegboard, as shown in a later photo.

Josh is marking a level line for the bottom nailer.

Nailers should run within 6" of the bottom, at the middle, and about 2" below the top.

Using a level, mark out the lines for all nailers. Mark for the screw holes about 18" apart along the nailers. Mark "left" on the front-left side of each nailer, just to avoid confusion.

Step 2: Attach to the Wall

If you're lucky enough to be building against a wood wall, simply screw the nailers to the studs. Drive one screw, long enough to grab at least 1" of the stud, in each stud.

We attached nailers to the concrete wall with $\frac{3}{16}$" × $1\frac{1}{4}$" Tapcon screws. You drive these hardened screws with a drill into small holes predrilled in the concrete. The advantage of small holes? They are easier to drill, but still no picnic.

When drilling for the Tapcon, hold the nailer in position, with the front left at front left, and drill one screw hole with the special Tapcon drill through the wood and 1" into the concrete—just enough for the screw to penetrate. Each size of Tapcon screw calls for its own drill; they're sold alongside the screws.

Building Smarts

Powder-actuated fasteners are a good fastening alternative for concrete. Simpler and safer than they sound (*if* you follow the directions …), these guys will blast a hardened nail into the toughest concrete. Place glue on the back of the nailer, as described later in the chapter, and then put on eye and ear protection and hold the nailer exactly where you want it. Hammer the end of the fastening tool, and presto! It's done. Make sure you have the nailer in the right place to start with, because you won't get it out. Note: If you have a lot of holes to drill, consider renting a rotary hammer.

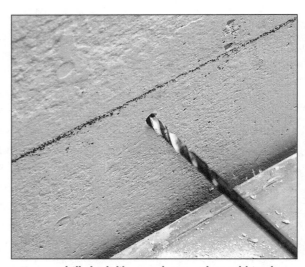

Tapcon drills look like regular wood-metal bits, but they have carbide cutters. We've removed the wood strip for clarity.

Using a Phillips screwdriver in a big electric drill, start this screw, and then drill the other holes on this nailer.

Pull out the screw, smear adhesive on the back of the nailer, and screw it into position. Repeat for the other nailers.

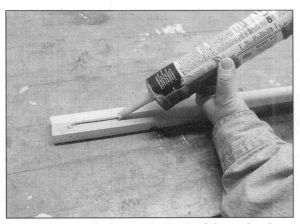

Construction adhesive on the back of the nailers lets you cut down on the hole drilling.

After all this drilling, it's smart to take a break, to allow the glue to set up nice and strong. No sense letting haste undo your hard work!

Step 3: Cut and Attach the Boards

Before it's installed, pegboard is weak, and that makes it hard to cut. I've found a jigsaw works best, but a table saw or circular saw would also work. Or have the building material store cut it to size.

With good (but unseen) support under the pegboard, it's easy to cut through a line of holes. To make our lives simpler, we bought pegboard in 4' × 4' pieces. This strip goes to the left of the one that's already on the wall.

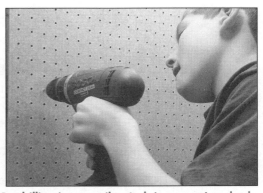

By drilling into a nailer, Josh is preventing shock from loosening the nailer. Horrors! That would mean more drilling in concrete!

Nailers (on back of pegboard)

Almost done! Josh is hand screwing the pegboard to the nailer, using ¾" flat-head sheet metal screws. They drive easily and will stop short of the concrete.

Nothing like pegboard for taking away every excuse for disorganization! This arrangement provides lots of storage for hard-to-store items like clamps, levels, and other large hand tools.

In This Part

Part 6

Kitchen Projects

You see it at every party: The kitchen is the heart of the house. But in too many houses, the heart has some circulatory problems. Before we overdose on these medical metaphors, let's prescribe some cures: Replacing a kitchen sink, with or without the fixtures, is described in Chapter 18. The process of tiling a kitchen countertop and backsplash is the subject of Chapter 19.

If the back of your cabinet shelves aren't meeting their potential for storage, Chapter 20 shows how to build and install big drawers in those cabinets. If the problem with your kitchen cabinets is more in the realm of appearance, don't leap automatically to the obvious solution: total replacement. Chapter 21 introduces a middle-ground solution to calcified cabinets: replacing the doors, drawer fronts, and wooden faces.

In This Chapter

Replace a Kitchen Sink and/or Fixture

Like the rest of your house, kitchen sinks and fixtures—spigots and faucets—have this way of wearing out. (If they haven't worn out, they are no doubt reminding you of the former owners' stale taste.) Sink and fixtures are usually easy to replace, although it does entail some overhead work. If you are replacing the sink *and* the fixtures, make most of the connections before mounting the sink. That will save wear and tear on your back—and your disposition.

Modern plumbing fixtures are surprisingly easy to work with, although you'll have to find the right connectors to mate them to the pipes under your sink. Look for knowledgeable folks at the store, and recognize that return trips to the store come with the territory of plumbing.

Sink projects can take several forms:

◆ In this chapter, we will install a sink and fixture in a partly finished tile countertop. Please see Chapter 19 for details on replacing the countertop.

◆ If you are replacing only the spigot and faucets, see "If You Are Replacing Just the Fixtures," later in this chapter.

◆ If you're replacing a sink with an identical size and mounting style, skip the section on sizing the cutout.

Seeking Sink Styles

Kitchen sinks are sold with three or four holes for fixtures. Depending on design, the faucets and spigots use one to three holes. You can put a sprayer, a soap or lotion dispenser, an air break for the dishwasher, or a filtered-water tap in the other holes. We bought a four-holer and capped one with a plastic cap; maybe later we'll put a water filter outlet in the hole.

Most fixtures fit a standard hole pattern, with holes 4" apart. If your fixtures fit a non-standard pattern, see Chapter 25 for details on connecting them.

Sinks come in several mounting varieties:

◆ "Self-rimming" sinks, made of plastic composite, cast iron, or stainless steel, have a rim that sits on top of the counter. They are easiest to install, but the rim always seems to need cleaning. Stainless sinks are light, so they need clips to hold them in place. Plastic composite and cast-iron sinks can be held in place with caulking.

◆ Tile-in sinks rest flush with the tile, or slightly below it.

◆ Undermount sinks rest below the counter. They are difficult to mount because you must cover the exposed edge of the counter.

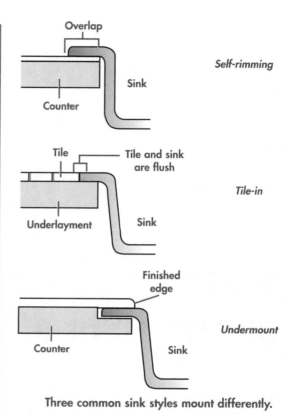

Three common sink styles mount differently.

If You're Replacing Just the Fixtures

If you're replacing only the faucets and spigot, but not the sink, plan on spending some time upside down inside the sink cabinet. A basin wrench, seen in Chapter 25, and flashlight on a stand will both come in handy. The basic sink connections are the same, however; the following photos show the necessary steps for faucet replacement:

1. Close the stop valves and loosen the fixture mounting nuts with a basin wrench or an open-end wrench. (Some faucet assemblies are mounted with a single nut; others use one or more locking rings.)

2. Remove the water-supply tubes at both ends. It's best to replace the tubes, but if they are in good shape and flexible, they may be reused. Note that water-supply tubes often have different sizes at each end: $\frac{3}{8}$" × $\frac{1}{2}$" is a common size.

3. Clean the sinktop. Use steel wool for stainless and nonabrasive cleaner for others.

4. If, after attaching the water supplies, they will fit through the appropriate hole in the sinktop, attach the supplies now. (See the later photo of this step.)

5. If the new faucet mounts through a single hole *and* the water supply tubes will not fit through the hole after they are attached, mount the faucet to the sink first, and then attach the top ends of the water supplies from inside.

Step 1: Locate the Cutout

In this section, we'll assume you're installing a self-rimming sink in a countertop that you can cut with a jigsaw. Some counters can be cut only by installers or manufacturers. If that's your situation, go to Step 2: Mount the Fixtures First. To make a cutout for the tile-in sink shown here, see Chapter 19.

If the sink comes with a cutout template, use it. Otherwise, mark the cutout as follows:

1. Stick wide masking tape on the counter, on the approximate sink location.

2. Place the sink upside down on the tape, centered on the opening, with at least 1½" clearance to the back splash, and parallel to the front of the counter. (Note: This method will fail with an asymmetrical sink. Measure the opening and mark the cutout instead of tracing it.)

3. Mark on the tape around the perimeter of the sink.

4. Remove the sink and measure the amount of overlap. Mark as shown in the diagram.

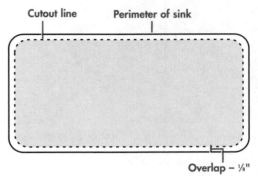

Measure the amount of overlap on the sink and subtract ⅛".

5. Drill through the countertop at the corners; then make the cutout with a jigsaw.

Step 2: Mount the Fixtures First

If you are installing a sink and faucet, do everything you can before mounting the sink. And read the instructions: Faucets vary widely in the way they are mounted and connected. Occasionally, manuals can be helpful, especially the ones written in English …

Attach the Faucets and Spigots

Attach the faucets, spigots, or the one-piece unit to the sink. The attachment may be made with a single ½" nut or a large lock ring, as shown. When attaching a metal ring to a metal pipe, plumber's grease will prevent rust.

A plastic nut holds this faucet body to the sink.

Attach the water supply tubes.

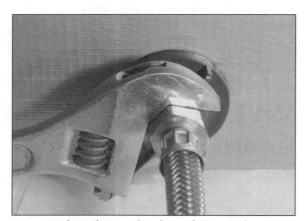

Tighten the supply tube with a wrench.

Attach the Dishwasher Air Gap

A dishwasher air gap is a safety measure. If the drain plugs, the dishwasher will dump its wastewater into the sink, not into the sink cabinet. As a fringe benefit, it puts a slug of hot, soapy water into the drain, helping keep it clear.

Attach ⅝" and ⅞" tubing to the air gap with hose clamps. Leave the hoses long enough to connect as shown in the diagram. Then attach the air gap to the hole in the sink.

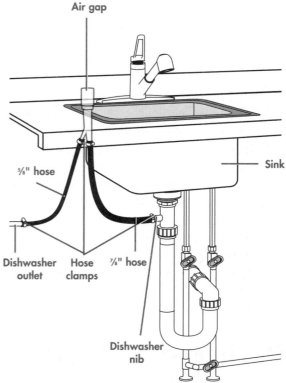

Air gap

⅝" hose

Dishwasher outlet   Hose clamps   ⅞" hose

Sink

Dishwasher nib

The air gap prevents floods if the dishwasher drain plugs.

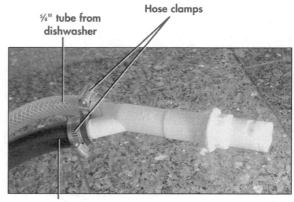

⅝" tube from dishwasher

Hose clamps

⅞" tube to dishwasher

The hoses on an air gap are tough to connect after the air gap is mounted to the sink.

Step 3: Connect the Tailpiece and Drain

The top of the sink is now connected. The type of drain connections depend on whether you will be installing, or reinstalling, a garbage disposal.

Disposal Duties

Disposals require a specific type of tailpiece connection, which attaches with three screws. If you have an existing disposal, it's simplest to use the existing attachment if it is in good condition. To replace the disposal, shut off the circuit, disconnect the wire, remove the disposal, and install the new one, following directions that come with it. To install a disposal on a new sink, attach the tailpiece, and then follow directions for the disposal.

Connect the Tailpiece

If you're not installing a garbage disposal, connect a tailpiece to the new sink with silicone caulk. Masking tape will protect the sink and tailpiece from the caulk, which can be tough to remove.

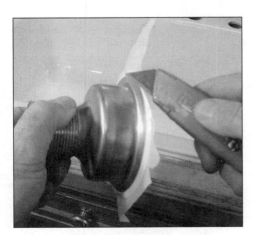

Trim masking tape away from the flange on the tailpiece.

Place silicone caulk on the bottom of the upper tailpiece and push it through the sink drain hole. Assemble the rubber washers and the housing, and then tighten the lock nut and wipe off extra caulk. When the caulk is dry, remove the masking tape.

A screwdriver or a big pliers tightens the lock nut on the bottom of the tailpiece.

Step 4: Mount the Sink

Now that you've made the cutout and connected the faucet, water supplies, and drain, turn your attention to mounting the sink. Various mounting styles for sinks are described earlier in the chapter.

The sink shown mounts in a tile countertop; you can do the tiling either before or after mounting the sink. If you tile first, you'll have to make a precise place for the sink. If you place the sink first, the faucet may get in the way of tiling. We brought the tile near the sink, placed and connected the sink, then finished tiling.

You can see the tile portion of this job in Chapter 19, and in the photo.

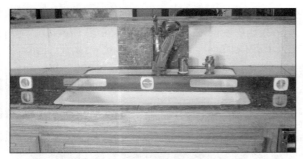

A long level checks that this tile-in sink is level (or slightly below) the tiles. Omit this step for a self-rimming sink.

Finally, it's time to place and fasten the sink. Stainless-steel sinks are lightweight and should be held down to the counter with concealed clips.

For plastic and cast-iron sinks, put the sink in its final position. Mask the countertop with tape, right next to the sink. Remove the sink and place silicone caulking on the countertop, then reposition the sink. Stopper the drain, fill the sink with water to weight it down, clean off extra caulk around the edges, and let the caulk set overnight.

Step 5: Connect the Drain and Dishwasher

At this point, you've made most of the connections in a comfortable position. It's time to dive under the sink.

Connect the Drain

Kitchen sinks use a 1½" P-trap, which can be adjusted in angle and length. The trap connects with slip nuts and big washers. If the drain parts do not reach, buy an extension tube.

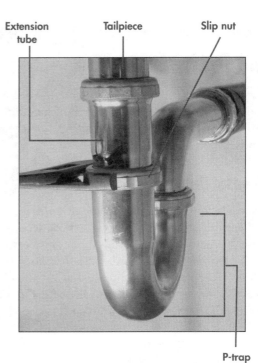

As you tighten the slip nut with pliers, make sure the big washer seats smoothly.

Connect the Dishwasher

The dishwasher air gap is already connected, but you need to connect the lower end of the tubes. Connect the ⅞" tube from the air gap to the Tee connector.

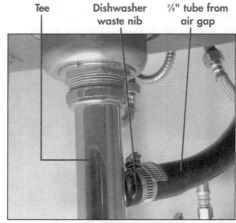

Wastewater from the dishwasher exits the air gap and enters this Tee connector, just below the tailpiece.

Connect the ⅝" tube from the air gap to the dishwasher outlet.

This copper pipe delivers dishwasher waste to the ⅝" plastic tube, which loops around and connects to the air gap on the sinktop.

Step 6: Connect the Water Supplies

With the sink in place, and the drain and dishwasher connected, make the final connections to the water supply tubes.

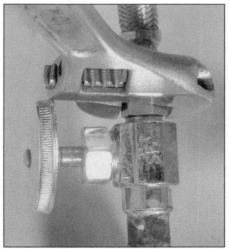

An adjustable wrench tightens the water-supply tube on the stop valve.

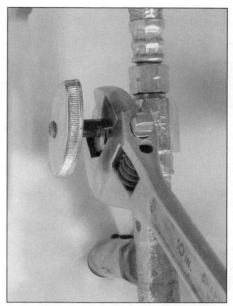

Tighten the valve bonnet nut to eliminate leaks around the stem.

Remove the spigot strainer so it does not catch rust or sediment from the pipes. Open the stop valves and check the faucet operation. Replace the strainer.

Feel the plumbing underneath, and if your hands stay dry, you're done! If not, check and gently tighten connections. Major leaks indicate that a washer is missing or badly placed.

This faucet proudly dominates the new sink. Thirsty?

In This Chapter

- ◆ Step 1: Make your plans
- ◆ Step 2: Dig out the old
- ◆ Step 3: Make a solid substrate
- ◆ Step 4: Laying out the tile
- ◆ Step 5: Cutting the tile
- ◆ Step 6: Laying tile
- ◆ Step 7: Got grout?
- ◆ Step 8: Trim time

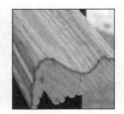

Chapter 19

Tile a Kitchen Countertop and Backsplash

Are you stuck with an entry-level kitchen counter? Been casting envious glances toward granite countertops or hankering after ceramic tile? Truth is, these counters are easier to install than you might imagine. And although one-piece granite countertops are beyond do-it-yourself territory, granite tiles are affordable and easy to install.

When it comes to improving a kitchen counter, many approaches will work. You can replace the countertop, the backsplash, or the sink. I'll describe the countertop and backsplash as one project, because that's how many people would approach the job. I'll describe the sink replacement as a separate project, again because it's often done that way. In reality, we did the whole shebang at once, because it reduced the overall level of chaos in the kitchen.

So what are you waiting for? Send the family on a long vacation (or plan on visiting a lot of restaurants) and get out your crowbar. Your countertop is about to get stoned (or at least tiled).

Step 1: Make Your Plans

Tiling is intense work, driven by the fact that rented tile saws are expensive, and mortar always wants to set. But there's no need to rush the planning stage. Visit a good tile store and ogle the stone and ceramic. Don't rush to judgment: This installation will be visible for years to come!

The Materials

Start by choosing your tile material. Hard glazed tile and granite (seen in the photos in this chapter) are both good choices, and both can be installed with the same tools and techniques. Marble is too soft for a countertop, although we did use it for the backsplash, on the wall above the counter.

In terms of tile size, larger is generally better, because it reduces the number of hard-to-clean grout lines. Handily, 12" × 12" is the most common size for tile, which not only reduces grout lines, but also fits nicely in the average, 24"-deep countertop. For the wall tiles, although almost anything that harmonizes with the counter would work, large tiles are easier to lay and grout.

Tile mortar, commonly called thinset, is sticky and rubbery. Protect your work area with masking. Thinset removes from most surfaces with a wet rag, if you catch it within an hour or so. Buy white thinset for projects with light-colored grout, and gray for dark grout. The theory is that mortar won't be too obvious if it shows through the grout, but mortar color isn't critical if you clean the joints as I describe later in the chapter.

Tile grout is sold with and without sand. Use the sanded variety for wider joints, and unsanded for narrow. Tile stores carry a wide selection of colors, but don't expect the final grout color to be a perfect match of the sample.

The Layout

Scan your countertop and backsplash, checking that they are reasonably square and level. Memorize this dimension: tile size + grout line, which will show the spacing for successive courses of tile. Then, starting from obvious corners and edges, determine where the grout lines will fall. There's no ultimate virtue in starting in one place or another. Strive for a balanced layout that is reasonably easy to lay.

Decide whether to lay the counter or wall tiles first. We started with the wall tiles, so we added ½" to the depth of the countertop. If you start with the counter, raise the wall tiles by ½".

Also determine how you'll finish the front and other exposed edges of the countertop, to cover the ugly edges of tile. I screwed an oak 1 × 3 along the front, and rounded off the top edge. I attached the edging to a ⅜" lip of plywood in front of the tile.

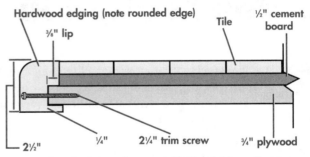

Plan ahead. This ⅜" lip provides a solid base for the hardwood edging, but you'll need to add ⅜" to the depth of the plywood base.

Whereas stone tile is usually square, ceramic tiles are often sold in special shapes used to trim the job. If you're planning to place tile on the edge, screw a temporary support board to the plywood in advance, to support the tiles while the mortar sets. Take tile edging into account when you measure and lay out the countertop and backsplash.

Bullnose: Used at the outer edge of the counter, or where wall tiles meet drywall or plaster.

Double bullnose: A bullnose tile for an outside corner.

Trim tile: Special tiles used to dress up the installation, with a different shape and/or pattern than the regular tiles. You can also cut tiles to serve as accents.

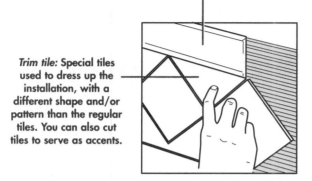

Edge tile: Oblong tile used for the vertical front of a countertop.

Base tile: Joins the wall to the countertop.

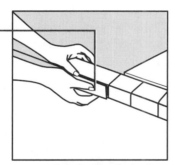
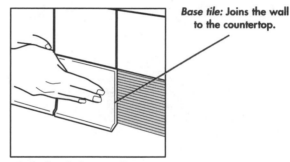

A variety of special tile shapes can help finish the installation. Make sure you get what you need when you order your tile.

Step 2: Dig Out the Old

It's true: Deep within the heart of most home-fixers lurks a destroying angel. Put another way, demolition can be fun, if you protect your house and yourself.

This homely countertop is about to die a sudden death!

Here's how to get rid of the old junk:

1. Clean out the kitchen, especially the cabinets below the counter.

2. Disconnect the sink: Shut off the water supplies (the two little valves on the small pipes or hoses that deliver water to the faucet). Disconnect the supply pipes or hoses. Disconnect the drain pipe. Cap the drain with a plastic bag so you don't breathe sewer gas. Look underneath the sink and detach the clips holding it to the countertop. (Review Chapter 18 for more on this process.)

3. Cut the countertop free from the caulking with a utility knife.

4. Look inside the cabinet for screws holding the countertop to the cabinet or wall.

Unscrew those you find, and then pry up on the counter and look for the other screws.

A reciprocating saw cuts a countertop for easier removal. A jigsaw would also work.

5. If you can, cut the counter at the sink opening, and then remove one side at a time.

6. Pull off the countertop. If you are going to remove the backsplash, attack it now.

This tile didn't fare well against this flat crowbar. The funky backing behind the tile will "take a long walk off a short pier" before we attach new wall tile.

7. Remove everything back to the studs (unless you are lucky enough to reach a very solid layer of drywall or plaster).

Step 3: Make a Solid Substrate

With the demolition done, turn your thoughts to making a strong, rigid *substrate*, or backing, for the tile.

For the Countertop

Strength is especially important under the countertop. The countertop substrate has two layers: ¾" exterior plywood ("AC" grade), topped by ½" of cement board (such as WonderBoard or Durock).

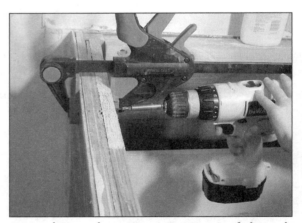

We're gluing and screwing a ¾" × 2" strip of plywood (oriented strand board would also work) to the top of the cabinets. The strip strengthens the counter mounting and gives a bigger target for your screws.

I recommend going overboard to reinforce the cabinets before attaching the plywood. Double up the top edges of the cabinets, as shown in the photo. Screw a 1 × 3 or 2 × 2 nailer to the wall to strengthen the back of the plywood. Make sure the reinforcements don't interfere with the drawers.

Building Smarts

There is some dispute about the ideal countertop substrate. I used techniques that have worked for me in the past, but some builders, experts, and manufacturers suggest the following:

◆ Placing building felt ("tar paper") or 4-mil plastic sheeting on top of the plywood to create a moisture barrier.

◆ Cutting the plywood periodically with a circular saw to prevent moisture buildup. (Although the technique is intriguing, the American Plywood Association noted the obvious when I asked: All this sawing would weaken the plywood. I skipped this step.)

◆ Screwing the cement board down in a bed of tile mortar. This seemed like overkill, because the only "person" who will be walking on our counter is Pupcat, our fur person. If you believe in overkill, Chapter 13 on tiling a floor explains the technique.

◆ Laying the cement board in construction adhesive—a sort of middle ground between laying the board dry, as we did, and setting it in mortar.

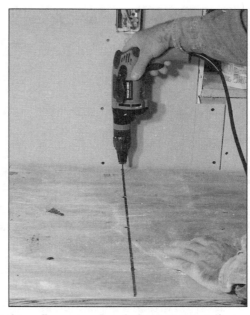

2" drywall screws, placed about 4" apart, fasten the plywood to the cabinet. The line marks the location of the cabinet edge under the plywood. See the new drywall on the wall? Live and learn. I screwed it on, then decided it was too weak, and replaced it with ½" oriented strand board (OSB).

Screw a layer of ½" cement board to the countertop plywood; this puts the tiles on something that expands and contracts at the same rate. Cement board is no fun to cut: Use a big drywall square, a utility knife, and plenty of blades (they get dull fast). Cut one side (the label on the cement board tells which), fold and break the board, and then cut the other side.

Screw the cement board to the plywood every 6½", using screws designed for cement board. Place the screws no closer than 1½" to the edges.

For the Backsplash

The backsplash substrate doesn't have to be as strong as the countertop substrate. I screwed ½" oriented strand board to the studs, and then screwed ¼" cement board to it.

The backsplash substrate is, however, more complicated, because it needs openings for outlets and switches. You may need to reposition the boxes so their fronts will be flush to the tile. Ideally, the box edges will also line up with the tile joints. If you're not confident doing electrical work, hire an electrician for this phase.

To cut the OSB or plywood for these openings, mark the openings, drill ⅜" holes at each corner, and then finish the holes with a jigsaw.

To attach OSB, I place a 2" screw every 6" along each stud. Notice the electrical boxes peeking through.

With the plywood or OSB on the wall, cut ¼" cement board to fit. To cut openings for electrical boxes, drill at each corner, cut the outline on both sides with a utility knife, and then tap with a hammer to fracture the board. When the cement board starts breaking, finish the cut with the knife.

Drill a hole at each corner to start a rectangular cutout for an electrical box.

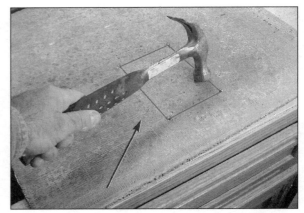

With the board well supported, tap the break lines with a hammer.

Screw the cement board to the wall with the same screws you used on the countertop. Now take a break. The prep work is finished!

Step 4: Laying Out the Tile

Tile layout is usually straightforward. Kitchen counters are 24" deep, so the common 12" × 12" tiles will lay out in two rows. Wall layout can present more layout challenges, but I recommend keeping things simple if you're new to tiling. Small pieces are difficult to design, position, and grout.

Ideally, grout lines would be small and rare. But if they are too small, they will accentuate any layout errors. We settled on ⅛" grout lines, so we bought ⅛" plastic spacers.

We used a *tile-in* sink, which lays flush to the top of the tile. To prepare for the more common *overlay* style, which fits over the top of the tile, place at least ½" of tile under the sink on all sides. In either case, the plywood and cement board should extend ½" under the edge of the sink.

A straight guide board, screwed to the front of the countertop, keeps the crucial front row of tiles straight. Don't use the edging, described later in the chapter, because you can't screw it at the exact height until the tile is already placed.

Step 5: Cutting the Tile

Your method of cutting tile for this project depends on the nature of the tile. Use these suggestions to guide your choice of technique:

◆ A "wet saw," with a water-cooled blade, will cut any type of stone or tile. Tool-rental outfits have these saws. You can see one in action in Chapter 13.

◆ A tile store may make straight or curved cuts for a fee.

◆ A tile breaker will make straight, but slightly rough, cuts in ceramic tile, but not in stone.

This tile breaker is an affordable solution to straight cuts in ceramic tile.

◆ A RotoZip tool with a tile-cutting bit will make curved or straight cuts in soft ceramic tile. It is, however, slow and *loud!*

I rented a wet saw and cut all the tile before starting to mortar. Tile cutting can get hectic, especially when you're scurrying to meet the rental company's return deadline. Mark the tile location and cut line on each piece before cutting. Masking tape is handy, especially when using a wet saw, which cleans off pencil marks.

Masking tape cuts confusion and is essential on dark tile. "3E2" means *third tile, east side, second row.* "[X]" marks the side to be discarded. The cut line is at center.

As you cut tiles, lay them in place, dry, using spacers to simulate the final layout pattern.

With one hand, Meg's holding the dry-fit tiles in place. With the other, she's marking a cutout for an electrical box. Working without a tape measure reduces errors.

Step 6: Laying the Tile

You can lay either the wall or the countertop first. We decided during the layout step to lay the wall first. We used a notched trowel, as seen in Chapter 13, to create a regular mortar bed for the tiles.

Building Smarts

You may be the one who bought the tile, but don't think you are in charge. The mortar is the boss, and like all bosses, it sets the pace. You can't rush things, but you can't fall behind, either. You get a certain amount of time to move the tiles, but then they won't want to move. Ditto for grouting: The grout moves nicely, and then starts to set. That's good, because you can't clean grout from the tiles until setting begins. The take-home message? Watch for changes in mortar and grout, and do each step at the right time.

Tiling the Wall

Mortaring is a skill that you'll learn with time. I find I get more control by using a couple of trowels, rather than just one. Here's the routine:

1. Lay enough mortar for at least four tiles. Place the mortar at the edges of the area you're tiling and pull it toward the center.

2. Spread the mortar with the flat side of the notched trowel, and then use the notched side to make the "toothed" effect that you'll see in a later photo.

3. Cut one leg from some spacers so they are T-shaped. Place these spacers on the countertop to support the wall tiles.

4. Push the first wall tile in place. Give it a twist and beat (whack it with something heavy) it to get good adhesion. Continue with other wall tiles, beating and leveling them as you go.

A 2 × 4 block taps the tiles down to get complete contact with the mortar. The mortar to the right has been "toothed" by the notched trowel and is ready for tile. As we lay the third course, you can see the narrow strips of tile cut for an accent course.

5. Lay any edging tiles as you go, using the same techniques. Rest vertical tiles on the face on the props you previously emplaced.

The beater block also checks that the tiles are flush. Adjust tile height as soon as possible, while the mortar is fresh.

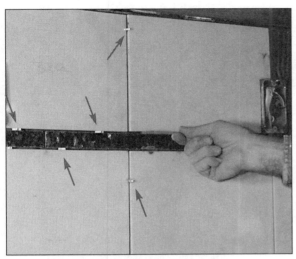

Plastic spacers (arrows) are not the only way to get good spacing. If you need a larger spacer to align tiles that vary in height, carve a wood shim. Don't let your grout lines sag!

Dave's Don'ts

As the mortar starts to set, start cleaning out the grout lines, as described later in this section. Mortar gets *extremely hard* over time, and you risk leaving hideous roughness along the grout lines if you don't clean promptly.

As you lay tiles, work first on the level and then on the orientation. With modern tile mortar, you have a minute or two to adjust height, and five or ten to adjust position. The longer you wait, the harder the adjustments become.

Tiling the Countertop

The wall is done! The countertop is easier, because it's mainly built with whole tiles.

Don't start at the center. It's easier to lay out mortar at the edges of the new area and then drag it toward the center.

Countertop tiles must also be beaten into place.

Laying the tiles flush is critical on the countertop. Notice how flat the 2 × 4 sits on the tiles? That's a sign of careful work.

A Quick Cleanup

One half-hour after you lay your first tiles, remove extra mortar between the joints, using first a screwdriver, then a rag, as shown.

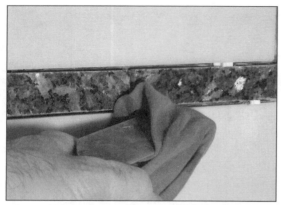

A rag wrapped around a trowel blade cleans out extra mortar. These gaps are for grout, not mortar! Notice the plastic spacers. Once the tiles are firmly set in place, I'll remove them. Wait too long and they get severely stuck!

All done and ready for grouting!

Step 7: Got Grout?

After the mortar sets for 24 hours, grout the joints. Grouting is a simple two-step. First you get the joints full. Then you keep them full while you clean off extra grout.

Mix the grout according to instructions, making sure no dry crumbs remain. Mix enough to cover only a few square feet so you don't rush yourself too much while you getting the knack.

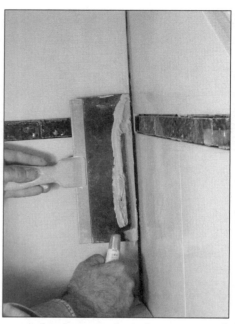

Corners are hardest to grout, so they are a good place to start. A big drywall knife and the ¼" tuckpointing trowel shown are ideal for filling corner joints.

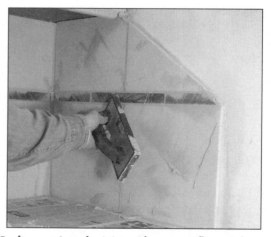

Push grout into the joint with a *grout float*, a dense, spongy tool made for this purpose. The diagonal streaks indicate that I used a diagonal stroke to prevent the float from digging into the joints.

When you have a chance, start cleaning the faces (*don't touch the joints yet!*) of the tiles with a trowel. After the grout starts to harden, start cleaning with a damp sponge.

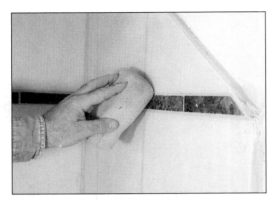

A damp sponge, regularly rinsed in water, removes extra grout while sparing the joints. If cleaning pulls out too much grout, wait a few minutes to clean. You may need haze remover, a product designed to get the last bit of grout haze off the tile.

Step 8: Trim Time

Let the grout set for 24 hours. If you have used tile to trim the front, just seal the installation as described in a moment. If you will put wood edging on the raw edges, cut it to fit.

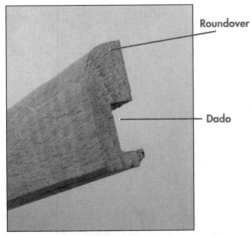

Roundover

Dado

I cut a *dado* (a rectangular slot) in the back of a hardwood 1 × 3 for the edging. Then I rounded the front with a roundover bit in a router.

A router is the perfect tool for shaping edging, but a table saw would also work for the dado. Or cut a ready-made molding to length.

Meet outside corners with a miter joint, as shown in the next photo.

Secure the edging with 2¼" trim screws (these are much stronger than nails) placed 16" apart. Drill a countersink so the screw head sinks ⅛" below the surface. Drill a second hole for the screw shank.

If you will use polyurethane glue, as recommended, protect cabinet faces with masking tape and newspaper or plastic.

Place the edging in perfect alignment, flush to the top of the tiles, with any corner joints lined up. Put polyurethane glue into the dado, and then screw the edging in place.

A clamp lines up the edging. You can also line up the joint with screws.

With the edging in place, sand it and fill the nail and screw holes with putty.

With a bit of sanding and some stain, this dot of putty will almost disappear.

Stain the edging either before or after installation. After the countertop cures for a couple of weeks, seal it with one of the sealers made for ceramic or stone tile.

You can see a photo of the finished countertop in Chapter 18.

In This Chapter

Chapter 20

Build and Install Drawers in Your Kitchen Cabinet

Got enough storage in your kitchen? Neither did we. We thought about "growing" our kitchen by drafting the driveway or enlisting the dining room. Those solutions, however, were expensive. We chose a middle ground in the war on kitchen clutter: drafting our base cabinets into storing more junk better.

To improve our old deep-shelf cabinets, which were known to swallow blenders and what-all, we built six big drawers, plus one for the garbage can. That allows us to group stuff in logical categories—and use the full depth of the cabinet. Result? No more cascades of pots, pans, and plastic plunging from the cavernous depths of our cabinets.

Step 1: Make Some Decisions

Big drawers are a good thing, but they take work. In this chapter, I've suggested several shortcuts and mass-production techniques; but if you don't want to build the drawers, cabinet shops, including some represented on the Internet, will build them for you. If you do order drawers, one caution: Make accurate measurements. Otherwise, you'll get drawers that are *exactly* the wrong size!

In any case, kitchens look best when the drawers are equally wide in each vertical stack. Good thing, because they are also easier to build: You'll work faster, and make fewer mistakes, when cranking out same-size pieces.

Drawer height depends on what you want to store. To store pots, pans, and plastic containers, we opted for 8" and 9" depth. Big drawers look and work better near the floor, so we put the 9" drawers on the bottom row.

Use the Existing Kitchen Face: Less Work, but Less Freedom

To build drawers without replacing the cabinet face, you have two options:

◆ Leave the existing doors on their hinges and place the drawers behind them. This is easier to build, but you'll need to open the door every time you pull out a drawer.

◆ Saw the doors horizontally to make drawer fronts, and screw them to the new drawers.

Putting on a New Face: More Work, but More Freedom

Replacing the cabinet face gives you more control over size or shape, at the cost of more work. If you're interested in this option, build the drawers as described here, and see Chapter 21 to build the cabinet face.

Building Smarts

Kitchen cabinets are constructed in two ways. In "face frame," as shown here, a frame surrounds the cabinet doors and drawers. In "full-flush," only the edge of plywood or particle board is visible. A face frame decorates the cabinet front, but narrows the opening. Full-flush construction offers more space inside the cabinets, but the drawer fronts and doors must be cut and mounted even more accurately, because there's only ¾" of room on the front of the frame. Cabinet construction determines many details about drawer installation.

Step 2: Make the "Sleds"

Drawers have a reputation as uncompromising critters, and no question accuracy is necessary, especially in aligning the drawers with the *drawer slides*—the hardware that lets the drawers move in and out.

This design uses a time-saving trick for perfect alignment. Instead of screwing the slides inside the cabinet—a dodgy, error-prone step—each drawer mounts to what I call a "sled." Attach the drawer slides to the sled, and then screw the sled to the cabinet. The sled does reduce the width of the drawers, but it also lets you install drawers in places that now lack wood to support the slides.

Make the sleds as wide as possible. In full-flush cabinets, they should touch the cabinet sides. In face-frame cabinets, the inside of the sled side goes flush to the drawer opening. If the face frame is too narrow for that, place the sled against the cabinet side.

Make the sleds about 3" shallower than the cabinet, to avoid hitting obstructions at the back, and to save a bit of wood.

Because this project was built to last, with heavy, strong drawers, I used full-extension drawer slides. These slides are not cheap, but they can carry 75 pounds or more. Although your cabinets are probably 24" deep, an 18" slide allows access to the entire drawer.

To make the sleds, cut the sled parts. With the sled upside down, fasten the bottom to the sides, and glue with yellow carpenter's glue.

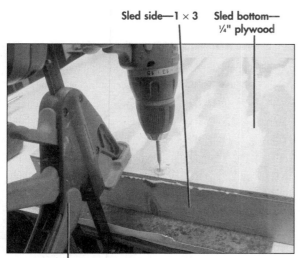

Clamp holds joint
while screwing

As I drill a screw hole in the sled, notice the glue squeezing out? That proves I've got plenty of glue. A wet rag quickly cleans this "squeezeout." These screws are strong, but 1½" ring-shank nails are faster.

Turn the sled over and clamp a spacer while the glue dries.

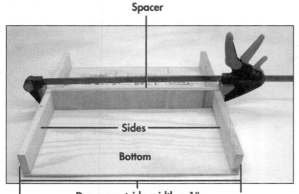

Drawer outside width + 1"
The temporary spacer holds the sled sides square.

Step 3: Make the Drawers

Once the sleds are built, turn your attention to the drawer boxes. I used ¾" plywood, but melamine-covered particle board works equally well.

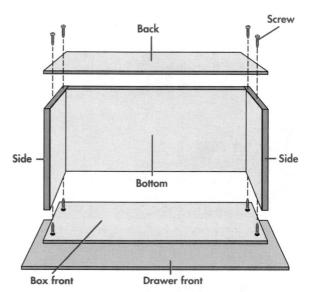

Each drawer box has five parts. All are ¾" plywood, except the bottom, which is ¼" plywood. The drawer front will be made later.

Screw through the front and back into the sides. The front screws will be covered by the drawer front.

The clamp holds parts during screwing; the square keeps the drawer side vertical.

Flip the drawer over and nail the bottom before the glue dries.

1½" ring-shank nails hold the bottom while the glue dries. Make sure to get the drawer square!

Step 4: Attach the Drawer Slides

With the sleds and the drawer boxes both made, fasten the drawer slides with the screws provided. (Screws with larger heads can jam the slides.)

Screw the Slides to the Sleds

Screw the slide's cabinet piece to the sled, touching the sled bottom. The end of the slide goes in one of two places:

◆ Flush to the front of a full-flush cabinet.

◆ Flush to the face of a face frame cabinet. (A later photo shows that ¾" of slide must stick out in front of the sled.)

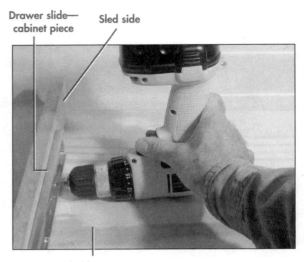

I'm screwing the slide to the drawer sled.

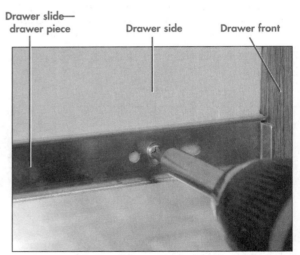

Screw the slide flush to the bottom of the drawer. This gives ¼" clearance between the drawer and the sled.

Screw the Sled to the Cabinet

Position the sled flush to the front of the cabinet carcase, or body, (for face frame and full flush). Screw the sled to the cabinet bottom or shelf, and to the cabinet sides.

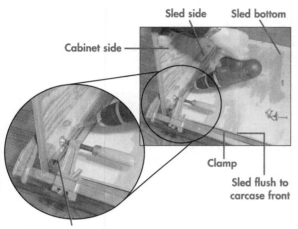

Cabinet side

Sled side   Sled bottom

Clamp

Sled flush to carcase front

Slide protrudes ¾" past sled—for face frame only

Screwing at an angle brings the sled down to the cabinet floor and makes a stronger joint (because more threads are in wood). The face frame goes on later.

Put It Together

With the preliminaries out of the way, engage the drawer slides. This may take a bit of fiddling, and my heavy-duty slides started out stiff.

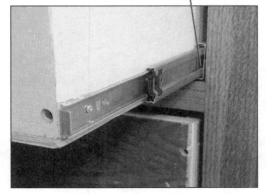

Drawer slide flush to face

Here's a drawer slide in action, right next to the new cabinet front. Those hideous screw holes will be hidden behind the drawer front.

Test the action on the slide. If it's too tight, adjust by removing some wood from the side of the drawer. If it's too tight, add a shim, such as a flat washer, under the slide.

Organization rules! No more kitchen kvetching when it's time to find a plastic foodsaver. With the lids stored alongside the containers, domestic bliss is assured!

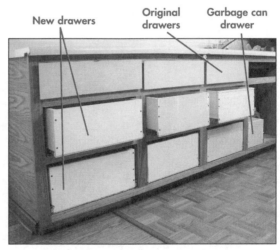

New drawers   Original drawers   Garbage can drawer

The cabinets have received new face frames, and these drawers are ready for their new fronts. I even built a drawer for that kitchen necessity, the trash can.

When done, either replace the existing fronts, or buy or build new ones. The process of building and attaching new fronts is described in Chapter 21.

In This Chapter

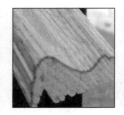

Build and Attach New Fronts for Kitchen Cabinets

Face it. The ol' kitchen cabinet faces are not looking so great these days. If you have a boatload of kitchen problems, and a truckload of money, you have a trainload of options on updating kitchen cabinets. The obvious choice is to replace the cabinets, knob, door, and hinge. But that's expensive, especially if you can't abide the looks of the cabinets you can afford.

A less-drastic alternative is to buy new faces for the existing cabinets. Aside from saving money and reducing the number of trees that get cut, you may benefit from higher quality: Old cabinets were typically made from strong plywood, not particle board.

But if you have some tools, some time, and some talent, you have other options. You can build some drawers, as we did in Chapter 20. And you can build an entire new front: doors, drawer fronts, and the cabinet face. That's our task in this chapter.

No question, this project takes some effort and some tools. But if you've been looking for an excuse to buy a table saw or a router, consider them part of the price of the project. You'll still save a lot of money, and beyond the "I-did-it-myself" glow of satisfaction, you'll acquire some awesome tools for your next project.

How long have these old cabinets been begging for retirement?

Step 1: Plan the Project

In this project, I replaced the cabinet fronts, the drawer fronts, and the doors. I had already added seven new drawers (see Chapter 20).

A new kitchen face is not something to jump into lightly. It'll cost time and money, and you'll spend for some take-out food. And the project will disrupt your life, so you'll need to plan your moves.

First, if you are embarking on any other kitchen projects described in this book, figure out a logical sequence for the work. If you'll be replacing the countertop (Chapter 19), use the old counter as a no-risk work surface while updating the cabinets. If you're working on the whole kitchen, subdivide the project so part of the kitchen remains functional as long as possible. If you're planning rewiring, get it done before finishing the cabinets or counters.

Our strategy on this project was to make the new faces, then the drawer fronts, and then the doors. The easiest way to replace the parts with something more attractive is simply to copy them: Measure all sizes and locations before demolition. You'll find certain dimensions repeated again and again, which may seem boring, but makes the project much more manageable. Keep the parts list in a safe place.

Choose wood according to your taste, your budget, and what is available in your area. I chose red oak for the doors, the *face frame*, and the drawer fronts. I used oak-veneered plywood, which is stable, cheap, and strong, for the panels (the center boards) of the doors and drawers, and to cover the cabinet ends.

You'll also have to choose hardware. Drawer pulls are mostly a matter of taste. But the easiest hinges are called "overlay" hinges. I would avoid European-style disappearing hinges, which are tricky to use. And even though they are hidden by a closed door, they look clunky when the door is open.

Step 2: Demolition Derby

With the planning out of the way, clear out the kitchen and get to work. Unscrew the door hinges and pry off the drawer fronts, and then remove the drawers. Hammer the face away from the carcase—the body of the cabinet. Then slip a prybar behind the face and gently pry it off.

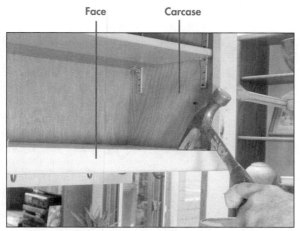

Face   Carcase

I'm using a flat prybar and a hammer to pry the face from a face-frame cabinet. I don't care about damaging the face, but I don't want to injure the carcase—or myself.

Grooves for cutting board

Slot for cutting board

With the face just about off, we're way beyond the point of no return! I'll replace the cutting board in a slot in the new face frame.

Building Smarts

While installing a hardwood face, cover any exposed cabinet ends with ¼" veneer plywood. Cut the vertical end piece of the face frame so it extends ¾" past the carcase. Cut a ¼" × ¼" dado in the back of this face-frame piece, ½" from the edge, to hold the end panel. Once the face frame is installed, cut the end panel ¼" long and slip it into this dado. Nail the end panel to the carcase with panel nails and cover exposed edges with molding.

Step 3: Build the Face Frame

Cut the pieces on your parts list from ¾" hardwood. Before *rip-sawing* to width, leave the boards about 2" long. After rip-sawing, remove sawmarks with a sharp hand plane. Then *cross-cut* to length.

Lay out your parts on big table and put them in position. I joined the face frame with *pocket screws*, which enter the back of the frame at an angle. Pocket screws make a quick, easy joint that's invisible from the front. You'll need a pocket-drill jig and the special drill bit that comes with it.

Make a pocket-screw joint with these steps:

1. Mark the joint on both pieces.
2. Clamp the piece that will hold the screw head in the jig.

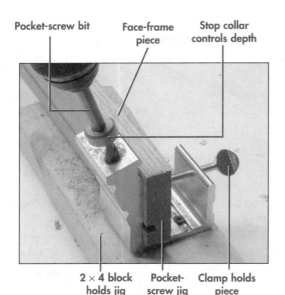

Pocket-screw bit | Face-frame piece | Stop collar controls depth

2 × 4 block holds jig | Pocket-screw jig | Clamp holds piece

The jig holds a horizontal piece of face frame while I carefully drill a screw hole.

3. Drill with the bit that comes with the pocket-hole jig. Go slow at first. Trust me: If you force the bit, it'll break!

4. Clamp the pieces and drill a second, smaller hole for the screw. Don't drill too deep!

Block protects wood from clamp | Clamp holds parts flush while drilling

Holes from pocket-screw drill

Pipe clamp holds pieces while drilling *and* screwing
A long bit drills for the pocket screw.

5. With the joint tight and the parts flush, drive a screw into the pocket.

Step 4: Attach the Face Frame

Once you've assembled the face frame, it's a simple job to attach it. Use 2¼" trim screws and *countersink* the screw holes so the heads are below the surface.

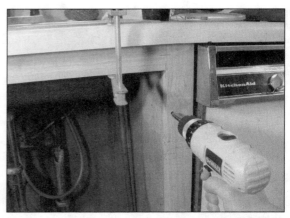

Work your way around the face frame, attaching it every 16" or so with trim screws. The clamp holds the horizontal rail tight to the counter.

Step 5: Make the Drawer Fronts

With the face frame in place, make the drawer fronts. Accuracy is still key if you want a good appearance.

To find the *size of the drawer front* …

◆ **Face frame:** 1" taller and wider than the opening (½" overlap all around)

◆ **Full flush:** ½" taller and wider than opening (¼" overlap)

Drawer Fronts: The Easy Way

If you have plenty of tools and time, make drawer fronts with the "hard-way" technique described later. Otherwise, use this easier approach to drawer fronts or for doors.

A clamp holds the parts while the square checks alignment of the "easy-way" drawer front.

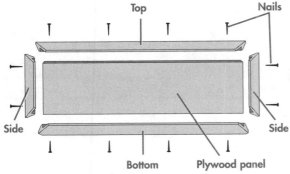

Four pieces of molding and one rectangle of ½" veneer plywood make an easy-way drawer front.

This corner molding nicely caps a drawer panel of ½" plywood.

Make 45° miter joints at each end of the corner molding. Glue and nail the front with 1½" hardened trim nails.

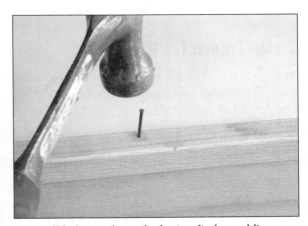

Drill holes so the nails don't split the molding.

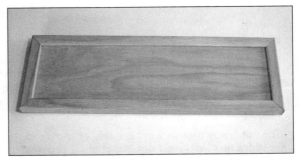

The easy-way front is finished or ready for decoration.

If the finished front seems too plain, use your imagination to decorate it. I screwed ⅛" × ¾" hardwood strips to the plywood. When you add decoration, make sure it will not interfere with your hardware.

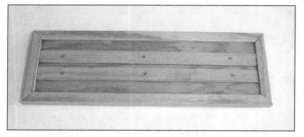

Here's the easy-way front, banded, stained, and ready to mount to the drawer.

Drawer Fronts: The Hard Way

More interested in a great result than in saving time? Then make the fronts from hardwood. Use 1 × 3 (actual size ¾" × 2½") for the frame, and ¼" veneer plywood for the center panel.

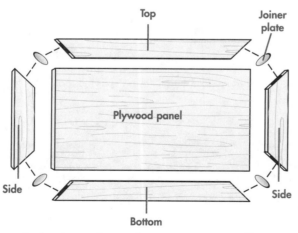

The hard-way drawer front is made of four solid-wood frame pieces, and one panel of ¼" plywood.

To make same-size parts, clamp a stop block to the miter saw.

Run the frame pieces through a router table to cut a ¼" × ¼" dado for the ¼" plywood panel. Or cut the dado with a table saw.

A router mounted in a router table cuts a dado for the plywood panel. A push stick that you can't see keeps my hands out of trouble.

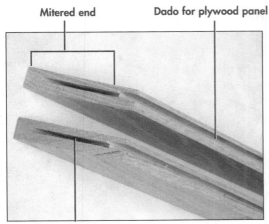

A close-up view of the door parts.

If you need to push the plywood panel forward in the slot, press 4-penny finishing nails into the dado from behind. Pull the nails after the glue dries.

With the drawer front assembled, turn your attention to decoration. I chose to rout grooves in the fronts, and to trim the edge with a cove router bit. You can also cut shallow grooves with a table saw or circular saw, or bevel the edges with a power planer, belt sander, or hand plane. If you leave the edges square, at least round them with a plane or sandpaper.

Finally, it's time to glue the frame. Glue one corner, let it set, and then glue the panel and the other three corners. I made the gluing jig shown in the photo, with one perfectly square corner. Clamping the frame parts against this corner ensures a square frame.

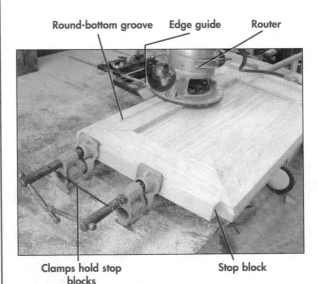

For decoration, I routed round-bottomed grooves in the drawer fronts and doors. The stop block stops the router at the end of the groove; the edge guide tracks the router along the edge.

With the first joint dried, clamp the last three joints. Gluing the panel into the dado makes a strong front.

Install the Drawer Fronts

Sand and stain the drawer fronts, and then install them with the help of a level and clamps. You can't be too careful about locating drawer fronts—the eye is very sensitive.

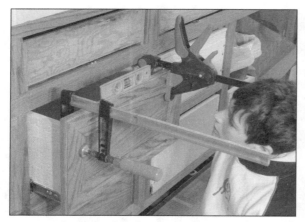

Josh checks that the drawer front is level.

Use clamps to keep the front lined up. Open the drawer and screw the front from inside, using four 1¼" trim screws.

The second drawer front is easier to mount, especially if you position it with a small panel nail (choose a color that matches your stain). The level confirms the height and angle as we drive in the nail. Then we'll screw from inside.

Step 6: Make the Doors

The doors are larger than the drawer fronts, but built the same way. Make face-frame doors 1" larger in each dimension than the door openings, to overlap ½" on four sides. Make full-flush doors ½" larger than the opening (¼" overlap). Use a plate joiner, or two 2¼" trim screws, to make the miter joints.

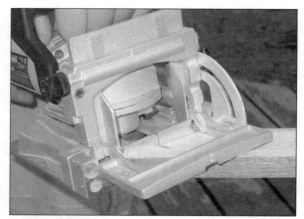

A plate joiner makes simple, strong joints. Adjust the depth so you can fit two slots in the end.

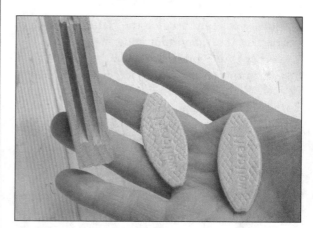

With two joiner plates, this will be a strong joint!

An old toothbrush is ideal for gluing the biscuit slots. Tap the plates into the slots with a hammer before assembly.

Clamp the doors like the drawer fronts, taking special care to keep them flat. Tighten clamps slowly and evenly until some glue squeezes out.

Sand, stain, and decorate the doors if you want. I lightly glued and screwed a piece of 3" × ³⁄₁₆" mullion casing molding down the center of the doors.

Using #4 × ⅜" flathead wood screws, I'm fastening the center strip.

After fooling with a variety of hinges, I fell in love with the ½" overlay hinge. It's solid but needs no *mortise*—cutout. First mount the hinges 3" from top or bottom on the door. Then hold the door in place and screw to the face frame. Use ¼" overlay hinges for full-flush cabinets.

These cabinets took a lot of effort, but were definitely worth it. You can see move views of these cabinets in Chapter 1.

The eye is a harsh taskmaster. Work accurately, and you'll be rewarded with cabinets worthy of a pro! These are easy-to-use "overlay" hinges.

In This Part

Part 7

Fun in the Bath

Want to remodel your bathroom? Get out the checkbook, or, more accurately, fill out a loan application. Between floors, walls, plumbing, and fixtures, prices can escalate until you drown in debt. But before you flush your bath-improvement fantasies down the drain, check out a piece-by-piece approach.

The projects include new racks for towels and other bath necessities (Chapter 22). Or sample a medicine cabinet you build yourself (Chapter 23). If the problem is plumbing, I show how to install a toilet (Chapter 24) or a pedestal sink (Chapter 25). And while tiling is covered in other chapters, I'd encourage you to consider tiling in your newly improved bathroom.

In This Chapter

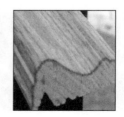

Install Towel Racks

No bathroom is complete without towel racks, and perhaps robe hooks or rings for smaller towels. Now that you can attach these racks to simple drywall anchors, replacing loose, rusted, or outdated towel racks is an inexpensive, rapid bathroom facelift. And although I don't show a toothpaste holder, soap dish, or toilet paper dispenser, the mounting technique shown for the robe hook also works for them.

Good-size home centers show bathroom accessories in a variety of materials (wood, chrome-plate, brass, and porcelain) and styles (modest, modern, gauche, and points in between). Selection is mostly a matter of personal taste; it's usually good to harmonize the material and style with the plumbing fixtures and walls.

Towel racks should be handy, but not in the way. In the bowling-alley bathroom we were working in, we hung 'em high, to leave room for pedestrian traffic. Ideally, for the sake of appearance, the racks would be mounted one above the other.

Step 1: Attaching the Mounting Plates

Attaching towel racks is simplicity itself, especially because they are sold with all needed hardware. First you attach the mounting plate to the wall with plastic drywall anchors. Then you fasten the rack bracket to the plate, hiding the plate.

To attach the mounting plates, follow these steps:

1. Mark the bottom of one end of the rack on the wall.
2. Assemble the rack bar to the end brackets (the brackets visible on a completed rack, not the mounting plates). Usually the brackets just slip onto the bar.

3. Place the rack, level, against your mark. Mark the bottom of the second mounting bracket.

4. Place a mounting plate with its bottom touching each mark. Drill through the screw holes into the drywall.

Drill into the drywall to attach the mounting plate.

5. Remove the mounting plates. With a drill bit that's slightly smaller than the plastic anchors, predrill through each hole in the drywall.

6. With a hammer, tap a plastic anchor into each hole.

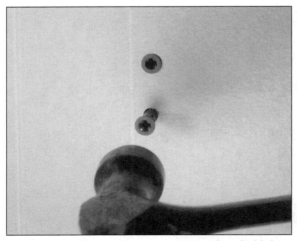

These plastic anchors are strong enough to hold the average towel rack in drywall or plaster.

7. Screw through the mounting plate into the anchors, and the mounting plates are finished.

If you want a stronger towel bar (got teenagers?), attach the mounting plates to the studs instead of the drywall:

1. Cut the bar to span between two studs, if necessary.

2. Drill through each hole in the mounting plates.

3. Drive the same screws supplied for the drywall anchors into the holes and continue with the normal mounting procedure.

Step 2: Tracking the Racks

Now that you can smell victory, finish the racks:

1. With the mounting plates in place, re-assemble the rack and slip the brackets over the top lip on each mounting plate.

2. The brackets we used (like most) attach to the mounting plates with a small screw at the bottom (seen in the photo of the robe hook, following). Tighten these screws, and then check that they grabbed the mounting plates.

After drilling 4 holes, turning 6 screws, and spending 15 minutes, this towel rack is positively positioned.

Step 3: Attaching Robe Hooks

A slightly different technology will attach other bathroom fixtures, such as toothbrush holders, cup holders, towel rings, and the robe hooks pictured here. Simply drill two holes, attach the mounting plate, and fasten the fixture to the plate.

With a hand or power screwdriver, tighten the screws in the mounting plates. The robe hook will slip down over the outside flanges.

Here's the robe hook, after about five minutes of light labor! The little screw at the bottom holds the hook to the mounting plate.

To fasten fixtures to hollow-core doors, don't use drywall anchors. Instead, use *winged anchors*—gadgets that expand like the wings of a butterfly after you push them through a big hole in a door.

In This Chapter

- Step 1: Designing the cabinet
- Step 2: Cutting the parts
- Step 3: Cutting the dadoes
- Step 4: Assembling the cabinet
- Step 5: Cutting the doors
- Step 6: Finishing the doors
- Step 7: Mounting the cabinet
- Step 8: Mounting the door

Chapter 23

Build and Install a Medicine Cabinet

It's one of the first things you see every morning, right after you slam the button on the alarm clock. And it's one of the last things you see at night. I'm not talking about your face—facial improvements are beyond our scope. I'm talking about the mirror on your medicine cabinet, and the cabinet itself.

Is your cabinet showing its age? Is it too small, poorly designed, or just plain ugly? You can replace the cabinet by buying a particle-board wonder, but it's rather easy to make a much better cabinet. Building your own takes work, but it also puts you in control of size, materials, and design. It's a great introduction to the art of cabinet-making. And you can admire the fruits of your labor first thing in the morning and last thing at night!

Step 1: Designing the Cabinet

Although over-the-sink is the standard location for a medicine cabinet, that's not enshrined in the Constitution—you can place the cabinet wherever it works.

How big to make the cabinet? I prefer a large cabinet, for two reasons. First, the large mirror makes a bathroom seem bigger. Second, well, look inside your medicine cabinet, and you tell me if it's big enough! The sample cabinet shown in this chapter measures 20" wide by 30" high on the outside, with shelves 2¾" deep. Because these cabinets are screwed through the back, as long as it covers two studs you'll find good fastening.

What materials are best? I used *melamine-coated* particle board, a standard stain-resistant material sold as sheets or shelves at lumber yards, but you could also use ¾" veneer plywood. The door frames are hardwood.

Building Smarts

Because you are the builder, you can make the shelf spacing as you wish. I like short shelves for the little paraphernalia that always accumulates in a medicine cabinet: tubes of medicine, nail clippers, tiny bottles. But feel free to change the spacing if this doesn't appeal to you. Just measure what you want to put in the cabinet and lay out the shelves accordingly. Similarly, if you anticipate storing big bottles in the cabinet, you may want to increase overall depth of the cabinet to 3½" or so.

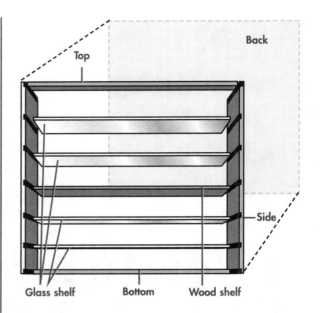

The following table lists the parts needed for a medicine cabinet that's 20" wide by 30" high on the outside, with shelves 2¾" deep.

Name	Material	Dimensions	# Used	Notes
Carcase top, bottom, wood shelf	¾" melamine	3" × 19"	3	
Carcase side	¾" melamine	3" × 30"	2	
Glass shelf	¼" plate glass	2¾" × 19"	4	Glass company cuts, rounds edges. *Measure when carcase is finished.*
Front edging	⅛" × ¾" hardwood	Cut to length after carcase assembled.	4	Can substitute edge banding.
Back	¼" plywood	19½" × 29½"	1	Cut after carcase finished.
Door side	¾" hardwood	2½" × 30"	2	
Door top, bottom	¾" hardwood	2½" × 20"	2	
Mirror front	⅛" mirror	19½" × 29½"	1	Glass company cuts; *measure when door finished.*
Mirror backing	¼" Masonite	Approx. 19" x 29"	1	Measure, cut after door finished.

Step 2: Cutting the Parts

We'll start by building the carcase, which sounds an awful lot like "carcass" because it's what cabinetmakers call the carcase—or body—of a cabinet.

With the blade guard lifted for clarity, I'm cutting a carcase side on a table saw.

After you *ripsaw* (cut lengthwise) the carcase parts, saw them to length. If you don't have a miter box, use a hand saw, a hand miter box, a table saw, or a circular saw.

Step 3: Cutting the Dadoes

This project depends on dadoes—rectangular cutouts—to hold other parts in position. On the sides, dadoes ¼" deep by ¾" wide hold the glass and wooden shelves. The sides, top, and bottom all get ¼" × ¼" dadoes to hold the back.

You can cut these dadoes with a router, a table saw, or a circular saw. To cut with a circular saw, clamp some guides to the pieces and cut repeatedly to make the width you need.

With a dado blade on a table saw, I'm cutting the dado in the sides to hold the back. A dado blade can be adjusted to various widths; the saw's blade height adjuster controls depth.

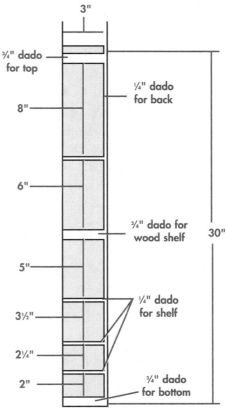

Dadoes on the side control the position of the shelves. All dadoes are ¼" deep.

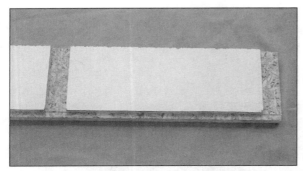

All dadoes are finished on this side, except those for the glass shelves.

Step 4: Assembling the Cabinet

With the dadoes finished, cut the plywood back to size and *dry-fit* the parts (assemble them without glue). If the carcase passes this test, start the gluing ceremony. Use regular carpenter's wood glue.

Follow these suggestions for a painless, accurate glue job:

◆ Carpenter's glue requires a tight fit. If you are short of clamps, use two 2" drywall screws per connection. Don't overdrive the screws and strip the holes.

◆ Have a wet rag handy for cleaning up glue *squeeze-out*. Squeeze-out is a good thing. When some glue gets squeezed out under clamp pressure, you know you've used enough glue.

◆ Spread glue with a scrap of wood or cardboard.

◆ Work quickly. Finish the assembly before the glue starts drying—15 minutes or less.

Glue, assemble, and clamp the sides to the top, bottom, and wooden shelf. Place the wooden shelf ¼" from the back so it aligns with the back dadoes. Clean glue squeeze-out. Nail the bottom in place with 1" ring-shank panel

nails (colored to match the stain you'll use on the cabinet). Space the nails 6" apart. Nail at an angle so nails don't poke through the melamine.

With the back in place and a square checking cabinet alignment, I'm clamping the carcase. I placed one clamp each across the top, the bottom, and the wooden shelf.

Leave the clamps for a half-hour while the glue dries. Slip the glass shelves into the dadoes. Lightly glue and nail the front edging to the front of the carcase and the wooden shelf, using panel nails.

Wood glue improves the joint under the front edging (shown ready to be glued). Use a scrap of cardboard to spread the glue.

With a clamp to hold the edging still, and a square to line it up, I nail the edging with panel nails. Clean up glue with a damp rag.

Step 5: Cutting the Doors

With the carcase done, it's time to start work on the door. The doors are built of hardwood, in this case red oak. I bought the "S4S" variety, meaning surfaced, or planed, on four sides. S4S is easily found at lumberyards.

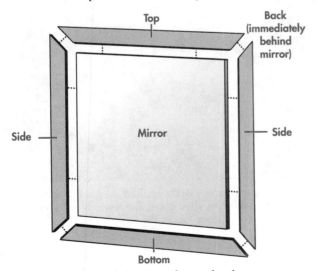

These six parts make up the door.

Using a push stick for safety, I'm cutting the door sides and tops. If you buy 1 × 3 (actual size ¾" × 2½"), you can skip this step.

Each end of the door parts gets a 45° *miter*, or angled, end cut.

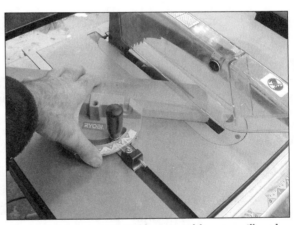

If you don't have a miter box, a table saw will make reasonable miter cuts. Note how far my hand is from the blade!

Building Smarts

To make a square door, the sides must be identical length; ditto for the top and bottom. If the saw manufacturer says it's safe, miter the ends of the top and bottom in pairs, stacked together. If you're using a power miter box, a clamp is critical for this cut.

Using the same kind of dado cutter as before, cut a stepped dado on the back inside of each door part. First cut a dado ⅜" wide by ¼" deep. Then cut a second dado ¼" wide by ¼" deep, as seen in the drawing.

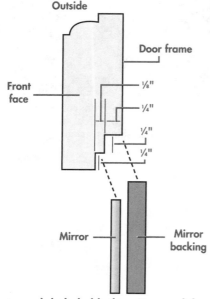

This stepped dado holds the mirror and the mirror backing. You'll see a photo later on.

Step 6: Finishing the Doors

Now it's time to glue and sand the doors, and then install the mirror and mirror backing.

Glue the Doors

The glue joints on the door frame are miter joints. Because they involve *end grain*, which glues poorly, we need to use a trick to get a strong joint. If you have a *plate joiner*, also called a biscuit joiner (a tool that cuts slots for *biscuits*—flat, rounded pieces of plywood), follow the tool's directions. Make two slots in each end of each frame piece, sized for size #0 biscuits. Larger cuts might come out the side of the frame.

With two #0 biscuits, these joints will be twice as strong as usual. Notice the stepped dadoes, described earlier.

Don't have a plate joiner? Screw the miter joints. Clamp the joint in position to a scrap of plywood. Predrill countersinks for one 2¼" trim screw on each side, making sure the screws will pass each other. Drill a second hole for the screw shank. Use urethane glue, such as PL Premium Construction Adhesive or Gorilla Glue, for a strong joint. Clean spilled glue with mineral spirits. Hide the screw heads with wood filler.

Gentle pressure, evenly applied, keeps the door square while the glue dries. Two clamps hold the door flat to the table.

With the door assembled, you can dress it up by using a router on the outside edge. Routers, which spin a router bit very rapidly, can put almost any shape on a wood edge, depending on your choice of router bit. When routing, always make several shallow cuts, not one deep cut.

This "plunge" router cuts deeper with each pass. (You can do the same with a regular router, with a bit more work.) I'm routing the door edge with an ogee bit.

Don't have a router? Here are other options for dressing up the door front:

- Cut shallow parallel grooves with a table saw.
- Hand plane a *bevel*, a slanting edge.
- Saw the bevel.
- Cut a stepped decoration using multiple passes on a table saw.
- Leave the edge square.

Sand the Doors

By now, the door should be impressive, but it will look a whole lot better after sanding. If you have a belt sander or the orbital sander shown, bring it on. Otherwise, use sandpaper and a sanding block—a flat tool or just a hunk of flat wood—and be sure to sand parallel to the grain, not across it. Start with medium sandpaper, and then change to fine and extra-fine grit.

These little random-orbital sanders work better and faster than you might expect.

Install the Mirror and Mirror Backing

With the door made, measure the openings left by stepped dadoes in the back:

- The mirror should be ⅛" shorter in each dimension than the inner stepped dado. Order a ⅛" mirror from a glass company, cut to this size.
- The mirror backing should be ⅛" shorter in each dimension than the outer dado. Cut this piece from ¼" Masonite.

After all this monkeying with routers, cutting a rectangular panel is easy! Notice the blade is set to reach ½" above the panel and that my hands are in the safety zone. A person could get used to having a collapsible, wheeled table saw, like this Ryobi model.

To insert the mirror and mirror backing, follow these steps:

1. Put 2" masking tape around the face of the mirror, within ¼" to the edge. The tape protects the glass from sticky caulking.

2. Place the door frame face down on a table.

3. Put the mirror backing in place and drill holes for #6 × ½" round-head screws at the very outside. Do not place a screw where it would hit the mirror.

4. Place a bead of clear silicone caulking designed to hold wood and glass into the mirror dado. The caulking holds the mirror tight in the dado.

5. Place the mirror face down in the dado and place the mirror backing on top.

6. Carefully drive the screws into the mirror backing, placed about every 6". Do not hit the mirror!

7. Remove the masking tape and scrape any caulking from the mirror with a single-edge razor blade.

Step 7: Mounting the Cabinet

With the door assembled, you can finally mount the carcase to the wall:

1. Find the studs behind the cabinet. Drill ⅛" holes until you feel solid wood. The centers of nearby studs should be 16" from the center of that stud, but check to be sure.

2. Mark the cabinet location on the wall and measure over to the studs.

3. Mark the stud locations inside the cabinet and drill ⅛" holes for the screws.

Drive 2" drywall screws into the studs, 4" from the top and bottom of the cabinet.

4. Hold the cabinet against the wall and drive the first screw, being careful not to drive it right through the back.

5. Use a level to hold the vertical, and then drive the second screw.

6. Drive the other screws. If the cabinet feels rickety, check that the screws caught the studs, and add a few more screws if necessary.

Step 8: Mounting the Door

With the carcase in place, fasten the hinges to the door. Place them about 2½" from the top and bottom, and carefully drive the screws, without drilling through the face of the door.

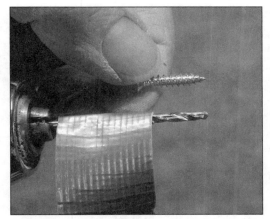

Wrapping a piece of duct tape around the drill bit will prevent you from drilling hinge-screw holes through the front of the door.

This nifty hole-centering device forces your drill to start at the center of the hole (otherwise the hinges may twist). A big nail also makes a decent indent.

Now mount the door on the cabinet. Have a helper hold the door in place while you drill one hole in the upper hinge. Drive this screw, put one screw in the bottom hinge, and then finish screwing the hinges.

Dave's Don'ts

Hinge screws can be tricky, especially the solid-brass ones provided with solid-brass hinges. I'm all in favor of solid brass, but the screws are too soft for hardwood. The steel screws that come with brass-plated hardware are infinitely easier to drive. I used butt hinges in this project, but the "overlay" hinges shown in the kitchen-face project in Chapter 21 may be easier to use. Make your decision based on esthetics and practicality—a fine-looking hinge is no good if it doesn't hold the door straight!

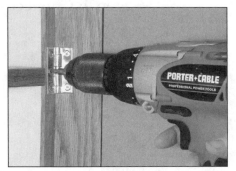

Add a magnetic catch on the side opposite the hinge, then drill and attach a knob and a catch. (Overlay hinges don't need a door catch; they are self-closing.)

If you like this cabinet, you can easily add a matching one to hold linens.

In This Chapter

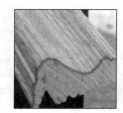

Chapter 24

Replace a Toilet

It's a fact: New toilets usually flush better than geezer toilets. And they may even harmonize better with your color scheme with harvest gold or avocado.

A third reason to replace a toilet is entirely practical: If the seal under the old toilet is leaking, water will eventually rot the wood framing underneath. That, my friend, is a drag, and it's a good reason to occasionally replace the seal under a toilet—something that, I guarantee, nobody does!

Toilets are usually shipped in two pieces: the bowl, which mounts to the floor; and the tank, which mounts to the bowl. You'll spend most of your time mounting the bowl.

Step 1: Out with the Old

It's usually easy to remove an old toilet. Shut off the water supply at the little valve, called a *stop*, beneath the toilet. If the valve handle sticks, loosen the big nut under the handle one quarter turn, as indicated in the following photo, close the valve, and retighten the nut.

Remove the water supply line—either a hose or a tube—by unscrewing the big nut at the valve end. In most cases, you'll be replacing this line with a flexible hose, but don't trash it yet. Bring the old hose to the store so you are sure the new water supply will connect to the shutoff.

Now pop off the decorative caps and loosen all bolts at the bottom of the toilet. (Look around; one may be hidden in back.) If the bolts don't want to move, try locking pliers. Don't worry if they break off; you'll be replacing them anyway.

Pull out the old toilet and cover the drain with a rag.

Dave's Don'ts

A toilet replacement can mushroom into a "more-than-you-bargained-for" project if you must replace the drain fitting and/or the wood supporting the toilet. If your old toilet is swaying like a porcelain hobby horse, the wood framing under it may be rotted. To do the replacement, you'll have to fix this framing, and that calls for digging into the floor under the toilet, or the ceiling below it.

It's harder to tell if you'll need to do serious work on the drain. You can get a hint from the overall condition and age of plumbing in your house. Consider also how well the old toilet flushes (although a drain cleaning may be the only thing standing between you and a straight flush).

No question, this could involve some work, but here's another way to look at it: If your house needs the work, somebody's gotta do it. If you're game, that somebody might as well be you. And by digging in, you stand to save a bundle on the repair! You'll find good advice on fixing floors and on ceiling repair, in *The Complete Idiot's Guide to Home Repair and Maintenance Illustrated* (see Appendix B).

Step 2: Preparing the Drain and Attachment

It's time to jump in—*not* literally—to the only tricky step: preparing the drain and attachment for the bowl.

Analyze Your Drain

The new toilet mounts to a floor flange that fits in a 4" (inside diameter) drain. The ideal toilet drain is a 4" closet elbow, connecting to a drain system that is sound, open, and strong. If you have a 3" drain pipe, install an expanding fitting to connect to a 4" pipe at floor level. This will, we regret to say, involve cutting into the floor—or the ceiling below. After repairing the drain, screw rot-proof 2 × 4 or 2 × 6 blocking around the drain, making a square box tight to the drain.

Building Smarts

If your toilet has been flushing without enthusiasm, the replacement is a great time to call in drain-cleaning wizards. You may save money in the long run. You will definitely save those anxious "will-it-or-won't-it" moments after the flush.

The Floor Attachment

Even if the drain passes inspection, you also need rot-free framing wood around the drain. If you can't tell whether such wood is present, try driving screws through the floor in the area that will be covered by the new toilet. If they grab solid wood, you are in good shape. If not, you need to tear into the floor and replace the framing.

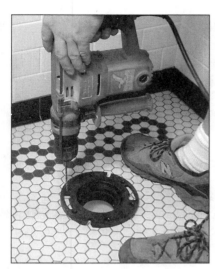

Using a monster drill called a rotary hammer, which drills by repeatedly banging onto the bit, Chris is drilling through tile to attach the new floor flange. The flange is a disk that slips inside the 4" drain pipe and rests on top of the finish floor.

These hefty stainless-steel screws are ideal for holding the floor flange onto the framing hidden in the floor.

Step 3: Preparing the Water Supply

If you're replacing an existing toilet, you'll probably connect to the existing supply valve, so you can skip this step, unless the valve is shot. If you've brought new plumbing to the toilet, a supply pipe should be coming out of the wall or floor at the back of the toilet. Stop valves with compression fittings attach to copper pipe, as shown, without soldering. If your supply pipe is another material, attach the appropriate stop valve to it.

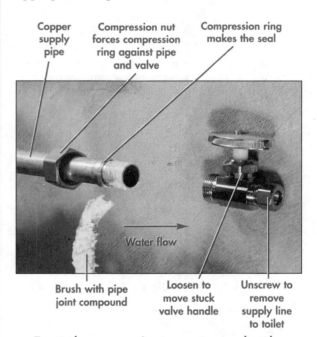

Copper supply pipe

Compression nut forces compression ring against pipe and valve

Compression ring makes the seal

Water flow

Brush with pipe joint compound

Loosen to move stuck valve handle

Unscrew to remove supply line to toilet

To attach a copper pipe to a water supply valve using a compression fitting, use pipe joint compound to prevent oxidation and grease the parts so they tighten smoothly.

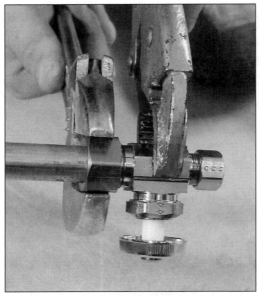

Locking pliers (or a wrench) hold the stop valve body, while the wrench tightens the compression nut.

Seal the Drain

Before placing the bowl on the flange, make a trial run, without any seals, to check if the bowl sits flat on the floor. If necessary, play around with the provided shims until the bowl is stable. (Cut the shims afterward so they will disappear under the bowl.)

A beeswax seal ring seals the toilet to the drain. If the new flange is not already greased (some come greased), smear some beeswax on it.

This grease—beeswax from a spare toilet seal ring—prepares for a tight seal between the toilet and the drain. Notice the mounting bolts, already in position.

Chris is pressing a toilet seal into place, tight to the toilet outlet.

Finish Attaching Bowl and Tank

At this point, everything is ready for a good, tight installation. Position the toilet over the mounting bolts, and tighten the nuts—but skip that Hercules act with the wrench—toilets can break!

Press the bowl down onto the seal. Put your whole weight on the bowl so it seats fully.

This bolt slips into the floor seal ring to hold the toilet to the floor. Notice the decorative cap, ready to slip over the nut.

Place the tank on the toilet and tighten the bolts holding the tank down. Tighten evenly, but don't break anything. The tank should come with the guts in place. If it doesn't, plumb them in according to instructions.

Tighten the floor bolts evenly. Place a small level on the tank to keep it level. Cut off the floor bolts with a miniature hacksaw, or grab a regular hacksaw blade in locking pliers.

Step 4: Connect the Water Supply Line and Finish

You have already connected the water supply shutoff (the "stop") before placing the toilet. Now simply attach a flexible hose between the stop and the toilet inlet.

Praise be to plastic! This plastic nut on the water supply needs only hand-tightening.

Insert the toilet seat bolts into their holes, tighten, and place the plastic covers on them. Open the stop valve and test flush the toilet. Caulk around the base with caulk that matches the toilet. Check for a leak at the supply pipe, and tighten if needed. You're done!

In This Chapter

- ◆ Step 1: Getting started
- ◆ Step 2: Connect the sink
- ◆ Step 3: Mount the sink
- ◆ Step 4: Finish up

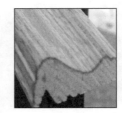

Chapter 25

Install a Pedestal Sink

A pedestal sink stands proudly on its own one foot, ignoring the little vanities found under the average bathroom sink. But a pedestal sink is only suitable when the wall behind it is in good shape. Still, pedestal sinks beat sinks mounted in vanities in one respect: There's no vanity to devour space in a small bathroom.

If your wall is scarred by pipes, do some drywall replacement before installing a pedestal sink. Use this opportunity to fasten a nailer behind the wall to support the sink, as I'll explain shortly.

Step 1: Getting Started

Like all sinks, this one requires hot and cold water supplies, and a drain connection. Kevin, a plumber with Lorentz Plumbing, Madison, Wisconsin, shares a handy trick for installing pedestal—and other—sinks: Make as many connections as possible with the sink on the floor. It's always nice to reduce upside-down-under-the-sink time, but pedestal sinks give you no choice: The connections will be partly hidden behind the pedestal after installation.

Your installation method depends on the condition of your wall:

◆ *If you must tear the wall apart* to repair the wall or the plumbing, securely screw two short nailers, made of 2 × 4s, across the area behind the sink. The nailers must be behind the mounting holes (shown in a later photo) on your new sink. Screw through the nailers into the studs. (If you are lucky enough to have studs where you need them, you're lucky enough to be buying lottery tickets!) Later, you will lag-bolt the sink to the studs or nailers.

◆ *If you do not need to tear into the wall,* mount the sink with spring toggles, as shown later in the chapter. Although a nailer is stronger, the advantage doesn't justify ripping up a perfectly good wall. However, make sure the drywall or plaster is both strong and good-looking, as it will be visible *and* be playing a supportive role.

Turn off the water supply, either at the shut-off valves under the existing sink, or at the main shutoff, if the shutoffs are absent. Remove any existing sink and make any repairs to the wall.

Unpack your goodies and take a look at the manual for the fixtures.

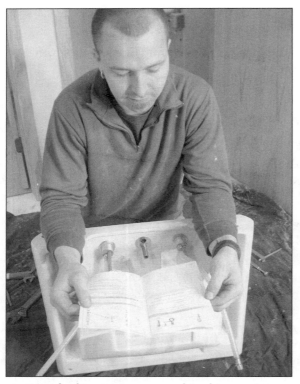

Isn't it refreshing to see a pro poking his nose into a manual? Kevin wants to check that he doesn't leave any essential parts behind. Some manuals are helpful, and others are not, but do give it a shot!

Step 2: Connect the Sink

With the sink on the floor or a table, start mounting the faucets and spigots. In the example shown, these separate pieces must be joined by tubes; most fixtures are one-piece, and thus are much easier to mount, as explained in the sidebar.

Connect flexible tubes to the faucet fittings.

> **Building Smarts**
>
> This faucet is more complicated than average, since it's made to fit sinks with nonstandard hole spacing. Fixtures for standard sinks, with holes spaced 4" apart, come already connected to the spigot. If you fear plumbing (and in their heart of hearts, most home-fixers do), buy a sink with 4" spacing, and jump to "Connecting a One-Piece Fixture," or see Chapter 18. One more suggestion: Put thread grease on metal nuts that attach to metal threads on fixtures. This will save aggravation and expense if you have to remove a fixture.

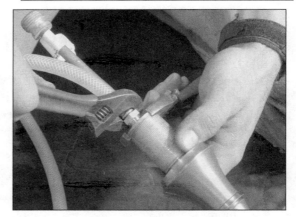

Tighten the tubes with two wrenches. The copper tube attached to the faucet receives its water supply from the house plumbing; the plastic tube delivers water to the spigot.

Mount the Faucet

Now mount the faucets in their holes. Some faucets seal to the sink with plastic O-rings. This one seals with plumber's putty.

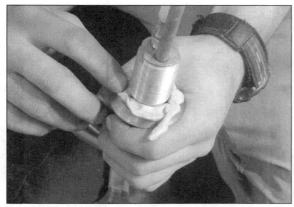

Form plumber's putty into a pencil shape and make a ring around the mounting location. Cram the tubes through the hole and tighten the lock nut from behind.

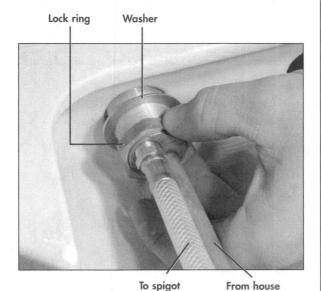

Lock ring   Washer

To spigot   From house
                 water supply

The lock ring and washer hold the faucet in place.

Basin wrench

A basin wrench reaches hard-to-reach nuts. The locking pliers prevent the faucet from moving. Make sure to get the faucet tight; it won't be accessible after you mount the sink.

Mount the spigot with a lock ring in the center hole.

Connect the Tubes

With the fixtures in place, connect the plastic supply tubes to the Tee at the bottom of the spigot. Then connect the water supplies (the flexible metal tubing seen in the photo) to the faucets. Leave the water supplies dangling.

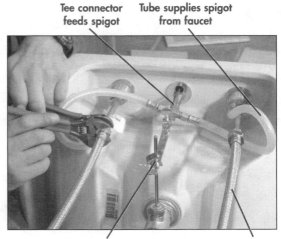

Tee connector   Tube supplies spigot
feeds spigot   from faucet

Linkage closes drain, connects to   Tube from
pop-up on sinktop   water supply

Two wrenches work against each other to make a tight joint without stressing the piping.

Connecting a One-Piece Fixture

To connect a one-piece fixture, start here. Connect two supply tubes to the inlets, using two wrenches as already shown. Then mount the fixture to the sink with lock rings or lock nuts, tightening with a basin wrench. Then continue from here.

Connect the Tailpiece

The last sink connection is the *tailpiece*, which connects to the drain. Place a ring of plumber's putty around the flange that enters the sink from above, insert the tailpiece from above, and tighten the lock ring from the bottom.

Using grease on the threads and plumber's putty on the sink side, Kevin attaches the tailpiece.

At this point, you have connected the spigot, two faucets, and the tubes connecting these parts. And you haven't spent a second on your back!

Step 3: Mount the Sink

You knew it had to happen. At some point, you'd have to lift this sink!

Test-Mount the Sink

Position the pedestal and place the sink on it, flush to the wall. When the sink is level, mark the mounting holes.

Center and level the sink on the pedestal. Hidden shims adjust the angle. Mark the mounting holes at the bottom outside.

With the sink in place, measure and cut the drain parts to length. Kevin cut the drain tubing with a tubing cutter, a special-purpose gadget with a cutting wheel, but a hacksaw will also work. See the photos of assembling a drain in Chapter 18.

Remove and Replace the Sink

Pull the sink away from the wall and drill holes for your fasteners. If there is framing behind the mounting holes, drill for two $5/16" \times 3"$ lag screws. Otherwise, use spring toggles, as shown.

If you don't have framing behind the wall, drill for this big spring toggle, shown coming out of the mounting hole.

With the holes drilled, return the sink to the pedestal. Drive in the lag bolts or insert the spring toggles. After you push a toggle through the wall, its wings will expand and lock on to the wall. Pull the bolt toward you as you start tightening, so the wings grab the wall instead of whirling inside it.

Don't tighten either a lag bolt or a spring toggle with your Tarzan routine—you could break the sink!

Step 4: Finish Up

With the sink finally mounted, a few connections will complete the job.

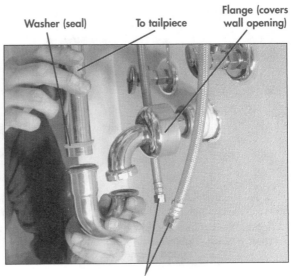

Washer (seal)   To tailpiece   Flange (covers wall opening)

Water supplies

Kevin assembles the drain parts.

To connect the drain pipes to the plastic drain pipe coming out of the wall, install an adapter. Goop the proper solvent onto the pipe, and then twist the fitting into place.

Tighten the drain assembly with locking pliers or a pipe wrench. Tighten evenly, holding the parts in good alignment.

Stop (shutoff valve)

Connect each water supply to the *stop,* the valve that shuts off the water from the house supply. An adjustable wrench will not scar metal like a pipe wrench.

Open the stops and test for leaks. Tighten any leaking pipes gently until you can't feel any water on your hand.

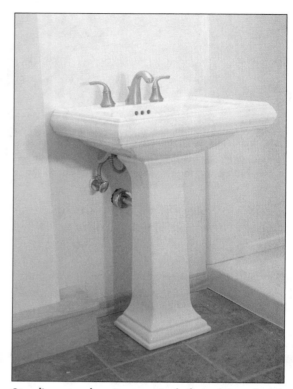

Standing proud on its own single foot, this pedestal sink is ready for business. "Kids, wash your hands before dinner!"

In This Part

Part 8

Electrical Matters

In this wired world, it pays to learn to tame electrons. If you have an el-hideoso or spark-spitting light fixture, see Chapter 26. Older homes may lack light fixtures in key places, like the middle of the living room. You could tape wires to the ceiling. Instead, why not learn to route wires through the wall and ceiling to a safe, attractive light fixture (Chapter 27)?

Speaking of ugly wires, do you have cable TV jacks wherever you want them? Now that cable often supplies Internet service as well as television signals, you may want more jacks. Running TV cable can be surprisingly easy; Chapter 30 shows how.

Older wiring systems, especially in a damp location, can often benefit from a safety upgrade. One good solution is to install an outlet with ground fault protection (Chapter 29).

If you've spent the time and money to make a beautiful kitchen counter, why not add lights under the kitchen cabinets (Chapter 28)? It's easy, it's cheap, and it's rewarding!

In This Chapter

Chapter 26

Replace a Wall Light Fixture

Have those old built-in lighting fixtures got you down? Whether it's a built-in lava lamp (now *there's* a horrid thought!), an el-grosso swag lamp, or a broken-down chandelier, built-in lights have a way of flaunting fading fads. But built-ins are not like death and taxes. You can replace them—without the pain of routing cable or the hassle of installing boxes.

If your house was wired before 1985, avoid electrical fixtures whose packages say they require 90°C wiring. Older wiring cannot withstand 90° temperatures, so old wiring to high-temperature fixtures creates a fire hazard.

Electrical work is usually pretty straightforward, but it has its own lingo, logic, and codes. Please read the sidebar spread on Basic Electrical Jargon and Safety in Chapter 27 before continuing. You can also find a helpful section on Making Electrical Connections in the same chapter. I can't possibly cover every conceivable wiring situation in this book, so I urge you to follow this commonsense rule: Don't get in over your head. If electrical work confuses you, this is not the best project for you. Let a pro handle it!

Step 1: Assessing Your Situation

Start by finding the fuse or circuit breaker powering the light: Ask a lackey to watch the light while you turn off fuses or breakers until the light goes out. Unscrew the fixture and gently pull it out.

Crossbar   Crossbar mounting screws

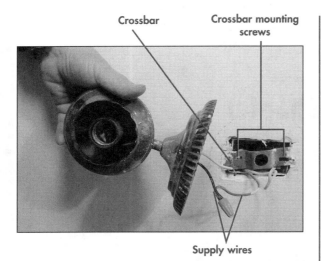

Supply wires

After a gentle pull, here's the scenery inside the old light fixture. We have already disconnected the white wires. Notice that the "black" supply wire is brown, with a splotch of white ... funky work!

Is the electrical box soundly connected to the wall or ceiling? If not, reconnect it using the techniques described in Chapter 27. If you are installing a ceiling light weighing more than 50 pounds, install a fan brace—a gadget that supports such a heavy light.

Building Smarts

Several tests in this chapter use an extension cord plugged into a grounded outlet. To start these tests, use a *circuit tester*, a pair of probes that lights when electricity is flowing through the tester, to check the extension cord. Put one probe in the small slot of the cord and one in the round hole. If the light lights, the cord is plugged into a proper outlet, and you can proceed. If not, consider buying *The Complete Idiot's Guide to Home Repair and Maintenance Illustrated* (see Appendix B), which has instructions on repairing this outlet.

Step 2: Which Wire Is Hot?

With the circuit still off, disconnect wires feeding the old fixture. If the old supply wires are long enough, cut them at the connector. If the wires are short, unscrew the connector.

To test that the black wire is the hot wire, follow these steps:

1. Plug a grounded extension cord into a grounded outlet.

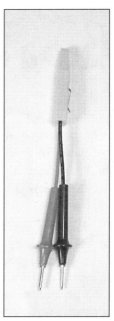

This circuit tester is a key tool for electrical work. Make sure it works—test it in a working outlet before trusting it.

2. Take the extension cord to the light box. Turn on the circuit breaker or fuse. Touch one end of the circuit tester to the round hole of the cord and the other to each supply wire. The tester will light when it touches the hot wire. Remember this wire.

3. Turn off the circuit breaker or fuse. If the hot wire is not black, mark it with black tape. Pull the black and white wires out of the box and push them to one side.

Step 3: The Ground Situation

Modern electrical wiring is "grounded" to drain off current in case something goes wrong. In systems connected with plastic-coated cable, the ground, technically the "equipment grounding conductor," is supplied by the bare copper wire.

Is the Ground Present?

To test that the bare copper wire is really grounded, touch the tester to the short slot of the extension cord and the bare wire. If the tester lights, the bare wire is a working equipment grounding wire.

If the equipment grounding wire is absent, the box may be grounded by *rigid conduit*, a thin-walled pipe that carries electrical wires. Only metal boxes (not plastic ones) are wired with rigid conduit. To check the ground in a rigid-conduit system, test between the short slot of the extension cord and the metal light box. If you don't get a light, the box is not grounded. An electrician can ground the box, but it's not easy, and in an older home, the new light might be the only one that's grounded!

Making Ground Connections

How the light box is grounded determines how you connect the ground wires.

For a system wired with *grounded plastic cable*, the incoming ground must be connected to the crossbar, the box (if it's metal), and the grounding wire from the new fixture. If your metal box does not have a threaded hole for a ground screw in the back, connect the ground wire to a green grounding clip.

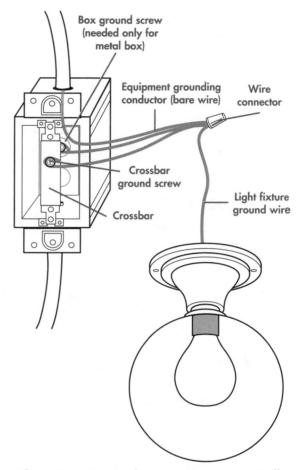

Box ground screw (needed only for metal box)

Equipment grounding conductor (bare wire)

Wire connector

Crossbar ground screw

Crossbar

Light fixture ground wire

The equipment grounding system must connect all metal parts except the hot and ground portion. (Only the grounding system is shown.)

For a metal box *grounded with rigid metal conduit*, connect bare wires to the box, the crossbar, and the grounding wire on the new fixture.

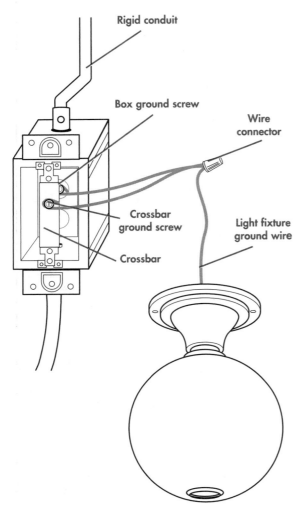

Rigid conduit

Box ground screw

Wire connector

Crossbar ground screw

Light fixture ground wire

Crossbar

Here's the grounding connection for a metal box connected by rigid metal conduit. (Only the grounding system is shown.)

Step 4: More Connections

With the ground system connected, use a wire stripper to remove about ½" of insulation from the end of the black and white wires. Using screw-on wire connectors, connect the …

1. Hot (black) supply wire to black fixture wire.

2. White supply wire to white fixture wire.

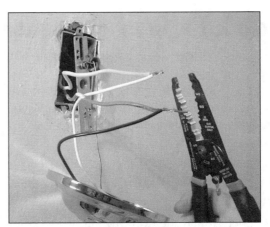

Twist white to white and black to black. Trim the ends to equal length and screw on a wire connector. We didn't bother flagging the brown wire with black tape because it was obviously not the white wire.

Step 5: Attaching the Light

With the hard work done, fasten the light in place.

If your fixture screws directly to the box (and does not use a barrel), fasten the fixture in place with two screws.

Many new light fixtures attach to a *barrel*—a small, threaded pipe that screws to a crossbar. Screw the crossbar to the box, thread the barrel into the crossbar, and attach the light.

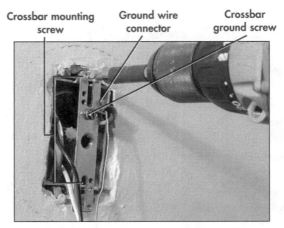

Crossbar mounting screw

Ground wire connector

Crossbar ground screw

With the ground and supply connections done, screw the crossbar to the box.

Thread the barrel into the crossbar, slip the light over the barrel, and screw the crown nut onto the barrel.

Screw the barrel so ¼" will protrude beyond the light housing.

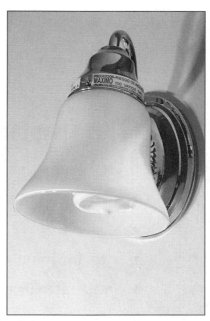

I think this fixture has timeless beauty ... but if I'm wrong, it can be replaced down the line.

Step 6: Testing, Testing

Turn the circuit on and check that the switch controls the light normally. Then make one final test: With the switch on, touch the circuit tester to the round (equipment grounding) hole on the grounded extension cord and to the body of the light. If the tester lights up, *you have connected a hot wire to the fixture body, a major violation!* Turn off the circuit, fix the bad connection, and recheck.

If the tester does not light, you are good to go. Enjoy your new light.

In This Chapter

27

Install a Ceiling Light and Switch

Got light where you need it? Probably not. No house seems to have exactly the right lights, in the right place, with convenient, safe switches. Even if a plug-in hanging lamp is where you want it, built-in wiring is safer, more convenient, and easier on the eyes. And it can, as in our example, be fitted with a dimmer switch.

In this improvement, we'll look at some basic electrical techniques, and then add a light near an electrical outlet. The hard part about running cable is getting through walls without destroying them; always try to run cable through an unfinished area, like a basement, attic, or garage.

Running cable through finished walls can be frustrating. Wires get stuck. The *fish tape* you use to pull wires through the wall gets stuck. Be creative. Visualize where the fish tape is going, and why it's hung up.

Basic Electrical Jargon and Safety

Working with electricity is not tricky, but it can be dangerous. If you are inexperienced or uncertain of what you are doing, consult a more thorough treatment, such as the chapter on electricity in *The Com-plete Idiot's Guide to Home Repair and Maintenance Illustrated* (see Appendix B). The following jargon and basic rules will help keep you out of trouble:

- *Hot wires* (usually black, sometimes red) carry incoming electricity.
- *Ground* (white, often called *neutral*) wires take electricity back to the utility.
- *Equipment grounding conductors* (usually bare copper, sometimes green) are a safety system that allows electricity to return if something goes wrong.
- *Supply wires* enter a box and bring electrical current.
- *Current* is the flow of electricity.

What size box do you need? To prevent overheating, the National Electric Code restricts how much junk you can jam into a box. The capacity, in cubic inches, should be marked on each box. Here's how to calculate the box size needed:

Each hot and neutral wire	1
All ground wires	1
Each switch and receptacle	2
All wire clamps	1
Add:	+ _____
Total:	

Multiply by 2 (for 14-gauge wire) or 2.25 (for 12-gauge wire). Result: minimum box volume required, in cubic inches.

Here are some electrical do's and don'ts:

- *Do* test your *circuit tester,* an essential tool that detects electricity when connected between hot and ground, in a working outlet. Don't trust—verify that the tester will protect you from live electricity. A tester is shown in Chapter 26.
- *Don't* use undersize wire or *fixtures* (lights or outlets). Most lights are wired with 14-gauge wire (connected to 15-amp fuses or circuit breakers). 12-gauge wires should be protected by 20-amp fuses or breakers. Read the breaker or fuse, and choose your wire accordingly. If you can't tell the difference, it's usually safe to use 12-gauge wire.
- *Do* shut off circuits before you work on them. Then test that the circuit is cold using a circuit tester.
- *Don't* fool around with aluminum wire, used in some houses built in the 1960s and 1970s. Aluminum is silvery-gray, whereas the more common and much safer copper is dull brown. Connecting to aluminum is tricky; it's smart to hire a qualified electrician to work on aluminum.
- *Do* make all connections inside boxes. Leave all boxes accessible and do not hide an electrical box behind a wall.
- *Don't* fool with electrical boxes containing a dense snarl of wires. These boxes, often found in a basement or near the circuit-breaker panel, may be powered by two separate circuits, and it's hard to be sure the power is off. Call an electrician.
- *Don't* get in over your head. *Any time you are thoroughly confused,* it's time to call in a professional electrician.

Step 1: Locate the Force

First find a source of power for the new light. An existing outlet is the most common source, but a switch is another possibility, *if both the black and white wires are in the box*. Also check for an *electrical box*—a metal or plastic box holding electrical connections—on the basement ceiling.

Once you have located the source box, follow these steps:

1. Shut off the circuit you think feeds the box. Test between each pair of holes in the outlet. If the tester is working, and it never lights, the circuit is cold, and safe to work on.
2. Remove the two mounting screws and pull out the old outlet.

On old wiring, it can be hard to distinguish the black wire. Here's how to tell:

1. Disconnect the wires from the outlet and keep them separate from each other.
2. Turn the circuit back on. Plug a grounded extension cord in a grounded outlet. Make sure your circuit tester lights when you touch the round hole and the small slot in the extension cord.
3. Bring the cord to the supply box. Hold one end of the tester in the round hole and touch the wires with the other end until you find the hot wire. Remember its location.
4. Switch off the circuit breaker or fuse. Now mark the hot wire, which will supply both the old outlet and the new light. Also mark other black wires that are connected in this box.

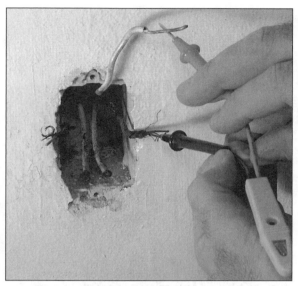

A circuit tester helps identify hot wires in an old box.

Step 2: Cut Box Holes

After ensuring that you have an accessible supply of electricity, follow these steps:

1. Locate the switch and light boxes. If possible, plan to fasten boxes to studs or joists (the ceiling beams). Find the studs and joists, which are usually 16" apart, by tapping on the wall or ceiling. Drill a small hole to confirm the location; the drill bit should hit wood in the stud or joist.
2. Cut access holes in the upper wall and ceiling, about 5" square, avoiding the framing. Square or rectangular holes are easier to patch. Likewise, separate holes, as already shown, are easier to repair than one big hole that meets at the ceiling corner.
3. Locate the light box. Generally, octagonal boxes are used for ceiling lights. Hold the box against the ceiling, mark the opening, and then cut.

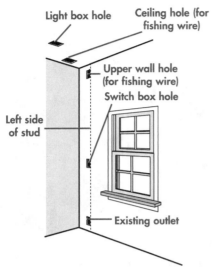

To mount a light in the ceiling, and connect it to a wall switch, I cut four holes: one each for the switch and light boxes, and two for routing cable. Think of these as fishing holes.

Measure the height of an electrical switch in the room. Place the bottom of the new box at the same height. Using a level, mark the new switch box cutout on the wall. (If you can't mount the box alongside a stud, buy a box designed to grab drywall; these are convenient but weaker.)

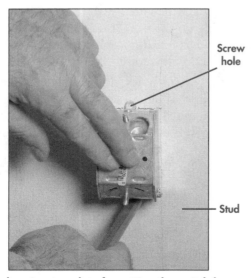

The box is a template for cutting the switch-box hole. Don't forget to mark the screw holes.

To start the saw blade, drill a ⅜" hole at each corner. Also drill for the switch-mounting screws at center top and bottom.

A jigsaw makes a fine instrument for cutting a box opening in plaster or drywall. Run a variable-speed jigsaw slowly to control dust. An extra-short blade will preserve cables already in the wall.

Building Smarts

When you route cable from point A to point B, don't worry too much about extra damage. If you're going to be fixing holes in plaster or drywall anyway, an extra hole or two shouldn't ruin your weekend.

Step 3: Fishing the Wire Through the Wall

With the box holes cut, turn your attention to electrical cable. If you are working on a 15-amp circuit (check the fuse or circuit breaker), use 14-gauge wire. Use 12-gauge wire for a 20-amp circuit. First drill holes to run the cable, and then pull cable between the box openings.

Drilling for Cable

Extra-long drill bits are essential for drilling these holes, and I advise using an 18"-long bit,

¾" in diameter from the start. In the example, you will drill only one hole, up through the *plate*, the framing on top of the studs, at a steep angle. In other situations, you might have to drill sideways through studs; the technique is similar to what's shown here.

Using a long bit, I'm drilling from the upper access hole up through the plate.

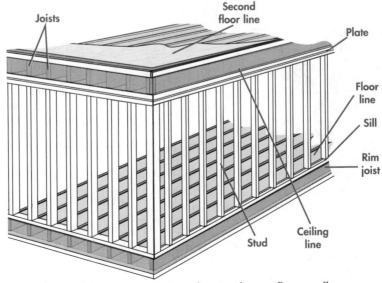

Here's a bit of typical house construction, showing how a floor, walls and ceiling are put together. The plate is two (or sometimes one) horizontal 2 × 4s resting on the studs. Joists are horizontal beams that rest on the plate. To get from the wall into the ceiling, drill through the plate.

Fishing for Cable

It's finally time to fish cables. One cable runs from the outlet to the switch box. The second cable runs between the switch and light boxes.

1. Uncoil a few feet of fish tape and work it down from the switch hole to the outlet.

2. Connect the cable to the fish tape and pull it up to the switch box hole.

🪚 **Building Smarts** _____

Be patient and creative as you fish. In extreme cases, you may have to poke two fish tapes through two holes, trying to hook one tape with the other. Eventually you'll get through, although you may have to cut more holes.

Use electrical tape to attach cable to the fish tape, a springy steel tape that pulls cable through walls. Extra hands are helpful: One person pushes cable into one hole, while the other pulls the fish tape from the other hole. Leave 15" of cable sticking out of each opening.

3. Push the fish tape down from the upper wall hole to the switch hole. Pull the cable up to the upper hole.

4. Run the tape down from the ceiling hole through the plate, to the upper wall hole, attach the cable, and pull it back to the ceiling hole.

Drill hole finds joist   Joist is marked

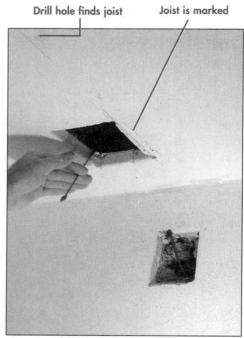

Success! We've gotten the fish tape through the plate.

5. Finally, push the cable into the light box hole. Cut off all cables, leaving 15" sticking out of the openings.

Step 4: Mount the Boxes

The hard work is now done, even though your place looks like the aftermath of Hurricane Fishtape. Take heart, things can only get easier from here.

A long drill bit reaches into the box as we prepare to screw it to a joist. Similarly, a long screwdriver bit is best for driving the mounting screws. Mount the box flush to the ceiling.

Handy boxes with sloped shoulders (arrows) are much easier than rectangular boxes because the cables won't snag on the plaster as you push the box into the opening.

Step 5: Repair the Damage

Once the cable is run and the boxes are attached, it's time to repair the damage, using a three-step process: 1) fasten backer boards across the opening; 2) screw scraps of drywall to the backers, and 3) finish the patch with joint compound.

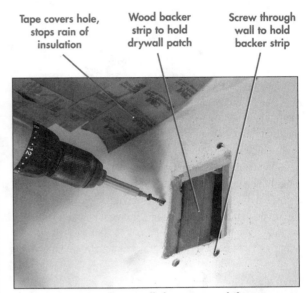

Tape covers hole, stops rain of insulation

Wood backer strip to hold drywall patch

Screw through wall to hold backer strip

Drill holes to reduce wall damage, and then screw through the wall to attach wood backer strips (roughly 1½" × 8"). (The tape is blocking a cascade of insulation from falling through the ceiling hole.)

Cut patches made of drywall and gently screw them to the backers. You may need shims (of cardboard, plywood, drywall, or roof shingle) so the drywall is flush to, or slightly below, the surface.

Duct tape contains the insulation as I work

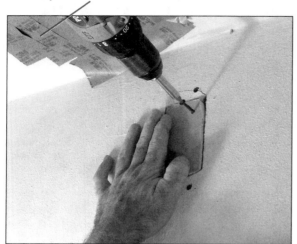

Screw the drywall patch to the backer without loosening the backer.

With the patch in place, apply drywall tape and trowel on a quick-setting compound. This stuff fills deep holes better than drywall joint compound, and then sets faster.

After one coat of drywall compound, the ghastly holes are disappearing.

Shift to normal joint compound after the quick-setting compound. Let the joint compound dry, sand lightly, and then put on a finish coat to match your wall.

I applied a finish plaster, which contains sand, because the surrounding plaster also contained sand. When you first put it on, this stuff looks awful, but floating quickly tames it.

Here's the repair, photographed in unforgiving shadowy light. I followed the steps in the sidebar, and even before the patch dried, it was almost invisible. A couple of coats of paint will make it practically disappear!

Building Smarts

Many older places have sand-finish plaster, a rough surface that can't be patched with spackling. Buy a plaster float and finish-coat sand plaster from a drywall supplier. Apply the finish plaster with a trowel. Wait 10 minutes, and then flick some water from a brush at the plaster and at the float. Move the float in a rotary motion. If the plaster is too soft, wait a few minutes. If it's too hard, use more water. Floating is magical: It flattens high spots and fills low ones—if you have the right tool, the right timing, and the right amount of water.

Step 6: Connecting the Fixtures

Finally it's time to make the electrical connections. Consult the following sidebar spread for some general information on electrical connections. Then read how to connect the three boxes in this lighting setup.

Making Electrical Connections

To wire a box, follow these steps:

1. Tighten the cable clamps (found only in metal boxes). You'll see two types of clamp; metal boxes may use one or both types.

Tighten the two screws evenly, and then insert the cable clamp into a round hole in a metal box. Turn the big ring to clamp the clamp to the box.

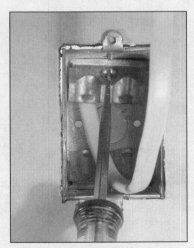

Other metal boxes use these built-in cable clamps.

2. Remove the cable sheath.

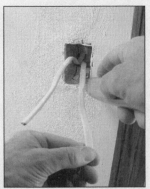

A utility knife will strip the outer sheath from cable. Don't cut the wires inside.

3. Strip ¾" of insulation from the wire ends.

A wire stripper removes insulation from the black and white wires. These nifty strippers will also strip the sheath.

4. Connect wires together: To join wires to each other, use screw-on connectors, sold in various sizes for various combinations of wires.

This screw-on connector makes a solid, insulated, but removable joint. The bare copper must be completely covered by the insulating plastic. Tug the connector to check the connection.

5. Connect wires to fixtures: The basic rule is that black wire goes to brass screws; white wire goes to silver-colored screws. Some electrical fixtures use *slip-in connectors* (round holes on the back in which you stick a stripped wire end). I prefer screw terminals, as shown in the photo. Strip the wire, make a hook, close the hook over the screw, and tighten.

Screw terminals, not the slip-in connectors, give a better connection to a receptacle.

6. Ground connections: The equipment grounding system should connect all bare wires, all metal boxes, and the metal body of every fixture. Grounding screws or clips connect the ground system to metal boxes.

Screw this green grounding screw into a threaded hole in the back of the box. No threaded hole? Use a grounding clip, sold in the same section of the building-material store.

Dim Wits

Now that we've seen how to make basic electrical connections, it's time to actually make some connections. We'll start wiring boxes at the dimmer switch, using screw-on connectors.

Connect the white wires from each cable. Attach one black wire on the dimmer to a black wire coming from the outlet. Connect the other black wire to the black wire going to the light.

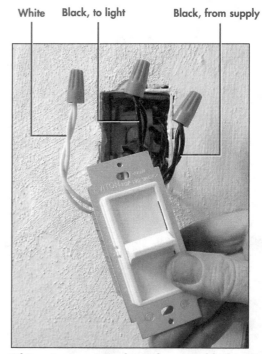

White   Black, to light   Black, from supply

White wires are joined together. One black wire connects to the supply, and one to the light. The equipment grounding (bare) wires are already connected and stuffed into the box.

To ground the dimmer box, connect both bare wires. If the box is metal, these wires also should connect to a short bare wire going to a ground screw or clip on the box.

Now screw the dimmer switch to the box.

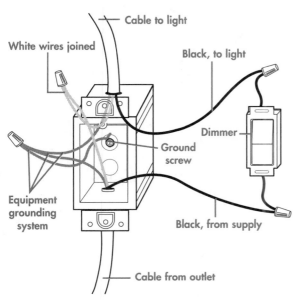

Make these connections at a dimmer box.

Rewire the Outlet

With the dimmer in place, let's get some power to the dimmer. Don't be tempted to connect all wires to screws of the receptacle. Instead, connect the wires to short wire "pigtails," which are then connected to the receptacle.

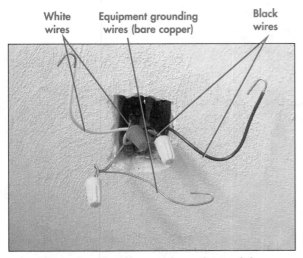

These pigtails will connect to the outlet, and the connectors will be pushed deep into the box. No bare wire grounds the box, because it's plastic.

With the receptacle connected, screw it in place and test it. A circuit tester must light between the short (hot) slot and a) the long (grounded) slot, and b) the round (equipment grounding) hole. The tester *must not light* between the long slot and the round hole!

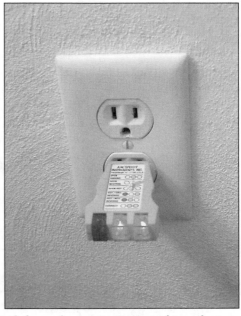

Much faster than a circuit tester, this outlet tester shows that the outlet is wired correctly when these two lights are lit.

This Light Is Lit

Finally we move to the last box—the one holding the light. First connect the wires, as shown in the photo. Although we are connecting a hanging lamp, similar steps will also connect another type of fixture, as described in Chapter 26.

The final steps in the process are easy:

1. Follow the instructions for mounting the light fixture.
2. Screw face plates on the receptacle and light switch.

3. Turn the circuit back on and make sure the switch operates the light.
4. Touch the circuit tester to the light body and the round hole of a grounded extension cord. *If the light lights, you have made a serious wiring mistake*—turn the circuit off and check that black goes to black, and white to white.
5. If the tester does not light, congratulations. You are finished! You'll see a photo of the finished light in Chapter 1.

At the light box, join two black wires, two white wires, and three bare or green ground wires with screw-on connectors. Then tuck the wires into the box and tighten on the crossbar.

In This Chapter

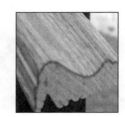

Chapter 28

Add Lighting Under Kitchen Cabinets

Although they don't rank as a necessity in the same way that running water does, undercabinet lights are a nice touch in a kitchen. They can be used to show off a fine countertop, illuminate your work area, or serve as mood lighting. You can buy a variety of undercabinet lights: halogen, fluorescent, low-voltage, and even rope light. Some lights mount from inside the cabinet, requiring you to pull wires through the wall. Others require a transformer, with a similar requirement for pulling wire.

Price and complexity increase hand in hand. Being lazy, in this chapter I opted for easy-to-wire halogen lights that screw to the bottom of the cabinet. Instead, I stapled the wires to the bottom of the cabinet, and then mounted a trim strip to hide the wires.

Step 1: Placing the Lights

My first thought was to locate the lights at the center of the cabinet. But because I wanted to illuminate the whole counter, which extends in front of the cabinet, I placed the lights forward of the center—away from the wall, in other words.

I held the light up to test the effect, and decided to mount it 2" behind the cabinet front.

Next I chose the side-to-side location. I decided to inset the side lights 8", and center the third light between those two.

Mark the side-to-side location on the underside of the cabinet.

Drill a hole and screw the lights in place.

Step 2: Getting Wired

With the lights in place, I turned my attention to wiring. In the system I used, each light came connected to a wire, which plugs into an extension cord that also came with the kit. The trick is to make the wires inconspicuous, by finding the least visible path for the cords that still follows the manufacturer's instructions.

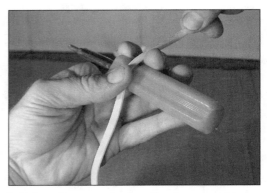

Pull the wires over the handle of a screwdriver to straighten them.

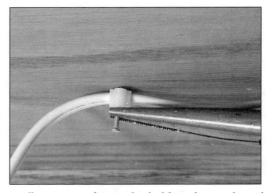

You'll save your fingers by holding the staple with longnose pliers when starting them. Notice that this staple has an insulated plastic head.

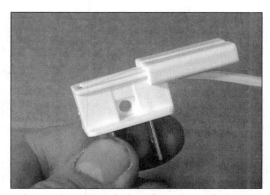

Cut the cord to the right length and attach the plugs by sliding the cap toward the left. A gentle squeeze with pliers helps at this point.

Big electrical staples can secure the coil of wire.

If the lights are too obvious (but remember, a week after you finish, you are more likely to dwell on the brighter counter, not the lights themselves), add a trim strip to the front of the cabinet, if you can find matching wood, and finish.

You'll see a photo of the finished installation in Chapter 1.

In This Chapter

Chapter 29

Upgrade to a Ground-Fault Outlet

Electrical systems have come a long way over the past 50 years or so, and one of the biggest improvements has been the introduction of equipment grounding systems. It's simple: Electricity wants to return to its source. Normally, that happens through the grounded (white) wires. But if something goes wrong with the white system, the juice still wants to return home.

In the worst case, that may happen through your body. But in new wiring, the return is supposed to occur through the *equipment grounding wires*. Equipment grounding, carried by bare copper wire, green wire, and steel *conduit* (steel tubes that contain wires), is good to have, but hard to install. You can get around this limitation, and improve safety in outdoor and wet locations, by installing ground-fault circuit interrupter (GFI or GFCI) outlets. These gadgets shut off the current when they sense a problem with the ground. So whether it's updating an ungrounded outlet in a kitchen or bathroom or improving electrical safety in an outdoor location, GFIs are good friends indeed.

Step 1: Location, Location, Location

A GFI is a fast-acting circuit breaker that senses small imbalances in a circuit caused by current leakage to ground and, in a fraction of a second, shuts off the electricity. The GFI continually matches the current going out to an electrical device against the current returning through the wiring. Whenever the amount "going" is significantly different from the amount "returning," the GFI cuts the electric power.

Where should you consider installing a GFI? Let moisture, common sense, and the electrical code rule:

- In a kitchen, especially above the counter
- In a bathroom
- In any outdoor location
- In a basement

We decided to update an existing outlet on a porch. You can also use the techniques described in Chapter 27 to install a new electrical box to hold a GFI. Please review that chapter first for some basic electrical safety information. If, after reading the relevant material, *you are still uncomfortable* working on wiring, hire an electrician.

The National Electrical Code requires a big plastic bubble (an "in-use" cover) over GFIs in exposed outdoor locations. I got around this requirement because my outlet was sheltered by a roof.

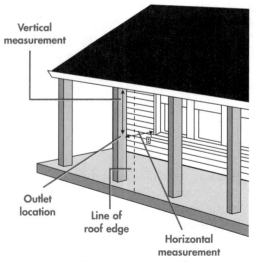

Do you need an "in-use" cover for an outdoor outlet? Measure vertically to the height of the nearest roof. Measure horizontally to a point directly under the roof overhang. If the horizontal measurement is less than the vertical, you need an in-use cover.

Step 2: Shut Off the Circuit

As usual, start this electrical project by cutting off the juice! Turn off fuses or circuit breakers and test the existing outlet to make sure it's off. If you're familiar with electrical work, the task is straightforward, but I'd suggest reading the discussion of testing a circuit in Chapter 27. It's good stuff. I know—I wrote it!

Before banking your life on a $3.59 circuit tester, check the tester by putting the prongs in a working outlet. Do this again after you test your circuit!

 Building Smarts

A modern circuit has three "legs," or conducting paths:

- **Hot.** Black or red wire that brings current to the box. Hot is in the smaller rectangular slot in extension cords and outlets.
- **Grounded.** White wire that drains current from the house. Ground is in the larger rectangular slot in extension cords and outlets.
- **Equipment grounding.** Bare or green wire, or steel conduit, that makes an emergency return path for current. Equipment grounding is in the circular hole in extension cords and outlets.

Turn off the circuit breaker or fuse that you think controls the outlet and test the outlet. Continue until you have turned off the right circuit.

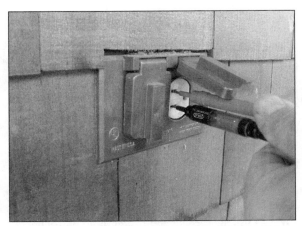

Using a circuit tester, check that the outlet is cold. Test between the hot slot and the grounded and equipment-grounding slots.

Step 3: Taking It Apart

Once you're sure you have the power off, dig into the box and unscrew the existing outlet.

Unscrew one screw at each end of the old outlet.

Pull the outlet from the box and look over what you find.

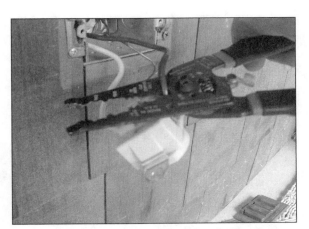

If the wires are long enough, cut them off at the terminal and restrip. Otherwise, unscrew the terminals and reuse the old, stripped ends.

If you see a nest of wires inside the box (this is rare), reread Chapter 27 for suggestions on what to do next. GFIs are bulky and take up a lot of room inside the box. If you choose to install a larger box—no easy task—consult Chapter 27 for box-mounting suggestions.

Step 4: Putting It Back Together

The easiest step is wiring in the GFI. Make sure to connect white to "neutral" or "grounded" terminals, and black to "hot." The back of the GFI should be labeled to guide you.

GFIs have two sets of terminals on the back. Bring your supply wires to the terminals marked "supply." To protect other outlets with the same GFI, connect them to the "load" terminals. To prevent confusion, the load terminals are covered with a plastic tape on a fresh-from-the-box GFI.

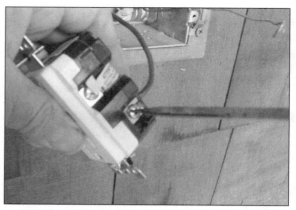

While I usually recommend avoiding slip-in connectors (round holes that lead to spring connectors) on the back of outlets, the slip-in connectors on GFIs use a secure, screw clamp.

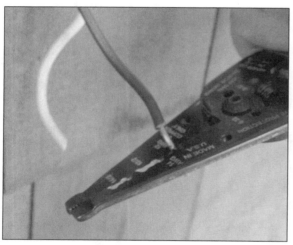

Strip about ¾" from the end of the wires. A "strip gauge" on the back of the GFI may tell you how much insulation to remove.

Firmly attach the ground wire to the ground screw. Notice that this wire loop is formed clockwise, so it will tighten when the screw tightens.

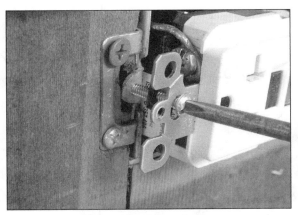

Connect the GFI to the box.

Install the spring cover. Be sure to buy the horizontal or vertical type, depending on installation.

If you have an outlet tester, use it to test the outlet, as shown. If not, a circuit tester should light between the hot slot and both the grounded and the equipment-grounding slots (assuming equipment grounding was present in the circuit). It *should not light* between the grounded and the equipment-grounding slots.

When these two lights are on, this handy tester assures you the outlet is wired correctly.

If the outlet fails the test, turn off the circuit, pull apart the outlet, and correct the wiring.

In This Chapter

Chapter 30

Run TV Cable Through Walls

Cable: It's not your father's television anymore. Cable may be bringing your Internet connection. It may be supplying the endless channels of digital cable. Or both. With everything from the next paycheck to the next basketball game riding on the cable, it's logical to want to bring cable to more rooms. The process can be easy—or a nightmare—depending on your luck and the construction of your house.

Parts for *coaxial cable*—so named because all the components are arranged around one axis—are widely available at home centers. Choose R6 cable, which gives a better signal than the older, R59 variety. Incidentally, the cable-routing instructions are also applicable to other functions, such as wiring doorbells, thermostats, or home Ethernet networks.

Step 1: Finding the Best Route

The most important decision of running cable comes first: finding the best route from the existing cable to the destination. If you can run cable through a basement, garage, or attic, you'll avoid tearing into walls or ceilings. The worst cable runs occur when walls do not line up from floor to floor, or you have to sidestep heavy beams and posts.

Expect to cause some damage in a complicated cable run. But with patience and cleverness, you should be able to get the signal where it needs to go. Then it's just a matter of repairing walls, a useful skill in any homeowner's bag of tricks. The wire-fishing techniques described in Chapter 27 can also be used to run coaxial cable.

Step 2: Getting from Point A to Point B

No question, the only hard part about working with cable is getting it where you want it to go.

Hold on tight! This right-angle drill—found in any electrician's toolkit—won't take no for an answer. I'm drilling through the ceiling of a cabinet that just happened to be under my upstairs destination.

The following tools are helpful for routing cable:

- Drill bits—the longer, the better. If you buy cable with the ends already fitted (as I suggest), 5/8" diameter is the minimum for easy cable routing.

- *Auger bits*, which pull themselves into the hole, work much faster than flat bits, but they are more expensive.

- A right-angle drill is perfect for working in tight corners. It's ideal for drilling from the basement into the first floor, for drilling between studs or joists, and for driving ridiculously long bits.

- Fish tape is a springy steel tape that electricians use to pull wire through walls.

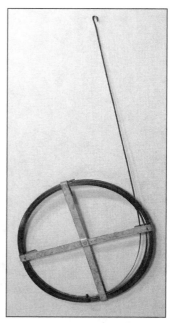

Don't go wire fishing without a fish tape! Fish tapes are the best tool you can find for pushing through holes in a wall. Some fish tapes have hooked ends to grab a second fish tape.

Dave's Don'ts

When you are drilling through a wall, you don't want to drill into an electrical cable. Here are some suggestions for reducing the electrical hazards associated with making blind holes in walls:

- If using a battery drill, turn off all electricity in the house.
- Use a grounded tool so the metal frame will conduct electricity to ground.
- Wear rubber gloves.

To route a cable from floor to floor, follow these steps:

1. To get to the floor below, cut an opening in the drywall near the floor and drill as vertically as possible through the 2 × 4 at the base of the wall. It helps to remove the baseboard before starting, but this does make for a bigger repair job.

2. To skip a floor (say from the basement to the second floor), drill up from the basement and down from the second floor into the same stud cavity—the gap between studs. Take the cable to the first floor and cut an opening in the wall. Push a fish tape from the basement into this hole. Tape the cable to the fish tape and pull the cable down into the basement. Push the fish tape down from the second floor and pull the cable up from the first floor.

A jigsaw or a hand drywall saw (shown in Chapter 4) work equally well to cut an opening for routing cable. A rectangular cutout is easier to patch.

To route cable along a wall, follow these steps:

1. Remove the baseboard by gently prying with a hammer and a crowbar. Cut out a strip of drywall just below the baseboard and drill holes through the base of the studs. Because you will hit nails, use a drill bit designed for metal.

2. Cut holes 24" apart, between the studs, low on the wall (where the holes will be less noticeable). Drill through one stud to each side, and then use a fish tape to pull the cable through. This trick works best with a 1" drill.

3. To get past a door or window, make your holes more than 8" above the opening.

To route cable into the next rooms, follow these steps:

1. Drill straight through one stud cavity and mount the new cable fixture in the drill hole.

2. Drill up and over, through the attic, or down and under, through the basement.

Step 3: Cable Connections

Once you've got the cable to its destination, the nasty work is done, and it's time to make connections.

If you don't already have a *splitter*, which allows you to connect several cables to a single source, install one. Splitters have various numbers of outputs.

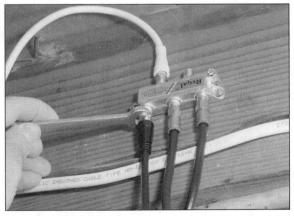

A light touch on the wrench makes a sound, durable connection. One cable brings the signal in; the others go to a cable modem and two TVs.

Building Smarts

The only job of coaxial cable is to bring you a signal. These pointers will help maintain a good signal:

◆ Don't crush or abuse the cable.

◆ Tighten connectors with a wrench, but spare the Hercules routine, which could cause damage.

◆ Avoid sharp bends. The bend radius should be at least 10 times the diameter of the cable.

◆ Stay away from house wiring. If you must run the cable near wiring, run it perpendicular, not parallel.

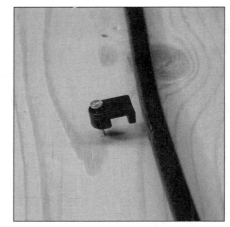

These purpose-made staples keep cable out of harm's way.

The male end (right) fits the female end. That little rod at the center of the female end carries the signal.

My advice is to buy ready-made cable, so you don't have to bother cutting cable and inserting end fittings. Buy more than you need, so you don't spend an hour fishing cable, only to find it 6" too short.

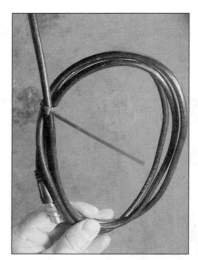

Cable ties are a great way to tame coaxial cable.

Connect one end of the cable to the splitter, and the other to the face plate. Secure the coaxial cable with staples every 2' to 4'. If the cable is too long, make a loose coil and tie it with cable ties.

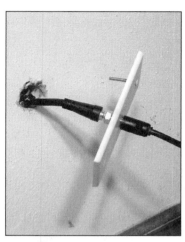

A ⅝" hole in the wall is all you need to route a cable into this outlet plate.

Tighten the fitting with a wrench, and then fasten the faceplate to the wall, using drywall *anchors*—gadgets that hold screws in drywall.

Step 4: Repairing the Damage

By now, you've got the signal to your cable modem or TV. So you've run out of excuses: It's time to undo the damage you did to walls and ceilings.

A key rule of drywall repair is to avoid any bulges on the surface, because they will cause havoc down the line.

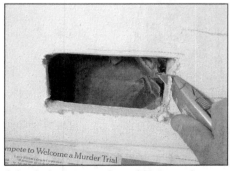

I used this hole to route the cable around a corner— the cable won't be visible here. The utility knife cuts away offending bulges.

Scraping with this drywall trowel completes the cleanup.

This hunk of wood goes behind the hole and is mounted to the drywall screws already in position.

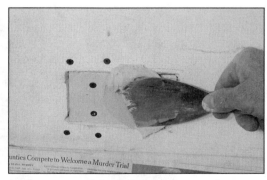

As I start to mud the hole, you can see the screws holding the drywall patch to the wooden backer. You don't see drywall tape because I pressed it into this patching after I shot the photo.

If you need more advice on patching these holes, consult Chapter 4 on drywalling and Chapter 27 on mounting a ceiling light.

The job is done! Sit back and relax with your 999 new channels!

In This Part

Part 9

For Decoration or for Fun

I used to think anybody could paint a room. Then I watched some first-timers, and realized that while most of the intended target gets paint, collateral damage too often plagues everything else. In Chapter 31, I offer some sage suggestions for making an easy project faster and easier. But why stop at painting? Chapter 32 describes molding replacement, a manageable job that can revolutionize the style of a room. And once you get the hang of hanging molding around baseboards, doors, and windows, why not take a crack at crown molding (Chapter 33)? It's truly the crowning touch in a room that you've worked so hard to beautify.

Replacing a fireplace mantelpiece (Chapter 34) offers a chance to show off your growing carpentry skills. If you've got a room that qualifies as a natural photographer's darkroom, you could install a skylight. But that's a big job, if it's possible at all. Instead, Chapter 35 describes a middle ground: a sun tube that can transport light to any dark room that's near a roof. Finally, if your kid is dreaming of a sleeping loft, see Chapter 36. Lofts make a great introductory project: With no drywall, no plumbing, and no wiring, you concentrate on structure and make a throne fit for a child-king!

In This Chapter

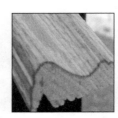

Chapter 31

Paint a Room, Painlessly

Many factors contribute to the psychology and esthetics of a room, but none is more potent than wall color. And dollar for dollar, hour for hour, nothing returns more results than whole-room repainting.

This job calls for a logical work sequence. If you finish one process before starting another—clean all the walls before starting to patch them, for example—you'll be less confused, make fewer mistakes, and waste less time hauling tools and handling material. There is no need to wear a mask with latex paint, although it's always smart to keep some windows open for ventilation.

Step 1: The Color Scheme

Choose paint color carefully, since color may be the dominant factor in a room's personality. Colors have moods. Whites can make a room feel large and cheery, or cold or forbidding. Darker, more pronounced, colors can make a room feel cozy, inviting, or artistic—or small, even cave-like.

Here are some considerations for color selection:

◆ What colors are in the trim, furniture, floor coverings, and artwork? Your paint should harmonize with these.

◆ Loud colors give a sense of energy, while softer, more neutral colors are more calming.

◆ Before selecting a bold color, make sure your family can live with it.

◆ Neutral colors slip into the background. As you paint, the room may seem stark or boring—until you add color with furnishings, art, and floor coverings.

- If your sense of color is as primitive as mine, take a look at the coordinated color combinations presented by paint companies.

- Dark paints are hard to lighten. To make a quick jump toward white on a wall that's now dark, put two coats of a good primer under your paint.

- Unless you enjoy redecorating, avoid the color of the week: Don't paint yourself into a corner by falling for a foolish fad.

- Don't judge a color based on a postage-stamp sample. Buy a quart of the color and test it on your walls. Or buy from a paint store that mails out larger color samples.

> **Dave's Don'ts** _____
> Most people use flat or "eggshell," a slightly glossy and easier-to-clean variation on flat, for walls, and semi-gloss paint for trim. Avoid full gloss enamel unless you have plenty of experience; it's difficult to avoid brushmarks.

Step 2: Going to Paint-Prep School

Once the decisions are made, it's time to empty the room and prepare for painting. When you empty the room, call in the Jettison Brothers—experts in trimming possessions. It makes a lot more sense to dump unwanted junk than to pack it up. At any rate, the preparation stage often takes as long as painting itself.

There is little sense in putting expensive paint over the dirt and grime that have accumulated on your walls. A strong cleanser like TSP substitute, sold at paint stores, removes grunge and roughens the paint, so the new paint gets a better toehold.

Masking—protecting surfaces from paint—is an excuse to be anal, especially if your paint-brushing technique ranges toward Jackson Pollock. First cover built-in or unmovable furniture, then windows and doors. Newspaper and masking tape are a good combination for masking small areas. For floors, tape down 3-mil plastic with duct tape or the special masking tape that sticks to plastic. Wipe away dust with a damp rag and press the tape firmly, so paint cannot seep underneath.

Strips of newspaper attached by masking tape should be adequate to protect trim unless you will be painting the ceiling, or are really wild with the roller. In that case, mask the entire opening with plastic.

If the baseboard will remain in place, mask it like the door top, after you mask the floor. (If you just tape the floor masking to the baseboard, it's sure to pull loose while you paint.)

Remove outlet and switch covers, stash the parts in a plastic bag, and stick masking tape over the electrical fixture. Turn off circuits and detach light fixtures from the ceilings and walls. Generally, it is safe to hang light fixtures on their wires, but if you're not sure what you're doing, get advice or call an electrician. Remove light globes, and protect the rest of the fixture in a plastic bag.

Protect the floor with heavy plastic tarps. Avoid 1-mil plastic. It's basically a square dry-cleaner bag, and is guaranteed to tear, or stick to your shoes, or both. Tape 3- or 4-mil plastic securely to the edges of your room.

Aren't you glad this isn't *your* house? Seriously, this room is finally ready for painting. The rolling scaffold allows work on the ceiling, where those fake beams (arrow) are about to fall victim to the capricious winds of fashion.

Step 3: The Patching and Texturing Ceremony

By now, your room probably looks so grim that—if you're like me—you're wondering who got you into this mess. But take heart: Things will get better fast.

Before painting, you're likely to need to patch the walls. It's a rare room without any cracks, rot, holes, or botched repairs that call for attention.

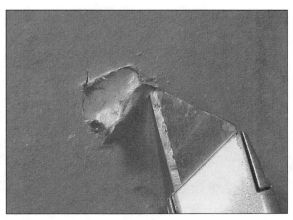

Before patching drywall, cut away any burrs above the surface. Otherwise the patching will make an ugly mound.

You'll see some slick drywall patching described in Chapter 27, or consult *The Complete Idiot's Guide to Home Repair and Maintenance Illustrated* (see Appendix B) for more advice on invisibly patching drywall.

Building Smarts

There are dozens of "miracle" ingredients sold for patching walls. I've had good luck with Patch 'n Paint and Spakfast, two nonshrinking patching materials that can even be painted (for a shallow patch) when wet!

With the patching done, you're set to add a texture, either to match an existing texture, or to liven up some drab walls. You can buy texture paint, add a texturing compound to paint, or make a generic texture with drywall joint compound. As a rough estimate, 1 gallon of joint compound, softened with water, will cover a bit more than 100 square feet. As you dilute the glop, test it occasionally until you like the texture that the roller makes.

I'm using a sidewalk scraper to load joint compound into a 5-gallon bucket. A small shovel would work just as well.

To mix the drywall joint compound, I made a hook from a metal rod and turned it slowly with a drill. A piece of 1 × 3 would also work for hand-stirring.

I am rolling drywall joint compound on the bare drywall that was left after I stripped an ugly texture from this ceiling. Trust me—you'll need goggles for this operation.

Step 4: Prime Time to Prime and Paint

After the patching and texture are dry (use a fan if you're in a hurry), prime all patched or textured areas, and then paint. Having done a duly diligent job of masking, I can use a roller, mounted on an extension pole, for almost all painting. A telescoping roller pole saves stooping, reaching, and most of all, wrist rot. It also lets you work from the floor instead of a ladder.

With good masking, it's even safe to roll paint inside this built-in bookshelf.

Masking also protects the bookshelf from a 2½" brush.

Step 5: Cleaning Up

Trust me, nobody loves cleaning up after painting. But there are some tricks that make it easier: like not waiting forever to clean brushes. Get to them before the paint has a chance to dry. You can throw out rollers—many people do—but a roller-cleaning tool will recover a lot of paint from them and make it possible to clean them. A brush comb cleans a big brush fast.

After the paint dries, tear up the masking. Keep an eye out for paint that seeped under the masking, and sand or scrape it off. Touch up the paint as needed, and then restore electrical fixtures, art work, and furniture. Consider replacing ugly heat registers, hardware, or lighting that detract from the overall appearance. Latex paint should be dry in a couple of hours. Then move back in and enjoy the fruits of your labors!

The roller-cleaner on this painter's tool can salvage a lot of paint from a roller. Once the paint is scraped back into the can, add water to the roller pan, roll the roller back and forth. Then scrape the roller with the painter's tool under running water.

Every painstaking detail is evident in the final product.

Building Smarts

Here's a painter's trick: If you'll be painting again in the morning, don't bother cleaning the roller. Drip some water on it, put it in the roller pan, and wrap the whole thing in a couple of plastic bags. The same trick will also keep brushes overnight.

In This Chapter

Chapter 32

Replace Moldy Molding

This chapter looks at an obvious but seldom-used method of improving the esthetics of a room: replacing the trim (molding) around the floors, windows, and doors. Look around: Did the builder hang the cheapest, plainest trim in the store? Did previous owners mangle, paint, or otherwise abuse that forlorn-looking trim? In either case, you can bring a room into the twenty-first century—or return it to the nineteenth—by tearing off the trim and starting fresh. While you're at it, you may want to consider other cosmetic improvements, such as replacing drywall or repainting. Both topics are covered elsewhere in this book.

Finish carpentry is not for the three-thumbed set, but it's not rocket science, either. You'll need only two uncommon tools: a $10 coping saw, and a power miter box. Also called chop saws, miter boxes start at around $150 (a bit less than you'd pay for the primo laser-guided Delta saw shown in this chapter). There are good reasons why miter boxes are becoming a standard tool among pros and handy homeowners alike. The reasons are accuracy—and more accuracy.

Step 1: Decisions, Decisions

Trim is entirely a matter of esthetics. In deciding whether to replace trim, consider this rule of thumb: Things that have bugged you for a long time will probably continue to bug you. I've begun heeding the "14-year rule": If something has irked me for 14 years, out it goes—even if it's nailed down!

Building Smarts

Before choosing a trim style, consider the esthetics of your house. If you're intent on establishing a new style and carrying it into other rooms, you have more flexibility than if you want to match an existing style in the house. Before choosing a molding style, visit a good building materials supplier to see which shapes, or "profiles," are available in your area—and in which woods. Don't ignore the price tag—some of this stuff doesn't come cheap!

Step 2: Removing the Molding

Molding replacement starts with molding removal. The cardinal rule of delicate wrecking is to remove one piece at a time. Work slowly, especially at first, and protect the house. If the molding resists removal, try slipping a wood chisel behind it and prying. Or drive some nails through with a nail punch. Then pry with two tools in unison.

Two levers are better than one. This flat prybar slips behind the molding to get started. Protect the floor and walls with wood scraps, and work slowly.

Remove baseboard and base shoe with the same routine. Start with the outer piece (the shoe), and then move to the baseboard. Protect your walls and floor as you work.

Step 3: Trim Basics

Trim calls for attention to detail, a heap of patience, and some good advice:

◆ Mark cuts with a utility knife or a sharp pencil.

◆ Make test cuts on scrap wood, especially when you're getting started. Angles can be confusing.

◆ Cut pieces a hair long, to give some adjustment room.

◆ Place nails next to each other; random placement looks funky.

◆ Predrill nail holes, especially in hardwood. To avoid splits, don't nail near the ends of boards.

◆ Hardened trim nails may go through hardwood without drilling, but drilling makes it easier to position the trim.

◆ Finishing nails should penetrate about 1" into the jamb or stud. Use a combination of 4d and 6d finish nails.

◆ Don't overfasten. Place nails about 18" apart.

Step 4: Finish Before You Start

Painting or staining trim before nailing saves gobs of time you'd otherwise waste protecting your walls and floor. Some people stain with a rag, because they hate cleaning brushes. Others prefer brushes, which do a better job of getting into crevices. Before using any finish, read the label.

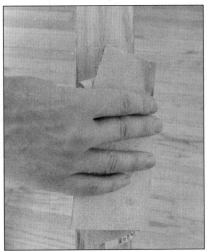

A quick swipe with fine sandpaper will smooth rough edges. To prevent splinters, it wouldn't hurt to wear gloves.

Apply stain or oil finish with a rag or brush, wait 15 minutes, apply more, wait another 15 to 30 minutes, and then wipe excess stain with a rag. Let the molding dry for a day so your hands and walls stay clean.

Usually you will choose a finish to match other molding. Prime bare wood before painting molding. Stained, varnished, or oil-finished molding is more complicated. To match a stain color, visit a paint store and take home some color chips. Then buy a small container and test it on scrap trim.

You can varnish a stained trim, but it's a chore to apply. A good alternative is called Danish oil finish. A blend of stain and varnish, this stuff stains and finishes in a couple of quick coats

and gets better with age. Plan on a repeat application after a couple of years. At any rate, the job will be cleaner if you paint or stain the trim beforehand.

Used with care, a power miter box can make the invisible joints that molding requires. Read the safety manual, keep your fingers clear of the blade, and clamp the wood while sawing. Hook a vacuum hose (arrow) to the saw to control sawdust.

Step 5: Starting Window Trim

Install trim in this order: windows, doors, and base trim. To trim a door, follow the relevant steps for window trim, described under Step 6: Side and Top Casing, and Door Trim, below.

Many modern windows are trimmed "picture-frame" style, with cheap, fast miter joints at all four corners. I prefer a more traditional construction using a windowsill, which carpenters call a *stool*. Dig that crazy jargon: Carpenters call the board below a stool an *apron*. And they call the little shoulder of the jamb a *reveal*.

Cut the stool from a knot-free ¾" board of the same species as your molding. Here's one formula for stool length: 2 × casing width + 2 × reveal amount + width between inside of window jambs + 2" = stool length.

For a standard ³⁄₁₆" reveal and 2¼" casing, add 6⅞" to the inside-the-jambs measurement. The depth of the stool is up to you. I found that 2" made the desired visual statement without sticking too far into the room.

If you have a router or a plane, dress up the front edge of the stool. In any case, sand it well.

Screw the stool to the window jamb with trim screws placed about 12" apart. Drill ¼"-deep countersinks, as shown, for the screw heads, using a bit slightly larger than the screw head. Then drill through the stool with a bit just larger than the screw. Finally, drill into the jamb with a bit smaller than the screw diameter. Use power-driven trim screws.

Coat one surface with wood glue, hold the stool in position, and screw into the jamb. You'll fill these ugly holes later.

Cut a piece of casing 2" shorter than the stool, with any attractive shape on the ends. Center this casing on the window, below the stool, with the thicker side up, and fasten with 2" nails.

The stool extends 1" beyond the casing. I finished the apron ends with a 45° miter, starting halfway down the apron (arrow).

 Building Smarts

Never finish pounding nails until the trim is perfect! With the heads exposed, you can easily fix mistakes. To adjust a piece, drill a new hole; otherwise the nail will find the old hole and return the molding to the same ol' location.

Step 6: Side and Top Casing, and Door Trim

Now that we have moved to the top and side casing, our instructions also relate to door trim. Side and top casings are usually nailed so ³⁄₁₆" of the jamb is visible. These *reveals*, or set-backs, increase the visual interest of the trim without requiring extra molding.

Mark the Reveals

Start fastening the casing by marking the ³⁄₁₆" reveals.

To trim multiple windows and doors, cut a ³⁄₁₆" *rabbet* (lengthwise cutout) in two edges of a wood block. Hold the block against the upper corners and mark the reveals.

Cut the Top Casing

The top casing goes into place first. Calculate the shorter (bottom) length of this piece: bottom length = 2 × the reveal + between-the-jambs dimension. Cut and tack the top casing in place.

To cut a miter joint, the outside of the molding must be longer than the inside. It's normal to swing the miter saw from side to side between cuts.

Instead of pounding a nail through hardwood, I'm drilling a hole slightly smaller than the nail. It's easier to drill the board on sawhorses.

Cut the Side Casings

Cut a 45° miter on one end of a molding. Place the mitered end on the stool and mark where the other end crosses the top casing. Cut square at this mark—it becomes the bottom of the side casing.

Working without a tape measure can be more accurate! Hold the molding upside down and mark the cut.

Put the first side casing back into position, check the miter joint, and recut it slightly if needed to tighten the fit. Then tack the casing in place and make the second side casing.

Fasten the Miter Joints

Tight miter joints are the only challenge in these moldings. I recommend using a plate joiner (also called a biscuit cutter), a specialized tool that cuts slots for little wood pieces called biscuits (named for their shape).

Building Smarts

If you don't have a plate joiner, use polyurethane glue (which is cheap and sold in tubes for caulking guns) in the miter joint, and then clamp it as shown in a later photo. Although polyurethane glue is extremely strong, you may have to carve the dry glue with a chisel—a small price to pay for a tight miter joint!

When both miter joints fit, remove all casings and cut slots for biscuits in each miter joint. To prevent the slot from cutting through the edge of the molding, use a #0 biscuit, the smallest sold for a standard plate joiner.

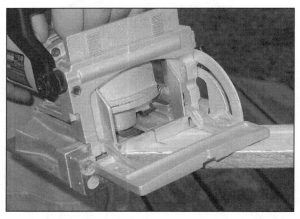

A plate joiner makes the tightest miter joints around.

Put carpenter's glue into the bottom of each plate joiner slot and insert the biscuit. Assemble the joint (some glue should squeeze out) and tack the casings back into position. Clamp the joint with a long pipe clamp (don't let it drop on your head!), a band clamp (a clamp made of flexible webbing), or just twist a band of webbing until it's tight. Compression tightens and strengthens the joint.

Finish nailing the bottom of the casings while you wait for the glue to dry. Polish the hammer face with sandpaper so it can "get a grip."

This band clamp adjusts to any size window, even where there's no room for a pipe clamp. Use moderate tension.

Finish Nailing the Casing

When the glue is dry, remove the clamp and finish nailing the casing. Work gently to avoid breaking the joints.

A nailset prevents hammer dents and sets nails ⅛" below the surface so you can putty them.

Lightly sand around nail holes to remove any high spots, and then fill them with wood filler, using the blunt end of a nailset. Quickly swipe away extra filler with a rag moistened in paint thinner or water (depending on the type of wood filler). Quick cleaning saves much sanding later on.

A pneumatic finishing nailer makes quick work of nailing. There's no need to drill beforehand, and you can usually get away without puttying the nail holes.

If you take your time, you'll have this kind of result in your miter joints.

This style of window and door trim skips the miter joints, but you still need accurate cuts.

Step 7: Base Trim Blues

With door and window trim out of the way, turn your attention to the *base trim*, which joins the walls to the floor. Base trim usually includes *baseboard*, the taller piece, and *base shoe*, a smaller piece that's shaped like part of an oval. Complete the baseboard before starting the base shoe.

The only trick to baseboard is to cope the inside-corner joints. Coped joints, unlike inside miter joints, stay tight over time. To cope, first fasten a square-cut piece into the inside corner, and then meet it with the coped piece. For a complete treatment of coping, see Chapter 33.

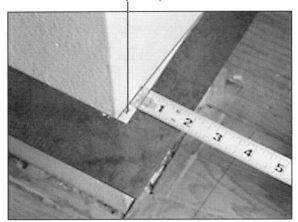

Out of square by this much!

Use miter joints on outside corners. If your corner is out of square, adjust the miter joints. On this weird corner, make test cuts on scrap wood first. This joint needed two 47° miters, not the standard 45° cuts.

Old nails show stud location

Scrap block protects floor

Put the baseboard in position, resting on a scrap of wood, and drill pairs of holes at the stud locations. You can usually find studs by looking for holes in the drywall where the old baseboard was nailed.

Nail the baseboard into the studs and sill (the horizontal 2 × 4 under the studs). Hide the lower nails under the base shoe.

With the baseboard completed, repeat the same steps for the base shoe. Putty all holes, touch up stain or paint, and you're done!

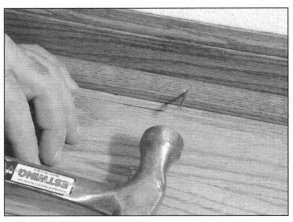

Nail the shoe horizontally into the baseboard, taking care not to scar the floor.

In This Chapter

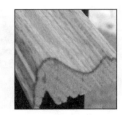

Chapter 33

Install Crown Molding

Crown molding—or cornice molding—is trim used where the wall meets the ceiling. This decorative touch can add a note of class and completion to a room. Because crown molding highlights irregularities in the wall or ceiling, use a long level or straight board to check that the walls and ceiling are straight enough so any gaps will be tolerable. Repair the surfaces before you start so the molding does not highlight the irregularities.

Crown molding comes in several sizes, made to complement different rooms. In our 12' × 10' dining room, 3¼", 38° molding looked just right. Crown molding requires sequence, patience, and jigs. Sequence, because it's easiest to work your way around the room. Patience, because it will be seen by a V-I-P, namely Y-O-U. And jigs, because you'll cut the molding in a homemade jig. I buy extra molding. Although I generally paint or stain molding first, if you don't stain the extra molding, you can always return it.

Step 1: I Been Workin' on the Nailer

Instead of nailing crown molding to the framing (the studs, plate, and joist), attach it to a *nailer*—a piece you attach to hold your nails. If you cut the nailer to fit the angle and size of the molding, it will practically fall into position on the wall.

Crown molding may rest at either 38° or 45° to vertical; cut this angle on the nailer, as described in a moment.

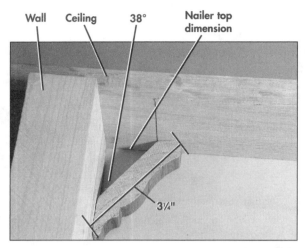

The crown molding is held in a frame representing the walls and ceiling. Measure the nailer top dimension.

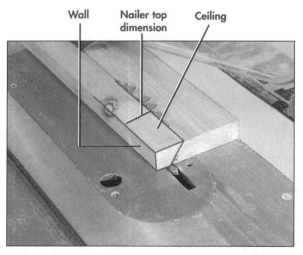

The nailer is cut at 38° to the top dimension. It will be fastened to the top of the wall in this orientation.

Position the nailers 4" away from the corners, to leave room for molding at the corners. Attach the nailer to the plate at the top of the studs with screws or staples 16" apart and slanting upward. Fasteners must grab 1" of the plate.

Step 2: The Nailing Sequence

With the nailer attached, turn your attention to the attaching the molding in the most efficient order, starting with corner A, as shown.

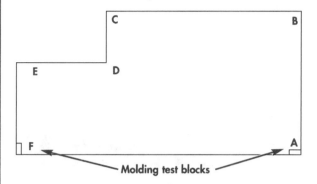

Molding test blocks

Most pieces of crown molding get a butt (square) cut at one end and a coped or mited joint at the other (all joints will be described later in this chapter). Use this sequence for fastening:

1. Cut two 4" scraps of molding and *tack* (lightly nail) them into position at corners A and F, along the walls shown.

2. Miter (angle cut) one end of a piece of molding longer than dimension A-B. Cope one end and test it against the block at F. When it fits, make a butt cut at the other end so the piece fits wall A-B.

3. Tack this piece to wall A-B, snug against the block at A. Remove that block.

4. Continue around the room, using scrap blocks for each coped joint.

5. Make a miter joint at the outside corner, D.

6. You can't test the coped joint on the long side F-A, because the molding would be longer than the room until you make the butt cut. If you are worried about cutting an accurate joint, cut side F-A in two pieces, joined with a *scarf joint*.

Step 3: Make a Cutting Jig

Crown molding joints are easy to cut—if you cut them upside down in a jig.

Crown-molding joints can be difficult to master, but this homemade jig makes them easy!

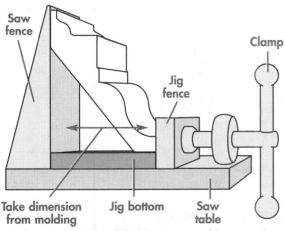

This scrap-wood jig holds crown molding upside down for cutting. To avoid sawing into metal, glue the jig without nails or screws.

Step 4: Coping with Coping

Coped joints are joints that won't pull apart over time, as inside miter joints tend to do. They are easier to illustrate than to describe; see the following photo.

Start a coped joint by sawing a 45° miter, with the molding upside down in the saw. The bottom edge (as the molding will be on the wall) is longer than the top edge.

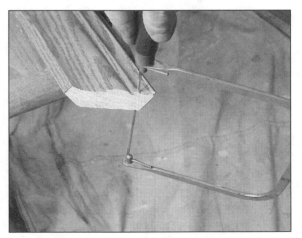

Angle the coping saw to remove more wood from the back; otherwise, the joint may not close. Clamp the molding; these joints are hard enough to cut when the wood is not wandering from Seattle to Anchorage! I've had this "Handy Andy" saw for 40+ years—since long before I knew about coped joints!

Tom's checking the fit on an inside corner.

This is a good, tight coped joint. The left piece has a butt cut, the right is coped. When the molding is nailed tight, this joint will close.

Step 5: Cutting Other Joints

Coped joints are only 99 percent of the battle in crown molding. You may also need outside miter joints, and scarf joints, used where two moldings meet on a straight wall.

Joining Outside Corners

Compared to inside corners, the miter joints used for outside corners are a snap—if the corner is square. To make these miter cuts, place the molding upside down in the jig. Cut so the edge toward the ceiling is longer than the edge toward the wall.

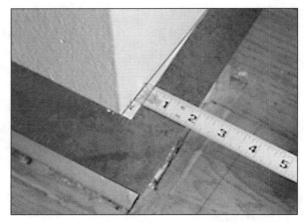

Use a square to check if the corner is square. If not, cut test miters on scrap wood; cuts on this corner must be more than 45°. (Photo shows base trim, but the principle is the same.)

Making the Scarf Joint

To join crown molding along a straight wall, use a scarf joint. Hold the molding in the jig shown earlier. Cut 45° miters at the left end of one piece, and the right end of the other.

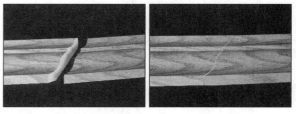

A scarf joint makes a nearly invisible joint. Lay pieces with 45° miters next to each other. Nail through the top piece to tighten the joint.

Step 6: Nailing It Down

If the nails don't pull the molding tight to the wall or ceiling, use larger finish nails (2½" or 3"). As a last resort, try skinny, 2¼" trim screws, with a countersunk hole for the screw head. These screws require more wood filler, but they really pull molding into position.

A pneumatic nailer makes short work of attaching crown molding.

When the molding looks right, drive the nails below the surface, and fill and stain nail holes as described in Chapter 32.

You can see finished photos of crown molding in Chapter 1.

Take your time when making outside corner joints. A lot of wood must meet, and if you rush, you'll be sorry!

The nailer in back holds the molding steady while you nail. Drill pilot holes for the first nails, which locate the molding. After that, you may switch to hardened trim nails, which go right through hardwood without a pilot hole.

In This Chapter

Chapter 34

Replace a Fireplace Mantelpiece

Every year, the proportion of the new American house that reaches the building site in a cardboard box seems to grow, all at the expense of skilled artisanship. The fireplace mantelpiece is a key victim of what you might call the "factory-built" syndrome. In modern home building, the venerable skills of cutting, fitting, and understanding proportions have all succumbed to the pressure to work fast and cheap. The problem is compounded by the oldest rule in fashion: Bad taste is always in style.

But have you considered how easily a mantelpiece can be replaced? A few boards, a few pieces of molding, and presto-chango, a whole new look! In this chapter, we'll replace the mantelpiece above a fireplace hearth. While the hearth happens to serve a wood stove, it's still the center of attention in the room. You could use the same techniques to adorn a regular fireplace. Call it your small contribution to a renaissance of craftsmanship.

Step 1: Fire It Up

Start the project with some planning, then some demolition.

Esthetics Rule

Mantelpieces are pure esthetics. While they may have to hold some knick-knacks, they don't have to keep out the cold, supply storage, or even be particularly strong. And that makes this project an opportunity for an artistic statement. Start your design by looking at the context: What else is in the room? Which wood, which color of stain or paint? Is the trim style classical, modern, or craftsman? While context is usually a valuable guide for design decisions, if you're unenthusiastic about the existing style, the sky is the limit in terms of design.

To broaden your design perspective, ogle the molding and hardwood at a good building-material store. Then examine fireplaces you like. How are they constructed? Which moldings are used?

In the example shown in this chapter, the design challenge was to complement, not overwhelm, the tile-work below the mantelpiece. I echoed the square tile pattern below, and the crown molding above, with a molding called dentil crown. I chose red oak to match trim elsewhere in the room. Otherwise I kept things plain, relying on good wood and good proportions to make an eye-pleasing result.

A bit of sanding, by hand or with a disk sander, will vastly improve the appearance of your wood, whether you will stain or paint it. If you do decide to use stained wood, doing the bulk of the staining a day ahead of time will keep your hands—and your house—a lot cleaner.

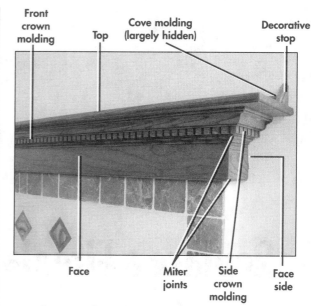

These are the visible parts of the mantelpiece.

Boring but serviceable, this mantelpiece did no justice to the marble-and-slate hearth and surround for this cast-iron stove.

Out with the Old

Start by removing the old mantelpiece and repairing any damage to nearby walls.

Patternmaking

You may decide to copy the dimensions of your existing mantelpiece, just using better wood. Otherwise it's smart to start by making a cardboard pattern.

A hot-glue gun assembles the cardboard pattern.

I chose to make the new mantel a couple of inches taller than the old. The need for 2" clearance between the mantel and the window trim set the overall width.

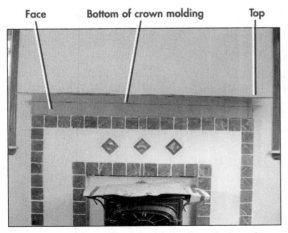

Face   Bottom of crown molding   Top

I wanted the visible part of the face (below the crown molding) to be slightly taller than the top row of tiles. Don't stop playing with the pattern until you like the proportions.

Step 2: Making the Frame

The old mantelpiece was attached to a 2 × 4 header that was lag-bolted to the studs. Because the header was in good shape, I decided to strengthen and reuse it. I added two $\frac{5}{16}$" × 5" lag bolts, which grabbed 2" of wood in the studs. For each lag bolt, drill a $\frac{5}{16}$" hole through the header, and a $\frac{1}{4}$" hole in the stud.

New lag bolts attach the header to the studs.

The header supports a frame, made of plywood or oriented strand board (OSB), that will form the internal structure of the mantelpiece. A plumb and level frame is essential for positioning the exposed mantel parts.

The frame front runs from the top of the tile to the top of the face. It is wide enough to hold the frame sides flush to the sides of the fireplace. It is thick enough so its front is flush to the front of the tile.

Screw the frame front to the header, with 2" screws.

Frame front | Shims | Header

Shims hold the frame front plumb, and flush to the tile, as I get ready to screw it to the header.

The frame front must also be level.

While the frame front holds the face, blocking supports the mantel top. Cut and fasten the blocking in two steps. Rip-saw the 2 × 4 so it will reach the top of the frame front.

1. Screw the back blocking to the header, positioned to hold the frame side flush to the side of the fireplace face.

2. Cut the front blocking thick enough to hold the frame front plumb.

3. Cut the frame sides and screw to the blocking.

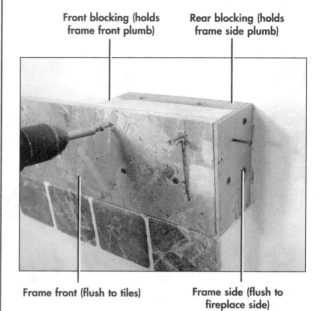

Front blocking (holds frame front plumb) | Rear blocking (holds frame side plumb)

Frame front (flush to tiles) | Frame side (flush to fireplace side)

The frame corner is finished. It's plumb, square, level, and ready to hold the mantelpiece.

Step 3: Making the Mantel

With the frame finished, it's time to make the visible parts of the mantelpiece: the top and the face.

A Tip-Top Top

Make the top from a single piece of hardwood. I used 1 × 8, and routed the edge, an optional but highly decorative step.

Using a cove bit, I'm routing the bottom edge of the top. The bit has a bearing that follows the edge.

Lightly mark the location of your blocking on the wall, so you'll know where to screw and nail the top.

Put the top in place and check that it's level in both directions. If the wall is uneven, *scribe* it (see the photo) and cut with a jigsaw.

Mantel top   Frame front   Pencil   Scrap wood

To scribe the mantel top to a crooked wall, find a scrap of wood that's as wide as the biggest gap between the top and the wall. Ensure that the front of the top is parallel to the wall. Hold a pencil against the scrap while moving the scrap along the wall. Cut along this line with a jigsaw, and the top should fit exactly to the wall.

Lightly screw the top to the blocking. (You'll be removing it later to fasten the crown molding.) Place the screws close to the back so they will be covered by the 1⅛" cove molding.

Face Lift

With the top in place, turn your attention to the face front and sides.

Cut the face and sides from hardwood, placing 45° outside *miter joints* at the corners. If you want, rout the bottom outside edges to match the top.

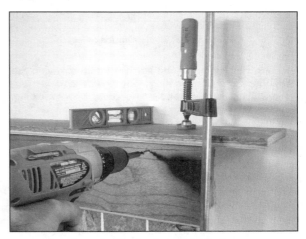

The clamp holds the face tight to the top.

Attach the face to the frame with screws placed where they will be hidden under the crown molding. Bring the miter joints together while you drive the screws: Shim the pieces if necessary to bring the joints tight.

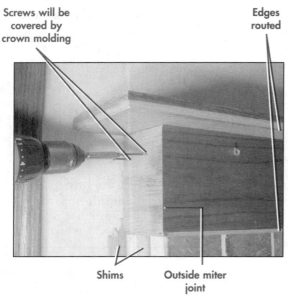

Check that the miter joint tightens while screwing the side. The shims position the side to tighten the miter joint. The 2¼" trim screws will be covered by crown molding.

Step 4: The Crowning Touch

It's time to install the crown molding. I chose dentil (toothed) crown molding, but plain crown molding would also work. The sidebar has suggestions for using crown molding.

 **Building Smarts**

Working with crown molding is tricky. Observe these tips:

◆ Cut molding upside down and backward in the miter saw.

◆ On outside miter joints, make the top of the molding longer than the bottom.

◆ Buy extra molding.

◆ Cut pieces a hair long. Test the joint and recut if necessary.

Chapter 33 has more information on working with crown molding.

To cut and fasten the crown molding, follow these steps:

1. With the top and face in place, carefully mark the underside of the top where it overhangs the face. Unscrew the top and place it upside down on sawhorses.

2. Clamp two blocks of 2 × 4 along the line you just marked.

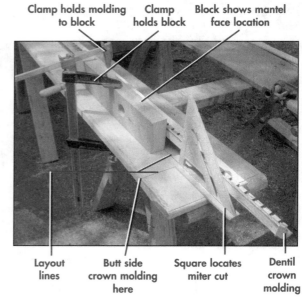

Assemble the crown molding on the upside-down mantel top. The layout lines show the position of the mantel face and side.

3. Cut an outside miter joint at *one end* of the long piece of crown molding. Cut the molding *upside down* in the jig, as shown in Chapter 33.

4. Lean the molding tight to the blocks and the top. Stand a square at the corner of the layout lines and nudge the miter joint until it touches the square. Clamp the molding to the block.

5. Move the square to the other end (see photo) and mark and cut the second miter joint.

6. Cut the mating miter joints for the side pieces. Leave the pieces at least 1" long at this point.

7. Check the joints and clamp them tight. Don't be bashful about recutting the joints until they are tight.

8. When the joints fit, cut the side molding square at the back of the top, as shown.

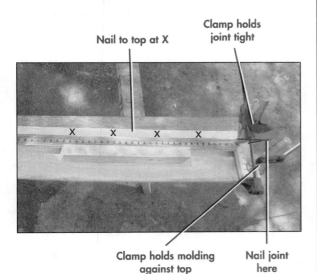

Accuracy and clamps are key to a tight miter joint.

9. Glue the miter joints and the joint between the molding and the top, and start assembling. Nail the molding to the top with hardened trim nails. (Cut short so they don't come through.) Assemble the miter joints with one 2" hardened trim nail from each direction.

Step 5: Finishing

When the glue dries, position the top without disturbing your hard-won miter joints. Redrive the screws used previously at the back, and nail the front of the top to the blocking.

Nail the top to the blocking with one 2" hardened trim nail every 18". Leave the nailheads exposed until you're sure everything is perfect.

Cut a 1⅛" cove molding 2½" shorter than the overall width of the top. Cut two 45° decorative stops of hardwood, and rout the edges. Nail the cove molding to the top, and then nail the two stop blocks.

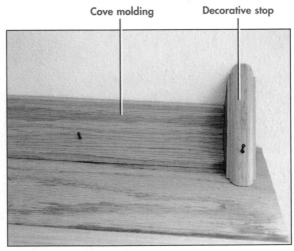

The top corner, finished.

A wood rasp softens the sharp corner.

Fill holes with wood filler and touch up the stain.

Here's the payback for good design and careful work! You'll see another view of the mantelpiece at the beginning of this chapter.

In This Chapter

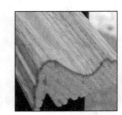

Chapter 35

Install a Sun Tube

Everybody loves the sun, but plenty of rooms are dark, particularly if they are surrounded by porches or additions. You might be tempted to install a skylight, but that's often a complicated project, and the trusses used in many modern roofs seriously restrict skylight width. And if the dark room is under a north roof, skylights offer only a limited benefit.

A new alternative called a sun tube offers several advantages. They are cheaper, vastly easier to install, and able to direct sunlight a few feet from a south roof to a room on the north side. We used a Velux Sun Tunnel; the company has a reputation for making skylights that don't leak, and we didn't want to take any chances!

Ruedi's looking a little down. This Swiss mountain climber is accustomed to caves. Natural ones—not his grotto-like kitchen!

Step 1: Placing the Tube

Ideally, the tube will run perpendicular to the ceiling and the roof, with an angle in the middle. The top unit should go on a south-facing roof, not shaded by a tree or building. However, we used 12' of tube to direct light from the south roof to a kitchen under the north roof, and it harvested a lot of light!

Theoretically, you could install a sun tube without having access to the attic, but since we did have access, we did some work up there. The manufacturer says you can install these tubes in two hours, but the first one will take longer.

Sun tubes come in 14" and 22" diameters, designed to fit joists and rafters that are 16" or 24" on center. A larger tube carries more light; and since the framing was 24" on center, we chose the 22" tube. Both tubes install the same way.

On the ceiling, place the tube between the joists, preferably centered in the room (as long as the tube will be fairly straight).

On the roof, place the top of the top frame at least 9" below the ridge, and not within 18" of a valley.

Step 2: Up on the Roof

On the roof, the top frame hole must be placed between two *rafters*, the framing that holds up the roof.

Holier Than Thou

To find the rafters *with access to the attic*, drive a nail up through the roof, centered between the rafters, at the approximate location of the top frame. To find the rafters *without access to the attic*, bang the roof with a hammer; the rafters are where the roof feels stronger. Cut a small hole with a jigsaw between the rafters, at the rough location of the top frame. Now look inside and locate the rafters exactly.

Hold the top frame straight on the roof and mark a circular hole inside the ring.

Cut the shingles away with a utility knife. Then cut the hole with a jigsaw.

Like a masked monster from an overheated attic, Ruedi attacks the shingles above the opening. No dummy, he starts removing at the top. Also no dummy, he uses the mask to protect against insulation fibers in the attic.

The roof is cleaned and ready for the top frame. The stairstep pattern lets us reshingle without slipping new shingles under old. If the top frame is farther from the ridge, the cutout should start getting narrower, not wider, toward the top.

Nail the top frame to the roof with 1¼" roofing nails.

Building Smarts

Reshingling is largely a matter of replacing old shingles with new ones. Get some new shingles and some 1¼" roofing nails (longer for a roof with several layers of shingle), and follow these tips:

◆ Old shingles are brittle; handle them carefully.

◆ Asphalt roofs are sealed with heat-activated glue. You can separate this glue with a trowel, if you work carefully. New shingles have black glue strips; use roofing cement to seal shingles away from the glue strips. Roofing cement is sold in tubes and gallon cans.

◆ Never line up vertical joints in successive courses of shingles.

◆ Cut new shingles from behind.

◆ Drive nails ¾" above the slot between shingle tabs.

◆ To slip a new shingle under an old one, work carefully, and seal the shingles with roof cement.

◆ If you must nail through the top of a shingle, cover the nailhead with roof cement.

◆ New shingles that are raised will lie down with the sun's warmth, sealing the cement.

Shingles, Again

The bottom of the top frame doesn't get a layer of shingles. Start shingling about halfway up.

The first shingles are cut to meet the top frame. If you're confident, make these curved cuts by eye. Otherwise use a cardboard template.

Cut here

Finish the roof with *capping,* shingles cut to cover the ridge. One shingle makes three caps.

Hammer 1½" roofing nails behind the glue line to cap the roof. Cover any exposed nailheads with cement.

Tube Time

With the top frame in place, turn your attention to the flexible tube. Tape the tube to the stainless steel lower ring. Pull the other end of the tube up through the top frame and temporarily attach it to the frame.

You are done on the roof for now. Time to move inside.

Step 3: In the Dark Room

Find the joists in your ceiling by tapping and drilling, and center the ceiling hole between them. Use the ceiling ring to mark your cut. Drill a hole for the jigsaw blade, and cut the hole, wearing eye protection and a dust mask.

The masked man is cutting the ceiling hole ¼" out-side the mark, to allow the trim ring to slip through.

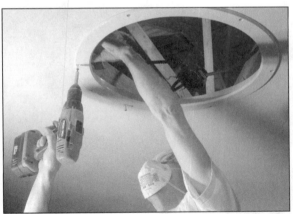

Screw the trim ring to the joists or the big nuts that come with the tube.

Slip the stainless-steel lower ring on the tube and bring it down into the trim ring. Screw the stainless-steel ring to the trim ring.

Step 4: Back to the Roof

Can you smell victory? You're almost through!

Pull the tube taut through the roof. When 3" protrudes, cut it off.

Locking ring

Bend the locking snap ring and seat it inside the top frame to secure the tube. Fold the short extra bit of tube down over the locking ring.

Slip the 4" stainless-steel upper ring inside the flexible tube to secure the snap ring and tube.

The roof work is now finished, and so is the job.

Screw the transparent cover to the top frame.

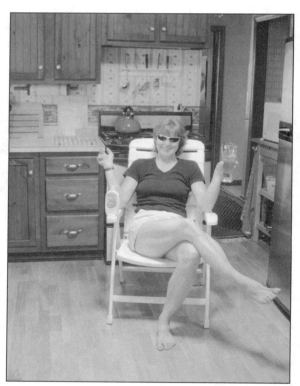

Ruedi did all the work, but it's Monika who's slathering on the sun-dope in her kitchen!

In This Chapter

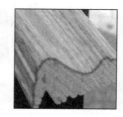

36

Frame and Finish a Sleeping Loft

Why build a sleeping loft? Maybe to add space to a small bedroom. Maybe to spice up a dull bedroom. Maybe because, as in this case, the family teenager plays a truckload of saxophones, and a sleeping loft would induce him to spend more time in the garage that he's claimed as his studio. That, at least, was the thinking of John and Michelle, wise parents who realized that "absence makes the heart grow fonder" was first uttered by the parent of a sax player ....

Having built a series of sleeping lofts, I've come to think of them as the ideal weekend project. Using basic tools—a circular saw and a drill (and a router if you have one)—you can delight the child in your life.

The basic limitation on lofts is ceiling height; I would not build one unless the ceiling is the standard 8', and even that makes for a snug fit. In an 8' room, place the bottom of the frame 50" off the floor; this provides 40" of room above the bed, and enough to put a desk or storage below it. To minimize height requirements, rest the mattress inside the frame, not on top of it. 2 × 6 makes a good frame; since few mattresses are thinner than this, 2 × 6 doesn't waste any more space than a 2 × 4 frame.

A sleeping loft requires serious support, provided by lag-bolting the frame to the studs (lag bolts are big screws with hexagonal heads). For simplicity, build the frame on the floor and have helpers hoist it into position.

Adjust your building strategy to the location.

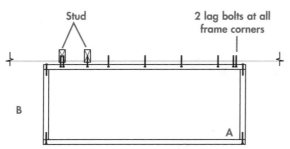

To attach to one wall: Place the ladder near A or B and add a 4 × 4 post at the other unsupported corner.

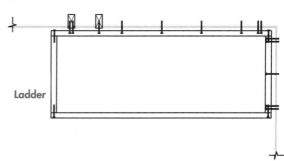

In a corner, a ladder supports the bed.

Step 1: Loft Placement

The room's floor plan usually governs the placement of the loft. We built in a corner, but you can also build into an alcove, or against one wall. While scouting your location, note the stud placement. Rather than placing a frame corner more than 8" away from a stud, move or enlarge the loft so the corners can be supported by studs.

Since corners are probably the most popular location for sleeping lofts, that's what we'll describe here.

Step 2: Structural Details

This loft design is a simple, straightforward structure with a touch of esthetics.

The Parts List

Before buying lumber for the loft, skip ahead to Step 3: Build the Frame to determine the length of the frame sides. If the stud spacing does not cooperate, you may have to extend the frame sides.

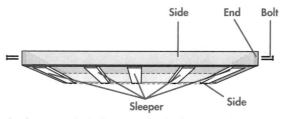

The frame and platform are built of standard framing lumber, with a few finishing touches. The diagram does not show the plywood platform or trim pieces.

The suggested parts list shows approximate sizes for a single-mattress loft:

Name	Material	Length	# Used	Comments
Frame side	2 × 6	92"	2	Measured on top of side. If ladder is at end, end is mitered at the ladder angle.
Frame end	2 × 6	42"	2	Length = mattress width + 3".
Ladder stringer	2 × 6	About 20" longer than top height of frame	2	Top and bottom mitered to be horizontal in use.
Ladder steps	2 × 6	22"	Approx. 1 per foot of height	See sidebar for step spacing.
Sleepers	2 × 4 or 2 × 6		Approx 1 per 2' of length	Bevel visible ends 30°.
Platform	½" plywood	4' × 8' sheet	1	Place any seams on a sleeper.
Guardrail uprights	2 × 3	Approx. 20"	2	Bevel ends at 30°.
Guardrails	2 × 3	Up to mattress length	2	Bevel ends at 30°.
Face trim	1 × 8 cedar	8' to 16', cut to fit exposed frame	1	Optional.
Top trim	1 × 2 cedar	Up to 24', cut to size	3	Optional.
Lag bolts + flat washer	⅜"	4"	About 2 dozen	
Nails	6d finishing nails	2" length	½ lb.	
Phillips-drive construction screws		1⅝"	1 lb.	
		2½"	1 lb.	
		3"	1 lb.	

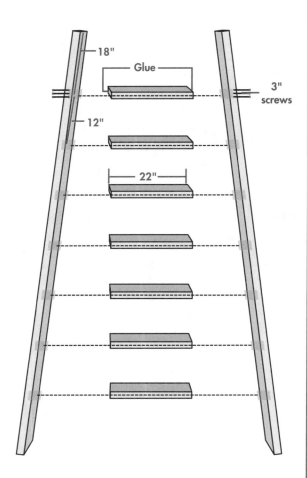

18"

Glue

3" screws

12"

22"

Angling for an Angle

To find the angle for the ladder stringers, brace a 2 × 6 in horizontal position and lean a second 2 × 6 next to it, as shown, until the angle will be comfortable to climb, but won't stick too far into the room. Or use 12°, as we did. You will use this angle to make the stringers. *If you attach the ladder at the end,* attach the frame end at this angle so the stringers bolt flat against it.

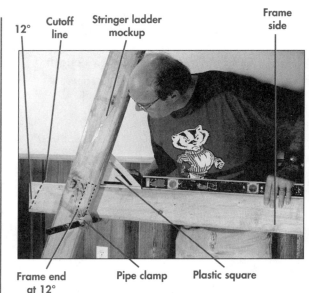

12° Cutoff line Stringer ladder mockup Frame side

Frame end at 12° Pipe clamp Plastic square

Measuring the ladder angle. That plastic square is ultra-handy for marking at 90° and other angles. For harmony, we'll cut the ends of the frame sides at 12° to match the ladder.

Step 3: Build the Frame

Draw horizontal lines marking the bottom of the frame on the walls, and find the studs. (If you drill for studs just above the line, you won't need to repair the wall.) Studs are usually located 16" on center. Mark every stud just below the frame line. As noted, you may have to adjust the size or position of the loft to get the corners within 8" of the studs, for support purposes.

The frame ends should be about 3" inches longer than the mattress width.

To find the frame side length, measure your mattress and proceed according to the ladder position:

◆ *If the ladder will attach to a frame side,* add 6" to the mattress length and cut both ends of the frame sides square.

◆ *If the ladder will attach to the frame end* (as shown in the photos), add 12" to the mattress length. Bolt the frame end between the frame sides at the stringer angle (12° in our example).

Bolt the Frame

With the frame parts cut, assemble it with two lag bolts at each frame corner. Check that all joints are square as you build. To place bolts along a side that will rest flush to the wall, drill ⅞" countersinks in the *wall face of the frame side.* (This recess allows the frame to rest against the wall.) See the sidebar for other suggestions on using lag bolts.

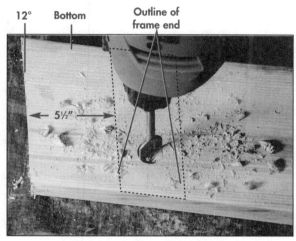

12°   Bottom   Outline of frame end
← 5½" →

Countersinks allow the side to rest tight to the wall. The side is shown upside down.

A socket wrench drives a lag bolt that attaches the frame end to the frame side. This face of the frame side goes against the wall.

Building Smarts

"Lag bolt" rhymes with "drag bolt," and for good reason. To use them right, use two or three drill bits. For ⅜" lag bolts, use these sizes in order:

1. A flat-bottomed bit for countersinking, such as the ⅞" Speedbor bit shown in an earlier photo, lets the bolt head rest below the surface. You may countersink other bolts to hide the bolt head and help the bolt get a deeper bite in the wood, but it's only necessary where the frame must sit flat to the wall.

2. A ⅜" bit lets the lag bolt slip through the piece you're attaching. (The bolt doesn't need to thread into the upper piece.)

3. A ⁵⁄₁₆" bit drills into the stud.

When you're done swapping these bits in and out of the chuck, you'll realize the virtues of the assembly line: Try to drill several holes before changing the bit.

Studs aren't always exactly where you expect. If you miss a stud, don't drill a big new countersink. Try drilling at an angle through the countersink; you'll often reach the elusive stud.

This project depends on lag bolts, and it's up to you to make sure they are strong. Do not bolt into knots, or so near the edge that you will split the frame. While driving the bolts, *make sure* they get a strong grab. Tighten firmly, but do not strip the threads. If you're not sure the attachment is sound, add another bolt or use a slightly longer one.

Bolt to the Wall

With the frame fully assembled, bolt it to the studs. I placed two lag bolts per stud near the ends, and one per stud elsewhere. Get two assistants to hold the frame while you place some bolts. Then clamp a temporary post or two to the frame until the ladder is attached.

I'm bolting a frame corner. Notice how the washer fits into the countersink.

Step 4: Make the Ladder

With the frame complete and attached, turn your attention to the ladder. Lean a ladder stringer in place, and cut to length, leaving at least 18" above the loft for a handhold while climbing. Cut both ends of the stringer so they will be horizontal once in place, so the bottom sits flat on the floor, and the top is horizontal. Now lay out the locations for equal steps (see sidebar).

We attached the stringers to the frame end. To fasten stringers to the frame side, cut out a triangular piece from the stringers so they lie flat against the side. One side of the cutout must be vertical, and the other side horizontal.

Finding Equal Spacing

In this project, you'll need to space several building components—the ladder steps, the sleepers, and the guardrails—equally across a set distance. Here's the general rule for calculating the spacing:

1. Measure the total rough length.
2. Multiply the number of components (steps, in this example) times their dimension, to find the total space they will occupy.
3. Subtract this number from the total length to find total gap space.
4. Add 1 to the number of components to find the number of gaps between components.
5. Divide the total gap space by the number of gaps to get the gap between the centers of the adjacent components.
6. Add the thickness of one component to the gap to find the center-to-center dimension.

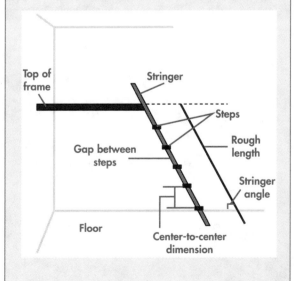

Here's how to lay out ladder steps, as shown in the following drawing:

1. Lean the stringer in position, at the chosen angle, and measure along the stringer from the top of the frame to the floor. Let's say this "rough length" is 80".

2. Estimate the number of steps, spaced about 12" apart: For an 80" stringer, let's check out 6 steps. So, 6 steps × 1½" per step = 9" taken up by steps.

3. Subtract from the rough length to find the total gap space: 80" − 9" = 71".

4. 6 steps + 1 = 7 gaps.

5. Total gap space / number of gaps = dimension of 1 gap: 71" / 7 = 10½" (10⅛" is close enough).

6. Gap + thickness of 1 step = center-to-center measurement: 10⅛" + 1½" = 11⅝", close enough to the 12" center-to-center spacing on standard ladders.

This method will also find the spacing of the sleepers and guardrail uprights, used later in this project.

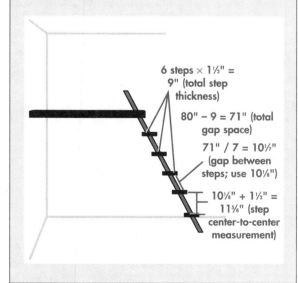

6 steps × 1½" = 9" (total step thickness)

80" − 9 = 71" (total gap space)

71" / 7 = 10½" (gap between steps; use 10⅛")

10⅛" + 1½" = 11⅝" (step center-to-center measurement)

Cut Dadoes for the Steps

To securely attach the steps to the stringers, cut ⅜" deep dadoes on the inside of each stringer. Use a router, or a circular saw and a chisel.

Do not rout freehand: Clamp a guide to the stringer. Our guide was a scrap of plywood, cut at the 12° angle used in the ladder.

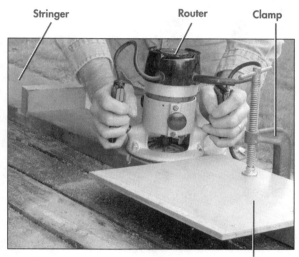

Stringer   Router   Clamp

Guide

The board guides the router to make dadoes for the steps.

For an accurate 1½" dado, put a spacer next to the guide after the first cut. Cut the other side of the dado, and then clean out the middle with the router.

Place a 1¼" spacer against the guide to make a dado that's exactly 1½" wide (dado width − bit diameter = spacer width).

A guide allows us to cut a dado with a circular saw. Set the saw to cut ⅜" deep, make multiple passes, and clean the bottom with a chisel.

Although you can't dado both stringers at once, the dadoes on both stringers should meet in the middle when the stringer fronts (arrows) touch as shown.

Assemble the Ladder

Starting from one end, glue and screw the ladder steps to the stringers. Check that the ladder is square as you work. Drill pilot holes about 1½" deep before screwing. Let the glue dry.

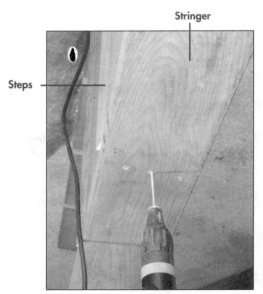

Clamp the ladder sides tight and fasten with 3" construction screws. Small countersinks will make the screw heads less obvious.

Attach the stringers to the frame and floor with 3" screws.

Step 5: A Nonpolitical Platform

With the ladder attached, turn your attention to the sleepers that support the plywood platform. Cut the sleepers to length, using a 30° bevel on sides that are visible, and attach.

Sleeper

I'm attaching a sleeper to each end of the frame, using three screws.

Use the formula described earlier to locate the inside sleepers, with a maximum gap of 20".

If the frame is square, cut the plywood ¼" shorter in each dimension than the frame, so it will slip into place without jamming. If the frame is not square (because you built in a nonsquare corner), allow more leeway, or custom-fit to the actual frame shape: Find a square corner, using a 3-4-5 triangle (as explained in Chapter 6). Measure the two legs of the 3-4-5 triangle, and mark what you have found on the plywood. Measure the other two frame sides, and the diagonals. Use these measurements to mark and cut the plywood.

Screw the platform to the sleepers with 1½" screws, placed about 8" apart.

Step 6: Finish Up

With the platform complete, it's time to deal with safety and appearance.

Make the Guardrail

Start with the guardrail, which is generally only needed along the long side of the bed. (Although it's hard to fall off the end of a bed, you certainly can put guardrails there if you want.) For the sake of appearance, cut 30° bevels on each end of the guardrail uprights.

Scrap block · Guardrail upright · Clamp

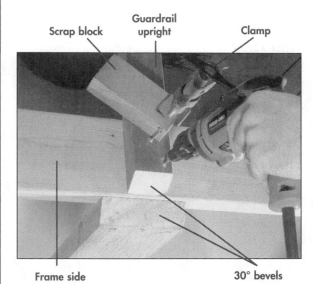

Frame side · 30° bevels

Center the guardrail uprights on the center sleepers, and fasten with three 2½" screws. The pipe clamp holds the joint tight as we screw.

Take care to hold the upright vertical while fastening, and place the screws in a regular pattern, because they will be visible.

Select strong, straight, fairly knot-free pieces for the guardrails. Hold the pieces in place, centered on the uprights. Choose lengths and spacing that will please your eye and prevent anyone from falling out of bed. Mark the uprights where they cross the guardrails. Remove the uprights, cut ½" deep dadoes, and replace.

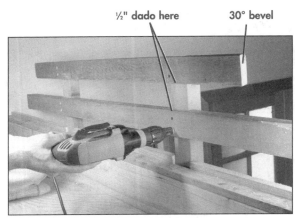

½" dado here   30° bevel

Dadoes on the uprights locate the guardrails, fastened with two 1½" screws per joint.

Trim Time

Trimming the frame is optional, but gives a big boost in appearance. We used cedar, but any attractive wood would work. The face trim should extend at least 1" above the frame side, to cover the top trim that you will soon attach.

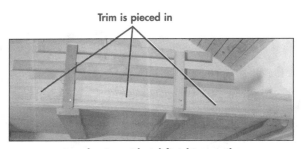

Trim is pieced in

Attach trim with 6d finishing nails.

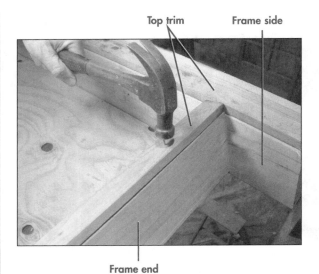

Top trim   Frame side

Frame end

The top trim is 1 × 2, cut to fit and nailed to the top of the frame. Note the angle on the frame end, used because the ladder is at the end.

And with that, you're about done. Check that all the screws are tight, sandpaper any rough spots, and paint or stain as desired.

Balanced and light looking, the loft is a fine addition to a small room.

Glossary

anchor A fitting used to secure something to masonry, drywall, and other hard-to-fasten materials.

auger A drill bit with sharp screw thread that pulls itself into the wood.

base shoe Small molding that joins the baseboard to the floor.

baseboard Molding at the junction of wall and floor.

beat (tile) To whack a tile with a heavy tool to push it into mortar. Often done with a 2×4 "beater block."

bevel An angled cut in wood, visible when looking at the edge, used to make a joint or decorate.

blind-nail To nail so the nailheads are invisible when the work is finished, usually on tongue-and-groove boards.

blocking Wood nailed to framing to support something else.

board, ledger Framing that connects a deck to the house placed parallel to a house rim joist.

box, junction or electrical An electrical box used to hold switches, receptacles, etc.

bridge Framing placed between joists or studs.

capping Shingles cut to cover a roof ridge.

carcase   The body of a cabinet.

circuit   An electrical loop connecting a source, a load, and the source.

circuit breaker   A safety device that shuts off a circuit when current gets dangerous, or when you work on the circuit.

circuit tester   A tool that lights up when a current is present.

cleat   A horizontal board fastened to a stringer to support treads.

compound miter   A cut combining a bevel and a miter.

conduit   A thin-walled metal pipe that carries electrical wires.

corner bead   An L-shaped metal or plastic strip placed on the outside corner of drywall.

countersink   To drill a hole so the head of a screw will be at or below the surface.

countersink bit   A drill bit that cuts a countersink.

crosscut   To cut wood 90° to the grain.

cut in   To prepare to roll paint by brushing edges and corners.

dado   A three-sided rectangular cutout used to make a joint.

disk sander   A sander that rotates a circular piece of sandpaper.

door, hollow-core   A door with two veneer surfaces and a hollow inside, usually used on the interior.

door, solid-core   A wood door without a hollow inside.

drum sander   A machine that rotates a wide piece of sandpaper to sand a floor.

dry-fit   To assemble parts to check fit before gluing.

drywall   Wallboard made of gypsum sandwiched between heavy paper.

drywall knife (drywall trowel)   A tool used to apply joint compound to walls.

drywall square   A large, T-shaped square used to mark and cut drywall or plywood.

elbow   A pipe fixture that changes direction, often 90°.

equipment grounding conductor   A conductor (bare wire, steel conduit, or BX sheath) that provides a safe return path for electricity if something goes wrong with the wiring.

face frame   A cabinet style with a narrow frame around the doors and drawers.

face screw   To screw through the visible face of a board.

face-nail   To nail through the face, so the nailhead remains visible.

fish tape   A stiff, springy tool used to pull wires through a wall.

fixture (device)   An electrical switch, light, or receptacle (outlet).

flashing   Metal that joins planes of a roof; or a roof to a chimney or a vent; or protects a ledger board on a deck.

float   A flat tool used to patch plaster, drywall, masonry, or concrete.

float, grout   A dense, spongy tool for pushing grout into tile joints.

flush   Surfaces that meet in the same plane.

framing   2" nominal-thickness lumber that forms the structure of a house (actually 1½" thick).

full-flush   A cabinet without a face frame.

fuse A device that prevents a circuit from carrying a dangerous current.

galvanizing A heavy zinc coating on steel to prevent rust ("zinc coated" is an inferior rust-proofing).

gauge A system for measuring diameter of wires, and thickness of sheet metal. Larger numbers are thinner.

grade Ground level.

grain, end Porous wood at the end of a board.

ground A safety system that gives electricity an "escape route" if a hot wire contacts something it's not supposed to, like a metal electrical box.

grounded conductor The wire (generally white) that returns electricity to the source in normal operation.

ground-fault circuit interrupter, GFCI (or ground-fault circuit interrupter, GFI) A device that shuts off the power if it detects current leakage.

header The beam across the top of the opening, like a window or door.

jamb The 1" wood enclosing a door or window; holds the hinges or sash.

joiner, plate (biscuit cutter) A tool that cuts slots for plates to strengthen a glue joint.

joint, coped A joint cut with a coping saw for an inside corner in molding.

joint, miter A joint cut with two miters, used to join outside corners, usually in molding.

joint, scarf A joint cut with two bevels, used to join two straight pieces of molding.

joist Framing that supports a floor or ceiling.

joist hanger A metal bracket that fastens joists to rim joists or other framing.

joist, rim A joist around the perimeter of a building or deck.

lag screw A heavy-duty wood screw with a hexagonal or square head.

latch side The side of a door away from the hinge.

load Anything that uses electricity in a circuit.

melamine Plastic coating used to cover particle board.

miter An angled cut in wood (visible when viewed face-on), used to form a joint.

mortar A mixture of Portland cement, lime, sand, and water; holds tile to substrate, and joins bricks, blocks, and stones.

mortise A shallow, rectangular cavity that allows a hinge or latch to sit flush; also a deep cutout used in a wood joint.

mud Slang for various mortar and wall patching materials.

nailer A board used to support something else.

O.C. (on-center) The distance between centers of repeated components, such as studs.

OSB (oriented strand board) A cheaper replacement for plywood, made of chipped wood.

penny A system for identifying nail length; larger nails get higher numbers.

Phillips screw A screw with a cross-shaped head, driven with a drill or a Phillips screwdriver.

pilot hole A hole drilled before screwing.

plate, bottom The framing under studs in a wall.

plate, striker A metal plate in the jamb that holds the latch when a door closes.

plate, top   The horizontal framing above the studs in a wall.

plumb   Vertical.

pocket screw   Concealed, angled screw that enters the back of a joint.

quarter-round   A molding shaped like one quarter of a circle, when seen from the end.

rabbet   A two-sided rectangular cutout used for joints or decoration.

rafter   An angled beam supporting roof decking.

rake edge   The slanting edge of a sloping roof.

receptacle   An electric outlet.

reducer (plumbing)   A fitting that changes pipe size.

reveal (set-back)   The shoulder in trim, used to increase visual interest.

ridge   The horizontal line across the top of a pitched roof.

rip-saw (rip)   To cut lengthwise, parallel to the grain.

rise   The vertical distance between two parts.

riser   A board that connects two treads in a stairway; has a vertical face.

romex   Plastic-wrapped cable, common in house wiring.

roof tar (roof cement)   A sticky goop used to seal holes in roofs.

rotary hammer   A heavy-duty drill that turns the bit and hammers it forward; used in concrete and masonry.

router   A tool that spins a router bit, to shape wood edges and faces.

run   The horizontal distance between two parts.

sand finish   A finish plaster containing sand; makes a regular, rough surface when floated.

sash   The movable wood or metal component holding glass in a window.

screw gun   A tool used to drive screws; sets depth automatically.

scribe   To mark a part to match an irregular surface: Hold the part in position, then mark a line an equal distance from the irregular surface.

seat   The ledge that holds glass in a sash; also the sealing component in a faucet.

sheathing   A thin structural layer used under siding and roofing (also called decking on a roof).

sill   The horizontal shelf at base of a window.

sink, tile-in   A sink that is flush to the surface of counter tile.

sinker   A cement-coated nail, thinner than a common nail; used to nail framing lumber.

slide, drawer   The hardware that lets a drawer slide.

splitter   A gadget that allows several TV cables to connect to a single source.

square   At a 90° angle; a tool used to mark or saw a 90° angle.

squeezeout   Glue that gets pressed out during clamping.

stop   Plumber's jargon for a shut-off valve, used under a sink or toilet.

stop, blind   Molding behind the upper sash in double-hung window.

stop, inner   Molding that separates the upper and lower sashes in a double-hung window.

stop, outer   Molding that holds the lower sash in a double-hung window.

stop, parting   A stop that separates two sashes in a double-hung window.

stringer   The slanting framing that supports a stair.

stud   The vertical 2×4 or 2×6 framing in a wall.

subfloor   The rough floor, laid directly on the joists.

substrate   Material supporting the thing you're attaching, such as tile substrate.

tack   To nail lightly to hold something in position temporarily.

tailpiece   A fitting that connects a sink to the drain piping.

tee   A fitting that connects three pipes in a T formation.

template   A pattern used to mark another piece for cutting.

tile, base   A tile used to join a wall to a countertop.

tile, bullnose   A tile used at the outer edge of the counter, or where wall tiles meet drywall or plaster.

tile, edge   An oblong tile used for the vertical face of a countertop.

tile, double bullnose   A bullnose tile for an outside corner.

tile, trim   Tiles used to finish a project, with unusual shape and/or pattern.

toenail   To nail at an angle, as through the bottom of a stud.

tongue-and-groove (T&G)   A board with a tongue on one side and a channel on the other; forms an interlocking floor.

tread   The part of a staircase you step on.

volt   A unit of electrical pressure.

water seal   A pool of water in a plumbing trap that blocks sewer gas.

watt   A unit of electrical power (equals amps $\times$ volts).

weatherstripping   A flexible material that seals a movable piece to a fixed piece.

wires, hot   Wires that carry incoming electricity.

wires, supply   Wires that run from the circuit-breaker panel to a box. Can be hot or grounded.

Resources

Whether you're looking for information on specific brands of tools or tips on how to build with tile, books, magazines, and websites are excellent sources of further information on home improvement. The following resources are a good starting point.

Books and Magazines

Ramsey. Dan. *The Complete Idiot's Guide to Building Your Own Home, Second Edition*. Alpha Books, 2005.

———. *If It's Broke, Fix It!* Alpha Books, 2003.

Tenenbaum, David J. *The Complete Idiot's Guide to Home Repair and Maintenance Illustrated*. Alpha Books, 2004.

———. *The Complete Idiot's Guide to Trouble-Free Home Repair, Second Edition*. Alpha Books, 1996.

The Family Handyman Magazine. A general-interest monthly, combining advice on projects and repairs; www.rd.com/familyhandyman.

Fine Homebuilding. High-level carpentry advice, written mainly for professional builders; www.taunton.com/finehomebuilding/index.asp.

Old House Journal. Good advice for encounters between owners and old places; www.oldhousejournal.com.

Workbench: Woodworking to Improve Your Home. Home-improvement projects that focus on teaching new techniques; www.workbench-magazine.com.

Websites

Note that while websites may change, all of these worked at the time of this writing.

General

Advice for do-it-yourselfers: www.handymanusa.com

Ladder safety: www.chess.cornell.edu/Safety/Safety_Manual/portable_ladder_safety.htm

General building information: www.doityourself.com

Tools/Equipment

Delta Machinery: www.deltawoodworking.com

Dewalt Tools: www.dewalt.com

Paslode nail guns: http://paslode.com

Porter Cable: www.porter-cable.com

Robert Bosch Tool Co.: www.boschtools.com

Sears (Craftsman tools): www.sears.com

Senco nail guns: senco.com

Flooring

Armstrong Floors: www.armstrong.com

Engineered wood floors: www.thisoldhouse.com/toh/knowhow/handbook/article/0,16417,216032,00.html

Floor tips: www.onthehouse.com/tips/flooring

Flooring varieties: www.wfca.org/flooringguide/guide.asp?tp=3&pg=6

Laminate floors: www.bobvila.com/FixItClub/Task/Repairing/LaminateFloorBasics.html

Refinishing wood floors: www.essex-silver-line.com/tips

Tile

Ceramic tile information: www.ceramic-tile-floor.info

Preparing a floor for tiling: www.handymanusa.com/questions/floortileq.html

Tile prep information: doityourself.com/ceramic/cwtprep.htm

Tile underlayment: www.usg.com/IC/products/C_BOARD/underlay.asp

Tiling technique: www.thetiledoctor.com/installations/ct_methods.cfm

Tiling tips: www.thisoldhouse.com/toh/knowhow/handbook/article/0,16417,221776,00.html

Other

Cable TV installation: www.cornerhardware.com/howto/ht051.html

Cable TV (more info) : www.smarthome.com/howto15.html

Deck-building simplified: www.rd.com/familyhandyman/articles/200106/fixit/main.html

Drywall cutting advice: www.taunton.com/finehomebuilding/pages/h00014.asp

Marvin Windows: www.marvin.com

Molding profiles: www.curvedmouldings.com/profiles.html

Wood substitute, a good weatherproof one from Correct Deck: www.correctdeck.com

Index

M

T

U

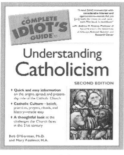